JOHN FEDDERS, SIX-FOOT-TEN AND VERY SMART, WAS A SUPERLAWYER HUNGRY FOR STILL MORE MONEY, POWER, AND FAME.

CHARLOTTE FEDDERS JUST WANTED A COMFORTABLE HOME AND A HAPPY FAMILY.

HIDDEN BY A VENEER OF COUNTRY CLUBS, PRIVATE SCHOOLS, AND A BIG WHITE COLONIAL HOME IN POTOMAC WERE SHOCKING SECRETS—A LIFE OF FEAR, VIOLENCE, AND . . .

SHATTERED DREAMS

"A HARROWING ACCOUNT."—*Time*

"A HELL OF A CAUTIONARY TALE."
—*Washington Post Book World*

"CHARLOTTE FEDDERS HAS HELPED US UNDERSTAND THE PLIGHT OF AN ABUSED WOMAN."
—*The Wall Street Journal*

Shattered Dreams

CHARLOTTE FEDDERS
and LAURA ELLIOT

A DELL BOOK

Published by
Dell Publishing
a division of
The Bantam Doubleday Dell Publishing Group, Inc.
666 Fifth Avenue
New York, New York 10103

To my husband, John Behm, and my father, Jack Elliott, men who know that tenderness and respect engender love.

—LAURA ELLIOTT

To my sons, Luke, Mark, Matthew, Andrew, Peter and John Michael, whose courage, strength, and unconditional love of me and one another have created and fulfilled a new dream.

—CHARLOTTE FEDDERS

Contents

Prologue

On February 4, 1985, Charlotte O'Donnell Fedders sat in the witness stand in a Montgomery County circuit court in Rockville, Maryland, waiting to testify how her storybook marriage had fallen apart. A soft-spoken, tall blonde, given to looking at her hands when nervous, Charlotte now clenched her fingers together, locked as tight as the weave of a new basket. She worried that everyone there could see how her entire body was trembling. Her hazel eyes filmed with tears. She blinked to clear them. She wet her lips, and felt moisture from her palms slowly seep into the Kleenex balled there.

She nervously realized she would have to lean forward, out of her bolted-down chair, to speak into the microphone. "My God," she thought, "a microphone." She shakily reached out to touch it and recoiled when she heard a stereophonic pop resound through the chamber.

What was she doing here anyway? Her presence in a divorce court signaled, at age forty-one, the end of something she had always wanted to be: a wife, pure and simple. But she felt she had no choice. That her husband had allowed her no choice if she and her five boys wanted to survive emotionally and financially.

Charlotte wore a modest wool plaid skirt with a gray blouse, turquoise sweater, and rose-colored blazer, and no discernible jewelry other than a necklace with a tiny gold charm representing an infant. She had purchased it after her fourth baby died and she never took it off. The baby was, in fact, her advocate with God, the angel she invoked when she called upon heaven for help, ever the simple, good Catholic. She had prayed the night before to her son to help her fall asleep and finally, finally she had.

Why was she so afraid? Divorce had become so common that attorneys and judges could almost conduct proceedings in their sleep. To look at her, she was nothing that unusual, just another upper-middle-class, unhappy, suburban house-wife, outgrown by her aspiring husband, and trying to piece together a new way of life by fighting for her estranged husband's help with it. A woman accustomed to belonging to a country club, sending her sons to private schools, at-tending formal parties with renowned VIPs, and living in a prestigious neighborhood in a five-bedroom house, to which a cleaning lady came weekly.

But Charlotte was different. Behind the comfortable pos-sessions, the enviable lifestyle, lay a secret. A shocking se-cret.

Across the modern, earth-colored courtroom sat her hus-band, John M. Fedders. John was a powerful and respected Washington attorney, the chief of enforcement for the Secu-rities and Exchange Commission, one of the most sensitive law-enforcement jobs in the federal government. He had also been a partner in one of the city's preeminent law firms before joining the SEC in 1981. He was an intellectually imposing man, indeed. He was also physically intimidating, since he stretched to six-foot-ten-inches tall.

John, too, seemed a prototypical Washington character—

a smart boy who had built his success on his own, driven by ambition and desire for money. He grew into a man preoccupied with climbing into the city's power circles, a man who neglected his family while doggedly fashioning his career, and thereby lost the purpose of his dreams in their pursuit. It was a common enough familial travesty.

But what made John different from other fast-rising lawyers was his living dangerously beyond his means, his seeming obsession with order and control, his chronic black moods, and his sometimes violent temper.

John also had hit his wife. Charlotte was afraid sitting in that courtroom because she had always been afraid of her husband.

Almost two years earlier, Charlotte had finally found the courage to force John to leave the house after he slammed his fist into her glasses, giving her a black eye. It was not the first black eye he had inflicted, but it was going to be the last. She couldn't stand it anymore, not the slaps, not his control over her and the children, not his compulsive cleanliness, not his stringent household rules, which included her helping him dress in the morning, or his moody silences, which could stretch for weeks.

After he left their home, however, John continued to make his mark at the SEC, recognized and profiled by the press for his crackdown on insider trading and corporate fraud. He hoped to be remembered, he would tell the judge during his testimony, "as one of the deans of the securities bar." And Charlotte recalls that John fantasized of climbing even higher politically. He had several good friends in the Reagan White House and, according to the *Wall Street Journal,* Attorney General Edwin Meese was considering naming him to be associate attorney general, the Justice Department's third-ranking job.

John was well on his way to long-lasting stardom in the nation's capital. There was nothing in his way; no one really knew about the alarming private side of this increasingly public man.

Meanwhile, as he soared, John did pay the mortgage and utilities on the family home he had left, but refused to give his wife more than $1,000 a month to support herself and their five sons, aged two to fourteen. John claimed that was all he could afford to send her on his $72,300 government salary. She countered that if that was the case, he should return to private practice, where he had once made more than $162,000 a year. After all, he had promised Charlotte when he joined the SEC that he planned to use Washington's revolving-door tradition and to leave the commission after only a few years, for a high-paying, private-industry job.

But John would not negotiate a compromise on alimony or child support, say Charlotte and her attorney, and so ended up in a court of law, in a public arena.

It would mean the end of his political dreams.

Sitting in the cushioned theater seats of the courtroom was Brooks Jackson, a staff reporter for the *Wall Street Journal*, a newspaper that had a particular interest in John and his work at the SEC and had written about John before. The reporter quietly scribbled notes as Charlotte testified that she had been a victim in her own home, growing more and more fearful and insecure—how, among other things, John had once almost pushed her over a banister as he beat her, had belittled her in front of friends and relatives, had refused to talk to her, had criticized her as being overweight and stupid, and had forced their family to not wear shoes in the house so they wouldn't hurt the expensive carpeting.

The next day, February 5, John was called to the stand. His voice cracked as he admitted under oath to having beaten his wife on several occasions. His testimony included: "I am ambitious. . . . I don't demand anything of anybody that I don't demand of myself. . . . There was no justification whatsoever [for having struck Charlotte]. . . . I am forever remorseful about it. . . . Yes, I demeaned her. I did a lot of stupid things. . . . We bred on each other. . . . I used to say this about our marriage—we had the capacity of building the Eiffel Tower in a day together, but we also had the capability of destroying it in ten minutes together."

Three weeks later, on February 25, the day their divorce hearing was supposed to reconvene, and, ironically, the date that twenty years before John and Charlotte had met, the *Wall Street Journal* ran a front-page article about their marriage and its shattered hopes. It chronicled the events of the trial, John's and Charlotte's testimony, and the pressures of John's trying to live like an affluent attorney on a bureaucrat's comparatively meager pay. It also quoted their eldest son, who had witnessed one of John's more brutal physical attacks on Charlotte.

Readers were shocked. In John Fedders, the city's overachievers discovered a disturbing allegory of themselves. He was a Washington Everyman, somehow gone berserk.

Wasn't domestic violence a heinous oxymoron, anyway? How could an educated, an otherwise honorable man, a man entrusted by the federal government to enforce a set of laws beat his wife? Did the very qualities that made him so successful at work, qualities so praised in the upwardly mobile American male, push him to be domineering and cruel at home? The city, and ultimately the nation, wondered, as John and Charlotte's distressing passion play was picked up in newspapers and news broadcasts across the country.

The day after the story broke, John handed in his resignation at the SEC.

In a daze, Charlotte listened to the conflicting public opining on her very personal agony, and to reporters' questions: Why didn't you leave him? You must have liked it; how else could you, would you, have stayed? Didn't you have the self-respect, the sense to get out?

No, she hadn't, Charlotte thought. But what would they have had her do, shove away all her dreams of happiness at the first hint of trouble, give up on the man she loved? She had tried for so long because she adored him, and she thought marriage was sacred. She also had been convinced that somehow his actions were her fault, and that if she changed, he would too.

And, when times were good with John, they were fairytale wonderful. Charlotte tearfully stated to the judge, when asked why she had remained with John for sixteen years. "He was just my life. I felt privileged to be married to a man of his stature. I felt I couldn't live without him."

On the outside, John was the knight that she and her affluent, Catholic school girlfriends had been taught to want —the handsome, ambitious breadwinner, through whom they could vicariously be successes. Charlotte also grew up believing, however, that she wasn't worthy of such a man; that she wasn't, well, thin enough, pretty enough, smart enough to attract him. So she had known that, if by some God-given fluke, she did catch him, she was going to do anything to make him happy.

"When I met John Fedders," says Charlotte, "I knew he was the one love of my life."

Part One

Growing Up Proper

We are not the first
Who with best meaning have incurred the worst.

Cordelia, *King Lear*

Charlotte Louise O'Donnell was born in Baltimore, Maryland, on August 14, 1943, to Charles O'Donnell, an ambitious medical student, and Helen Smith, a nurse who had given up her work and converted to Catholicism when they married in 1940. Charlotte was the first of five daughters, little girls who were to be pampered and protected as their father had never been.

Charles, in fact, had had a difficult childhood, one that steeled him against hard knocks, taught him to ignore the rules, and pushed him to want success as only a totally self-made man can want it. He was driven, smart, and aggressive.

He grew up poor in Long Island, during the Depression, the eldest of seven siblings. When he was sixteen, his father died, leaving Charles the head of a young, hungry household. He dropped out of high school and moved to Baltimore to live with relatives and to work in a can company. He also learned the machinist and lithography trades, yet never gave up on his dream of practicing medicine.

In 1937, after passing a high school equivalency test, Charles started working on a degree in chemical engineering at Johns Hopkins University. Halfway through that curriculum, he walked into the University of Maryland's medical school and announced that he wanted to attend. The dean told him that he had only half the necessary credits and to come back in two years when he had them. Charles asked if he came back in a year with them all if he could be admitted. The dean jokingly agreed.

Charles O'Donnell came back to the dean's office the next fall. With the help of his wife, his mother, and his aunts, he had managed to pass a crushing overload of courses and had the credits. The dean honored his promise and O'Donnell's career was launched.

It's a story Charlotte and her sisters recited with relish and pride, just as they recounted all of the doctor's accomplishments—which became many.

Charles received his medical degree in 1944 and opened his general practice a year later in Towson, a suburb on the northern fringe of Baltimore. To enhance his finances, he also became a county medical examiner, the medical director of the county jail and a juvenile facility, and physician to a hospice and nursing home. Those duties plus his house calls kept him working on weekends and late into the night.

By 1950, when he was thirty-three and Charlotte was seven years old, the doctor had built an imposing brick Colonial home on York Road, Towson's main thoroughfare, in which he also had his office. He gained status around town, and was afforded privileges such as parking on the fire lane of Immaculate Conception Church, so that he wouldn't have to wait with the rest of the congregation to get out of the parking lot following Sunday Mass.

But even with his monetary success and growing celebrity, Charles wanted more power, prestige, and influence than simply being a good diagnostician in Baltimore County could bring.

He strode into Maryland medical politics armed with his Long Island street savvy and knack for snowballing. His climb was swift and consummate. Within six years of his graduating from medical school, his colleagues voted him president of the Maryland Academy of General Practice. In 1952, he became the youngest president of the Baltimore County Medical Association. His honors would eventually include chairmanships in organizations affecting medical policies across the country—the Southern Medical Association, the American Medical Association, and the American Academy of General Practice.

Not bad for a poor boy who technically finished neither high school nor college.

Helen was terribly proud of him, proud to be his wife, proud to succeed through him, despite the fact she had advanced to head nurse at Baltimore's Sinai Hospital before quitting her career. Her own upbringing in a tiny North Carolina town had been poor, and the promise of stability and opportunities for their children meant a great deal to her. She repaid him by being where he wanted her, when he wanted her, the perfect, patient, obedient wife.

Each night, when Charlotte was a toddler, her mother bathed and dressed her in a clean, frilled dress and took her to the bus stop to meet Daddy. He was their hero, their linchpin, their definition. They were his cheering squad, his sparkling accoutrements, his responsibilities.

The dynamics of the O'Donnell family didn't change as more daughters came. It remained a pretty mobile, with its pieces moving only slightly independently, always anchored tightly to their center—Charles. That probably was a reality of most American families of the time, but somehow the hierarchy in the O'Donnell clan was even more pronounced, their deification of him eventually more constricting for his children.

Because his office was in the basement, the family's daily routine and meals circled around his schedule. Helen often had to juggle answering the office phone, which also rang in the kitchen, as she prepared dinner. Once a month, Charlotte and her sisters helped her mother write the doctor's bills and stuff them into envelopes for mailing. Generally, their table conversation was what the doctor wanted to talk about. And he expressed his views in a confident tone.

His opinion became family doctrine. The O'Donnell girls remember that they hesitated to express their own sentiments largely because their eager-to-please mother rarely challenged him. They emulated her and showed their father extraordinary, sometimes fearful, deference, which kept him at a distance.

"I probably saw more of my father than most children with a nine-to-five father," remembers Charlotte, "but he was always doing something else. He ate lunch with us, for instance, but he was always on the phone. When you set the table, you put out the napkins, the silverware, the glasses, and the phone with several lines.

"We were always aware of the patients downstairs. When I jumped on the middle step, my mother would warn: 'There are patients in the office.' And she'd say: 'Don't do that, it will upset your father.' I don't think she was passing the buck. I think she was being honest. I never saw them argue, but I think she used to buffer things for us.

"So we tried never to upset him. We never argued with him. He would sit at the dinner table and give a political monologue basically. He hated Communists and used to tell us to be nurses rather than teachers because if Communists took over they'd have their own teachers, but they'd still need nurses. He also always told us to register Democrat but to vote Republican in the elections. He did that because the Democrats had more exciting primaries than the Republicans and he loved the fun of politics.

"I never questioned anything he said. Sometimes I might doubt what he told us to do, but only to myself. I would think, 'He's my father, he's a man, he must be right.' The only time I did question him was to argue about abortion. He was for it in some cases because of his medical training. I was totally against it at the time because of what the nuns were teaching us at school, but I lost that one fast. He could just make you feel very silly in what you were arguing.

"I don't know why I was so nervous around him, because I can remember being spanked only twice. Once was with a belt and once was with a forsythia branch I had had to cut myself when I was probably eight or nine years old. I remember thinking I deserved it because I had embarrassed him in church by giggling or something. Un-ladylike, un-Godly behavior would embarrass him because everyone knew us.

"He was never really violent or threatened us with it; we just felt that kind of punishment was possible. I never saw him yell at my mother. It had more to do with the tone of his voice. I just knew that I never wanted to make a mistake around him. I was always trying to please my father because I was afraid that if I did something wrong, he would stop loving me."

More than anything else, the O'Donnell daughters remember their father's quick temper, made more intimidating because of their unfamiliarity with him. Perhaps Dr. O'Donnell was victim to the tragedy of many motivated, overachieving parents; perhaps his professional persona was so ingrained that he couldn't easily shed it when he was with his children. In Dr. O'Donnell's case, he needed to be hard-nosed to survive medical politics. He probably had no idea how his vindictiveness toward an adversary could frighten his daughters.

"I just didn't know Daddy that well," remembers Charlotte's younger sister Martha O'Donnell. "I wasn't scared of him like, 'Oh, my God, he's going to do this to me'; it was more the kind of scared you feel when you're on a first date and you don't know the person. And you'd see him get mad at other people, so you didn't want to have him get mad at you. He'd get furious at hospital telephone operators. God help them if they disconnected him or sent him to the wrong party. He'd ask where they got their diploma in stupidity and blah, blah, blah. It was a real belittling kind of thing.

"Dinner conversations would revolve around his day and how he had *gotten* somebody. That was what you were supposed to do, *get* someone who had crossed you. He wanted us to do the same thing, because he was protective of us. If I came home and told him about something bad a nun had said to me, he'd say, 'Now, you go back and say this and this and this,' and I would start crying and say, 'Daddy, I can't do that.'"

The youngest of all the sisters, Dotti Matthews, had similar feelings: "I was definitely afraid of him but not because he directed his anger towards me as much as just being afraid of his anger in general. I saw him throw a license plate at a dog once, and you'd always know when he had been looking for keys when you saw everything on the kitchen counter knocked onto the floor. It was never a slow boil with him. All of a sudden you'd realize that you had done something wrong."

And yet all three remember how important their father's approval was to them. He was a community leader. People called out to him on the street, "Hey, Doc." If they could gain his respect, they had achieved something big.

"It was nice if our mother signed our report cards, but it was really something if Daddy did. We were all very proud of him and it meant a lot if he did something for just us," says Martha. "He'd hand out a silver dollar if you got honors, which was very exciting."

"I remember feeling that I had really earned something when he put his arm around my shoulder," says Dotti. "It felt like heaven."

Charles certainly was capable of showing affection for his family. He nicknamed Charlotte "Schatz," German for "treasure." When she was away at camp for the first time, he sent her a telegram telling her that he missed her. But such moments were few because of his frantic schedule.

Most of his displays of love were saved up for big, lavish spectacles, displays befitting a family man of means. His gifts to Helen, for example, were glittery and presented with ceremony—once he surprised her with an ornate chandelier for their dining room, purchasing it and having it hung before telling her.

Each summer he sent his wife and daughters to Ocean City, Maryland, for at least a month. The doctor stayed in the city during the week to work, but when he came down, he'd fix huge Dagwood-style sandwiches for lunch, take them body-surfing and fishing, and treat them to a stellar night on the boardwalk their last weekend at the beach.

"Those were very festive moments," says Martha.

There were trips to Niagara Falls, the World's Fair, and Montreal, and five-star outings to New York City, replete with tickets to Broadway shows—*Flower Drum Song, The Music Man,* and *My Fair Lady*— and dinners at the Latin Quarter nightclub, where stars such as Merv Griffin performed. When in New York, they stayed at the Sheraton and only in large rooms that passed his wife's inspection.

Just as Charles preferred to wear only expensive Countess Mara ties, he wanted his family swathed in the best dresses that money could buy. Each Easter, for instance, the doctor paid for complete new outfits for his girls: suits, shoes to match, and hats, plus a corsage for each. He sent them to shop at some of Baltimore's finest stores, such as The Tweed Shop and Peck & Peck.

Charles's attitude was simply that only the best would do for his daughters. That included the best private Catholic education in the city. All five of the girls attended the prestigious Notre Dame Preparatory School from first grade through high school, where tuition was an average of $600 a year per child.

"There was a real largess about him," says Dotti. "The

sky was the limit. When we went out for a good meal, we could have steak, lobster, anything. We knew that if we could please him there was this reward at the end of the rainbow. But it was feast or famine with him. There was very little middle ground. It was either grandiose or you were tiptoeing around. There was no day-to-day support. That was Mommie."

Perhaps Charlotte best summed up the children's relations with their parents in two poems she wrote in the innocence of sixth grade.

My Mother

I love my mother, truly I do
and I know my mother loves me too.
Every morning when I leave for school
I love the way she waves goodbye.
I don't know why God
gave me such a sweet mother
And I guess that's why I really love her.

My Dad

My father is a doc, he works round the clock.
I love him, really I do,
although I don't see him as much as you.
He is really very nice, like fathers usually are.
And I really love him by far, by far, by far.

So the basic family unit for the O'Donnells was Helen and the girls. In many ways, their mother was as simple and giggly as her offspring, willing to play and tease with them. They could dress her up as Ringo when the Beatles were idols and challenge her authority gently. Once when she complained about their rooms and all the stuffed animals the children had, she awoke the next day to find five dozen fluffy creatures lined up against her bedroom door.

Another time she admonished them not to take their heads off their pillows before 10 AM the next morning because she and the doctor were tired. The girls were up and downstairs long before the appointed hour, watching cartoons on television. When their mother stormed in, she found each of them had a pillow wrapped around her head.

"What could I do but laugh?" asks Helen happily.

She made all their lunches and tucked notes into the bags of the girls who had tests or special events that day. Nothing fancy, just small words of encouragement. Helen was the one who took them to Mass each morning during Lent, and packed donuts and orange juice in the car for the ride to school afterwards. She had no friends other than the couples she and Charles saw together socially. She didn't belong to bridge or garden clubs. Her life was her family.

"She was the best mother," says Charlotte, "because she was always there. She taught us all the words to her favorite musicals and we'd dance in the kitchen and sing in the car. I wanted to be just like her when I grew up."

"She was just a great mom who could solve any problem, fix any wound, never told you no," says Martha. "I never thought my mother was a creep when I was a teenager like most girls do. There was never anything that was too much for her to do in terms of cooking, baking, decorating, or entertaining. She just loved it."

In fact, their mother could make home so appealing that Charlotte rarely wanted to go out. She preferred the company of her family, especially since she could be a reticent child. "Charlotte was definitely shy with people she didn't know," recalls her mother. "But she was just the sweetest, gentlest child. When she was two or three I could put her in a chair and say, 'Mommie has to go upstairs for a minute, you stay right there.' And she wouldn't move, and be happy as can be. I never had to say anything like 'Stay there or I'll shake you.' She just naturally wanted to please."

In her quest to help her daughter be the best she could be,

however, Helen may have contributed to Charlotte's growing insecurities. "My mother tried to build me up," says Charlotte. "She'd always say, 'Don't you look pretty.' But she'd also say, 'Always wear makeup, you never know who you might see. Don't bite your fingernails.' And I don't have a real feminine walk. I remember once in the den her showing me how I walked. She looked like a gorilla as she did this and I was so embarrassed. I thought, 'Oh, my God, I can't look that bad.' "

But for the most part, life at home was happy, even if sometimes restrained. The most traumatic event of Charlotte's young life was when her sister Martha was badly burned. Charlotte still blames herself for the accident.

"It was February 14, 1953. Valentine's Day," recalls Charlotte. "I was nine. I was fixing breakfast for my parents and Martha pushed a chair up to the stove to watch. She was only two. She was wearing a little green cotton dress and an organdy pinafore. That pinafore touched the electric burner and shot up in flames. She ran out into the hall, screaming. My parents heard and ran downstairs. They rolled her up into a throw rug she was standing on. She was hospitalized and sick for a long time. They thought she was going to die at one point.

"They never yelled at me. They never said anything. But I felt just terrible, that it was all my fault. How could I have been that stupid? How could I have not thought to roll her in the rug myself? I buried it, never talked about it until 1971, when we were at the beach, and my mother was absolutely appalled when she heard me break down over it, so many years later.

"You see, it had just never occurred to her that I might need to be reassured. That generation had a whole different way of parenting. They didn't have Dr. Spock. We spend all this time worrying about what to say to our kids, but they didn't back then."

The terms "interpersonal relations" and "emotional well-being," after all, just weren't household words in the 1950s. Helen and the doctor were basically everything that the culture demanded of them at the time. He was supposed to be ambitious, wasn't he? Didn't his being successful mean that they were happy? He provided for his family, provided royally, in fact.

It was simply an era that pushed men to be preoccupied with their careers and their financial success. As a result, a lot of fathers didn't have the time or impetus to spend many unstructured hours with their children—hours necessary to provide enough intimacy for a child to know a parent as a person, not just as an authority. Many of Charlotte's contemporaries grew up naive about men in general and dependent upon male jurisprudence. Charlotte, in particular, wasn't confident enough to try a relationship in which she had a truly equal voice.

But there is no question that his children were important to the doctor. In his backyard, Charles planted a dogwood tree for each daughter. And in his medical office, under the glass on top of his desk he had a collage of their pictures, plus the following poem:

Children Learn What They Live

If a child lives with criticism, he learns to condemn.
If a child lives with hostility, he learns to fight.
If a child lives with ridicule, he learns to be shy.
If a child lives with shame, he learns to feel guilty.
If a child lives with tolerance, he learns to be patient.
If a child lives with encouragement, he learns confidence.
If a child lives with praise, he learns to appreciate.
If a child lives with fairness, he learns justice.
If a child lives with security, he learns to have faith.
If a child lives with approval, he learns to like himself.
If a child lives with acceptance and friendship, he learns
    to find love in the world.

2

O Lord, I am not worthy
That Thou shouldst come to me
But speak the words of comfort
My spirit healed shall be

And humbly I'll receive thee
The Bridegroom of my soul
No more by sin to grieve Thee
Or fly Thy sweet control.

On May 14, 1950, Charlotte stood with twenty other six-year-old girls singing the hymn "O Lord, I Am Not Worthy," their translucent voices rising like the sound of wind chimes in the chapel of Notre Dame Preparatory School. All were dressed in stiff, white dresses, and were crowned with waist-long white veils, the picture of purity. Within a few moments each would walk to the altar and receive Holy Communion for the first time, an important rite of passage for Catholics, and one that would affect Charlotte more than most. While many of her schoolmates would eventually reject a great deal of the Church's teachings, Charlotte would not. The hymn "O Lord, I Am Not Worthy," in fact, became her favorite. In many ways, Charlotte would remain as innocent as she earnestly promised God to always be that day in 1950.

As the priest placed the blessed wafer, or Host, on her tongue, Charlotte believed she received the body of Christ into her own, and through that sacrament became one momentarily with God. She felt very special, very holy, very lucky as she walked back to her wooden pew to say her small prayer of thanks.

Several weeks before, Charlotte had been made fit to receive Communion by going to confession for the first time. She had climbed into the dark, wooden confessional, pulled the heavy red curtain closed, knelt, and waited nervously for the priest sitting in the adjacent chamber to slide back the door covering the grate, and press his ear toward her. She had recited her litany of faults quickly, fearing a long conversation with the priest would make her classmates, waiting their turn in a line outside, think she had been very bad, indeed.

Now, kneeling in the pew, with the last bit of the Communion Host dissolving in her mouth, she felt completely cleansed. Charlotte imagined her soul to be a shiny white canvas and any sin to be a black spot on it. Confession and Communion had absolved whatever smudges a well-behaved six-year-old could possibly have accumulated, and she was momentarily in a state of grace. If she died right then, she would have to spend only a short time atoning in purgatory. All she had to do to remain this pure was to avoid fighting with her sisters, coveting their toys, disobeying her parents, saying a bad word, watching too much television, or eating too much. It was a lot to remember. But she knew she could do it.

Charlotte felt a bit more blessed than others anyway be-

cause she was born on the eve of a Holy Day of Obligation
—the Assumption, the day the angels carried Mary up to
heaven in a cloud. Because of the proximity of her birthday
and that special day, Charlotte chose the Mother of God as
her special patron. She prayed to her exclusively, somehow
trusting her more than God or His Son or the other saints.
Like many good Catholic girls, she had a foot-high statue of
Mary in her bedroom, and each May, which was Mary's
month, she would adorn it with azalea clippings from her
yard.

Her family was hardly fanatical, but Catholicism was a
constant, daily influence in the O'Donnells' lives. Each night
the girls went in to kiss their parents good-night, and typically the doctor was on his knees in evening prayer, often
with a nightcap of Scotch on the bedstand. Grace was said
before each meal. The family ate and drank nothing on Sunday before Mass, and on Fridays abstained from meat, in
remembrance of Good Friday. Those were basic require-
ments of Catholics before Vatican II, the papal conference in
1965 that relaxed many of the Church's rules, as well as
changing the Mass from Latin to modern languages.

But under the influence of Notre Dame's nuns, the
O'Donnell girls tried to make their family more devout.
During October, for instance, the month of the rosary, they
persuaded their parents to try to recite its Holy Mysteries (a
twenty-minute process) together each night. Often on a long
car trip, they did say the rosary. A Saint Christopher medal
hung in the car for protection as well. And when the family
vacationed in Canada, they went out of their way to visit the
Basilica of Sainte-Anne de Beaupré, where the doctor and
Charlotte climbed thirty stairs to the altar on their knees in
penance.

All the O'Donnells wore Miraculous Medals, oval gold
medals that showed the Blessed Mother stepping on a serpent. At the top of each piece of paper the girls used for
schoolwork, they wrote "JMJ," for "Jesus, Mary, Joseph,"

to remind them that all aspects of their lives were to be dedicated to the Lord.

All these things contributed to Charlotte and her sisters' believing that they were constantly watched by Him, His archangels and angels, their personal guardian angel, the saints, and all the heavenly host. Dotti can remember leaving candy and flowers out for Saint Cosmas and Saint Damian, who she was sure strolled through her bedroom at night. She hoped that they'd look out for her in gratitude for her gifts. It was both a comforting and frightening thought, since the children believed that any little mistake would be immediately seen and condemned by all the persons of heaven.

Each girl had a cruxifix above her bed, a holy water font by the bedroom door, and a statue of Mary on the bureau; all of which were decorated with palms from Palm Sunday. They could not throw the palms away because they were blessed. So, the palms stayed up until Ash Wednesday the following spring, when they took them to church to be burned and used for ashes in that holy day's service.

Charlotte was tutored to gaze daily at the cruxifix and to recall Christ's bloody and painful death, his "humiliation" and "heartbreak," so that she would remember that any sin she committed was not simply a harm she did to herself. She was inflicting more pain and suffering on Christ, who had endured so much for her already. Not only was she bad if she sinned, she was ungrateful. A child who always wanted to please, Charlotte took all this to heart. Guilt became a familiar feeling.

Most of the O'Donnell girls' religious training came at Notre Dame, with the nuns, with daily religion classes, and yearly retreats. It began with the *Baltimore Catechism,* the book used to teach Catholic children the basics of their faith. It was written in singsong questions-answers, and the nuns required their students to recite passages to them.

"We studied religion every day," Charlotte remembers. "It was the major subject. You'd stand up to answer and every word had to be exact. There were no discussions or questions. The dogma was set and we were supposed to just memorize it.

"If you didn't get it right, it was a terrible thing. I remember the first time I raised my hand in a class in first grade was to answer the question on when Communion came in the Mass. I got it wrong and the nun made me feel so stupid that I don't think I ever raised my hand again until high school."

The nuns drilled such rote memorization in order to discourage individual thought, because it led to trouble. Charlotte and her classmates were also cautioned to comply with the commands of the Pope and priests, who were more holy than their congregations and who understood more clearly the word of the Lord, and to avoid "near occasions of sin" —"any person, place, or things that might easily lead us into sin."

"It didn't give us a lot of credit for strength of character," says Charlotte, "that, given the slightest opportunity, we'd commit a sin." Her religious beliefs contributed to Charlotte's deepening lack of self-esteem. They also paralleled the intellectual and emotional dependency she was learning at home, where she was encouraged to accept her father's opinion as gospel.

She certainly never challenged any Church edict, even to the point of refusing to look at a King James Bible when her family traveled and stayed in hotels. The King James version was the Bible of the Episcopal Church and wasn't embossed with the imprimatur, a mark in the front cover that told Catholics a book had been approved by the Catholic Church.

"In my mind in those days, it was almost like looking at a dirty book," says Charlotte.

Such compliance to orders was part of being a good Catholic. Obedience and respect for authority, then, were prime virtues and methods of living a holy life and thus deserving God's favor. Charlotte's *Baltimore Catechism* says: "Besides our parents, the fourth commandment obliges us to respect and obey all our lawful superiors . . . to refuse to obey anyone with true authority, as parents, teachers, etc., is to refuse to obey God and to reject His will."

But Notre Dame's girls rarely had to think for themselves anyway, on matters ranging from their dress to performance of movements during Mass. They wore prescribed uniforms and when they went to chapel, at least once a month they went in procession, led by nuns who were armed with clickers. Click-click-click, time to genuflect, click-click-click, time to stand.

Following the rules, however, was not just something to do out of fear of hell; there was a promise connected. If you abided by the rules with faith, you would see the kingdom of heaven. The Catholic Church is relatively unusual in the Christian religion in that it does offer practices that more or less carry specified guarantees.

For instance, indulgences—collecting money for "pagan babies," regular Bible study, making pilgrimages—bought time out of purgatory. Those who made sincere confessions, followed the penance prescribed by the priest ("Usually all I had to say were a few Hail Marys," says Charlotte), and promised never to commit the act again gained absolution. Novenas, a set of prayers said nine days in a row following certain procedures, were more likely than regular prayers to bring the desired answer. Using relics of saints—bone chips, pieces of their clothes, or articles they touched—while praying would also give entreaties extra clout. And special blessings brought special protection. Charlotte always looked forward to February 2, when the priest blessed her throat to guard her against sore throats and choking.

Taken simply, these sanctified rites pretty much guaranteed that the devout who practiced them would be shielded from harm and rewarded with good things. A trusting, non-quizzical child, Charlotte basically accepted every word and interpreted the message conversely as well—if something bad happened, you deserved it, because you must have done something evil to make God turn his back on you.

"Until my marriage broke up, I honestly believed," says Charlotte, "that if I was good, prayed, went to confession and to church, obeyed the Ten Commandments, and devoted myself to my loved ones that nothing bad *could* happen to me. I was convinced that bad things only came as a punishment for some fault in me."

Mea culpa, mea culpa, mea maxima culpa. It was an idea that has plagued her much of her life.

Of course, women were far more susceptible to evil and to causing evil than men, according to the scriptures. Eve was the one who directly disobeyed God by taking the fruit of knowledge from the serpent. She then coerced Adam into tasting it. This idea was dramatically brought home to Charlotte by a woman she knew who had to leave her own relatives to live with friends because she was pregnant.

"She was with [them] only until the baby was born," Charlotte recalls. "Then, it was given up for adoption. It told me that if you got pregnant you had to hide until the whole thing was over because it was your disgrace. It wasn't the man's fault if you got in trouble, it was the woman's for letting something happen."

A concept of Catholicism that would have a profound effect on Charlotte was the idea of turning the other cheek and patiently enduring injustices. The eight Beatitudes promised the poor in spirit, the meek, those who mourn, hunger, and thirst for justice, the merciful, the clean of heart, the peacemakers, and those who suffer persecution that they—not the proud, the rich, or the successful—would see heaven.

Charlotte's catechism included the following: "Love is purified, increased, and perfected by suffering. . . . God sends everyone all the sufferings they need on earth to cleanse, strengthen, and perfect their love. But most people waste their sufferings. They do not want them, complain about them, and try to escape them. . . . Our cross is everything that happens to us during the day that we do not like. . . . Crosses heal us quickly if we accept them and even love them the way our Lord did."

The virtue of trusting endurance was especially associated with the Mother of God. Mary always forgave, was always patient. She was the female figure the nuns taught Charlotte and her classmates to emulate. "Imitate that which Christ treasured in her: her simplicity, her devotion and love, her obedience," reads one of Charlotte's Catholic manuals.

Each May, Notre Dame paid tribute to Mary, holding a special procession. As the students reverently marched through campus to a statue of the Blessed Mother, they recited the rosary and sang hymns about the Virgin. Then, the May Queen, dressed in a full-length white dress, climbed a white ladder twined with blossoms and crowned Mary with a wreath of spring flowers.

The day Charlotte graduated from Notre Dame she asked her parents to drive by their church in Towson before going home. She wanted to place the spray of red roses she had received during the ceremony on Mary's altar in a special supplication. She knelt and dedicated her life to the Virgin, asking for her motherly protection, murmuring a prayer such as this one from *Youth Before God* by Reverend William J. Kelly:

Holy Virgin Mary, mother worthy of all love, give us a heart like yours, strong in its decisions and of unshakable loyalty.

A heart full of love that radiates forth good will and is not hardened.

A pure heart which lives in the flesh without living for the flesh.

A noble heart that quickly forgets its wounds and is ever ready to pardon.

A sensitive heart that shares in the joy and sorrow of others.

A heart gentle and kind that judges no one and never ceases to have confidence in others.

3

Notre Dame sits atop one of Baltimore's highest hills, nestled in a staid residential section on the city's northern border, shady and still. Its campus is convent-quiet, a place seemingly designed to inspire strolling and contemplation. Solitary stone benches are strategically dispersed amid unruly hedges and under tall, old trees for privacy. Sacred statues are tucked into modest, protective gardens. The narrow walkways eventually wind their way up gentle slopes to the tall, red brick administration building, where a gleaming white statue of the Blessed Mother awaits, hands outstretched reassuringly.

When Charlotte was in school, Notre Dame was the city's best private Catholic girls' institution. Part of that prestige came from the fact Notre Dame's college and prep school shared the Charles Street campus at the time, infusing the lower school with space and programs generally afforded only a college. Also, the student population was decidedly upper-middle-class, earning the school the nickname "Snob Hill."

Indeed, Notre Dame was part of a Catholic enclave that could seem snobbish and insulated to the outside world. The campus was buffered on one side by another small but landed Catholic college, Loyola, and on the other by *the* neighborhood for well-to-do Catholics, Homeland. Across Charles Street and up a few blocks was a newly constructed neo-Gothic cathedral that would become the center of the Church's politics in Baltimore, the Roman Catholic Cathedral of Mary Our Queen, its 128-foot-high stone tower looming huge on the horizon.

Unlike their brethren in some Eastern industrial cities, Baltimore's Catholics had integrated themselves into power and affluence early. The colony of Maryland, after all, was started by Lord Baltimore, a Catholic Englishman. The city became the site of the first American Roman Catholic cathedral and home of the first American archbishop.

Baltimore's diverse religious and cultural groups, however, were tight-knit and territorial. Laborers of different nationalities stuck to their own in residential areas rimming the docks and mills, and nothing much changed as they achieved affluence. Rich Catholics did move to the cool, uncrowded northern climes of the city, along with successful merchants of other religions, but they remained sequestered together.

Yet, side by side these elite neighborhoods and the adjacent Notre Dame and Loyola campuses created quite a privileged and comfortable stronghold, in which Catholics with proper credentials were an accepted part.

Notre Dame's hills, then, were far away from the everyday stress and struggle of the city's harbor, from which most of this wealth came. Far away from the ethnic groups that found work there, as disconnected from the throb of the city and its discomforts as clouds are from the surface of the earth.

On the campus itself there was little to tell the students about real life. The School Sisters of Notre Dame had started their academy in 1848, and one hundred years later the nuns still wore medieval garb—floor length black dresses with white bibs and stiff, elbow-length hoods that looked like bells sliced down the middle. Charlotte remembers them smelling musty and that the habits were so starched that the nuns had difficulty returning the embrace of any student courageous enough to touch them. She also remembers one nun telling her with an unusual show of pride that she brushed her teeth with Ivory Soap instead of expensive toothpaste.

The nuns meant to cultivate innocents like themselves. They believed that their responsibilities stretched beyond academics and religious topics to instilling patriotism, recruiting new sisters, and strengthening the moral rectitude of their charges.

Each day began with the Pledge of Allegiance and morning prayer. Convocations occasionally included a lecture on fighting Communism. This was the age of Eisenhower, and pride in country stuck with Charlotte.

"I can still tear up at 'God Bless America,' " she says. "That attitude just came along with thinking we were in the best school, the best religion, the best country."

The morning prayer time more often than not included a plea for "vocation," that youngsters suited for the cloth would recognize their calling. But if the girls didn't want to join the order, they were at least going to be properly decorous. The nuns chastised them for sitting in immodest poses, such as legs crossed at the knees. (Legs were to be demurely crossed at the ankle.) The nuns also encouraged students to join the Legion of Decency, a group Charlotte belonged to that promoted "modesty in dress, decency in entertainment, and the reading of clean literature." Prom dresses were required to have straps. A perceived penchant for promiscuity or using a bad word could bring expulsion. Being transferred to public school was an oft-heard threat.

Charlotte entered the first grade with twenty other well-behaved, well-heeled, "private-school material" Catholics and stuck with them through high school. She never really knew many Protestants, let alone anyone of a different race or creed. It was a cloistered, provincial way to grow up.

"It was very secure, very safe, and a beautiful environment," she says simply. "It was like a big family. I was very happy there."

Except for when she accompanied her father on house calls or to the nursing home, Charlotte saw little more of the world through her family life. The O'Donnell daughters were sheltered and coddled at home as well. Maids, for instance, came daily. "There was someone there to clean, cook, iron, or baby-sit every day except Sunday," remembers Dotti. "And there was always someone there for parties. We were never expected to do more than keep our rooms. They did everything else. It wasn't until college that I learned how to wash dishes.

"We were basically prepared to be princesses," she jokes.

According to Charlotte's high school diaries, most Saturdays she stayed in bed well past 10 AM, catching up on sleep she had lost the night before, giggling with girlfriends who had slept over. She spent weekend nights going with them to such movies as *Tammy, Tell Me True* and *Gidget Goes Hawaiian.* No scary or racy fare for these girls.

She did help her mother bathe, dress, feed, and shuttle the four babies who came after her, but Charlotte did not hold a job until after she graduated from college. Her parents paid for a trip to Bermuda with three girlfriends following high school graduation, and for two trips to Europe during college. In addition to these trips and family excursions, Charlotte traveled to West Virginia's exclusive resort The Greenbrier with her aunt and uncle.

"I think maybe part of the reason I had so much trouble later on in life and in my marriage," says Charlotte, "was that I had led such a simple, happy life that I just wasn't prepared for anything bad, for any kind of turmoil. Of course, it wasn't the real world. But I just expected life to be this lovely forever."

Yet, despite the material ease and financial success of her family, Charlotte never felt that she fit in anywhere. "We never had a normal neighborhood life in terms of having kids running in and out of the house from next door," she remembers. "We didn't know any of the kids around us. Our house was much larger than those around it and faced away from the neighborhood onto York Road, which is a very busy street. We were Catholic, most of them weren't, and they went to the local public schools. We did join the neighborhood pool, but we never felt comfortable there.

"It didn't matter that much when we were at home because we had each other. The five of us were so close in age —there's only a nine-year span—that we played with each other."

Charlotte, however, didn't feel entirely at ease with her Notre Dame friends, because the majority of them lived in Homeland, the city's Catholic promised land, and had been *born* into Baltimore's upper-crust society. She lived in the suburbs and was the daughter of a self-made man. No matter how important Dr. O'Donnell was in medicine or his neighborhood, Charlotte felt that he just didn't have the same social stature many of her friends' fathers had.

It was not a prejudice entirely of Charlotte's making. It was an attitude of the city's high society. Like the rich in many industrial towns on the East Coast, Baltimore's elite, blessed with the prestige of blood line as well as cash, often snubbed the newly arrived, successful professional, such as Dr. O'Donnell, as being merely an illegitimate half-brother, his offspring as pretenders. Charlotte could never shake the fear that her friends saw her as a second-class citizen.

While she waited for the public bus to go home, Charlotte watched her classmates walk across campus and disappear under the tall oak and pine trees of Homeland. Their homes were mainly built in the 1920s and were large, fieldstone or

brick, Tudor or Colonial in style, imitating the subdued
grandeur of English country manors. They had latticed windows and tall ceramic chimneys, and wide, manicured
lawns. The pristine neighborhood even had a string of man-
made ponds, with fountains in their centers.

"Some of the girls would schlepp us in to go ice-skating
on those ponds," says Charlotte. "It was very nice and all,
but we definitely didn't belong. Homeland is a closed system. The biggest dream for most of the girls I knew was to
move back to the neighborhood with a suitable well-bred
husband and to send their children to the same private
schools they attended. I never felt deprived, just inferior."

Much of her inferiority complex came from Charlotte's
unfavorably comparing herself with her friend Lawre, the
daughter of the president of the construction company that
had built the Chesapeake Bay Bridge. Her Tudor house was
one of the most stately in Homeland.

"My father was her father's doctor and the two families
were very friendly," remembers Charlotte. "Each New
Year's Eve we went to someplace like the Belvedere Hotel.
We'd get very dressed up and have an elegant dinner. We
always had an apartment at the beach just a block or two
away from theirs. Her father took mine hunting and deep-
sea fishing.

"But I always felt a little unworthy of Lawre's friendship.
My father couldn't really afford to treat her father to things.
They belonged to the Baltimore Country Club and we belonged to Hillendale, which was fine by me, but it was
smaller and out in the country and my parents really wanted
to join the Baltimore Club. It took them a long time to be
accepted as members. I don't know why. They knew the
right people."

Charlotte took on a kind of handmaiden role to her
friend, partly in deference to the doors her family could
open for Charlotte and her parents, and partly following the
ancient female ritual of pretty girls, like Lawre, leading a

pack of not-quite-as-pretty friends. It was a role Charlotte instinctively and willingly imposed on herself and one that helped gel the passivity she was learning at home and at school.

"I guess Lawre really was my closest friend. She was very nice to me, always. But she was socially there and very popular. I just followed along behind her. She was a debater, president of the athletic association, and a member of the holy group around school. I was never an officer in anything.

"She was pretty. I went through some really plain periods. She never had a hair out of place; mine was always flyaway. She never had a weight problem and I was always fighting ten pounds. I wore glasses, she didn't. And she always had dates. No one ever asked me out in high school, which didn't do much for my self-confidence.

"None of this was her fault. It was *me* making myself insecure. I just never felt good enough."

But Charlotte had always doubted her attractiveness. In fifth grade, at Camp Happy Valley, she carefully filled out all details about herself in the camper's handbook—age, address, family names, etc.—except for her height and weight. And at five-foot-nine inches she was taller and therefore often bigger than most of her high school friends, something that made her self-conscious. In her 1959 diary, she wrote: "I have lost about ten pounds. I weigh only 143. I feel really good."

Her mother tried to help Charlotte feel prettier and once enrolled her in a modeling seminar at Hutzler's, a local department store. She learned to walk down a ramp, turn, and go back. In all her full-length photographs following that, Charlotte stood with her feet in a perfect balletic V.

Her insecurity blossomed fully when she was a teenager, however, and it came time to find dates for school events. Charlotte was shy anyway with anyone outside her gaggle of girlfriends. But she was positively terrified of the opposite

sex. She simply didn't know any males. None of her friends
had brothers. She didn't know any of her neighbors. The
only time she had really seen boys up close was at the Mil-
brook Cotillion in the seventh and eighth grades, where she
had been sent to learn the box step and waltz. And that had
been a small disaster. She was so tall that no one asked her
to dance.

"Poor Charlotte was a bit of an oddity in that group,"
says Nancy Long, a high school and college classmate. "She
never felt attractive because she was gawky and wore glasses
and her hair was straight. It didn't help that most of her
friends dated regularly. I think she really envied the girls
from Homeland because they were petite and always well
put together and very, very popular with the boys."

Charlotte became a bit obsessed with the problem, record-
ing in her diary all the dates her friends had and pining after
any boy who talked to her at a party, writing: "I wish he
liked me at least a little," "He has had more prayers from
me," "I somehow feel that God might not want me to go
out with him," and "Frankly, I don't know why I even try."

In Charlotte's senior year, her parents arranged an escort
to Notre Dame's spring "Soiree" and hosted a late dinner
party for her and two dozen friends afterwards. Charlotte
had a marvelous time but was depressed that her date didn't
seem to. She prayed that he would ask her to his prom
several weeks later, but he didn't.

Finding an escort for her senior prom turned into a minor
crusade. She enlisted the help of all her girlfriends and finally, after several boys were called and had declined, Charlotte snared a date, the son of a well-to-do ophthalmologist
who also happened, not coincidentally, to be a friend of her
parents. He went to a prominent private boys' school,
Gilman. He called before the dance to ask Charlotte which
family car she wanted him to drive—the convertible or the
Continental.

"I was dumbfounded," Charlotte chirped to her diary. "But I chose the convertible."

They had a good enough time that she invited him to Notre Dame's White Dance, held the evening of her graduation. Then they went their separate ways. But not before Charlotte had asked him for one of his Gilman varsity letters, which she lovingly sewed onto her own white cardigan.

"I had to work so hard to get that blind date for the prom," says Charlotte, with a sigh. "It was really embarrassing. He never asked me out. No one in Baltimore ever asked me out. All my friends dated. If a boy was nice to me, then I'd spend a great deal of my energy for the next month liking him, thinking about him, or driving past his house, looking for his car, a boy who never even called me.

"That poor boy who took me to the prom called me a couple of times and I was head over heels. I don't know how I got that letter. I guess I asked him about it enough that he thought, 'Shut the broad up and give her a letter.' I was so proud of that thing. I even took it to Bermuda with me. You would have thought it was a serious boyfriend's letter sweater. It was my sweater, his spare letter. I just wanted someone so badly.

"I guess all that rejection contributed to my feeling so lucky when I finally found John Fedders. I felt so unworthy of him, like it was all a big mistake. I'd think, 'Nobody tell him, don't let him find out that he's really too good for me.'"

4

Charlotte did date one other boy before she met John Fedders—Dave, a Dartmouth history and language major who cared enough about her to take Catholic instruction, in preparation for converting if things got serious. But Charlotte felt that he just didn't quite match the O'Donnell family standards. Despite his attending an Ivy League school, Dave was not well-off financially, and the O'Donnells feared he was too much of a dreamy idealist to ever be as good a provider as the doctor had been.

Charlotte met him the summer after her senior year at Notre Dame, following a vacation in Bermuda with three school friends. The week was hardly as liberating as it might have been, but Charlotte wasn't quite as naive when she came back. She and her friends had had their first cocktail and actually had a date with some Navy officers they met at a beach party organized by the hotel. They went to see the Talbott Brothers, a legendary duo on the island, and then Charlotte received her first good-night kiss.

Of course, she and her friends were nevertheless up early

the next day for Sunday Mass. They hardly needed a chaperone. One of the group later became a nun.

When Charlotte returned, her family met her in New York City. They traveled through Quebec and then stayed for a week at Stonehurst Manor, a resort in Conway, New Hampshire. Dave was waiting tables there, earning money for college.

He introduced himself to the O'Donnell girls when he brought them dinner and later that night saw Charlotte playing bridge with her family. He sat down to watch and gave her some advice. Charlotte began referring to him in her diary as "Rave Dave." Soon, the two were playing Ping-Pong and pool and going to movies—*The Absent-Minded Professor* and *Jungle Cat.* Their eighteen-month romance stayed as innocent as those first dates.

"Dave was tall and blond and very, very nice," says Charlotte. "Stonehurst was a quiet, peaceful place, so we did things like playing cards and going to a square dance the resort hosted. I even helped him wash the dishes a couple of times. And we would just sit and talk and talk. He was the first boy I had ever really talked to.

"He taught me how to hold hands and to send little messages to each other that way. It was very sweet and very platonic. I remember once sitting in our living room. He was in a chair and I was sitting on the arm of it, sort of leaning against his shoulder, talking to my parents, and my father pulled me aside and told me that I was putting myself in an 'occasion of sin.' That's about as passionate as it ever got between us."

Yet, for a while, at least, Charlotte did think about Dave as being a serious beau. She wrote about him often in her diary. She was very happy that, when Dave visited her family during Christmas vacation, he attended Mass with them. She was careful to flash the Dartmouth charm he had given her for her bracelet when she had a picture taken with a Baltimore department store Santa Claus. She was also ecstatic when her parents let her go to Dartmouth's Winter Carnival. When Dave left following a visit, she wrote: "I hated to say goodbye. . . . I came into the room and cried. I really like him but C'est la vie! C'est l'amour! I hope he gets home okay."

But their relationship was not to last.

"There were two things that contributed to our breaking up," says Charlotte. "One was that Dave didn't have much money and his father was really sick, so that there was pressure on him from his family to quit school to save money. I used to write my mother and tell her to pray with me that his parents would let him follow through on his dream to study abroad. Dave had a lot of legitimate problems and could be sad when he wrote or called. I just wasn't mature enough to deal with it.

"The other main thing was that he wanted to be a college professor or an interpreter, neither of which brought in a lot of money. My parents didn't think he was going to be successful enough financially. I don't know how many times my father said that it's just as easy to fall in love with a rich man as it is with a poor man.

"So I sent Dave back his ring while he was abroad. It was a skunky, rotten thing for me to do. But I just couldn't do it face to face. I was afraid of his blowing up or of me backing down.

"It's just that I knew it wasn't right. In those days dating was serious. You thought immediately, 'Do I want to marry this man?' And if you didn't think so, then you shouldn't waste his or your time.

"All I ever wanted to be was a wife and mother. To marry a man who could give me children and a comfortable life, filled with love and little strife. That was my dream. So finding that man was very important. I went to college just because it was the thing to do. My parents just assumed we'd all go."

Charlotte remembers that they also assumed she'd study

nursing, which Charlotte dutifully did. The only other course she had ever considered was being a stewardess, but she dismissed that idea quickly because of her weight. Charlotte says she never really enjoyed nursing. "I was always afraid of doing something that would cause someone to die," she says.

The college Charlotte chose, however, was hardly prime hunting ground for husbands. In 1961, she began studies at Saint Joseph College, another all-girls' Catholic institution, buried in a tiny hamlet in the foothills of Maryland's Blue Ridge Mountains. There was literally one stoplight in the town of Emmitsburg, and four hundred girls in the school. They were all good Catholics who, like Charlotte, wanted good Catholic boys for husbands. They didn't even consider traveling to Gettysburg College, in the nearest big town, "because it was a state university and non-Catholic," Charlotte says with a laugh.

Fortunately for some, Mount Saint Mary's, a small all-boys' Catholic college, was ten minutes away by the school's bus (Saint Joe's girls weren't allowed to go over to "the Mount" by themselves). But Charlotte wouldn't meet another man who was interested in her until she spotted John Fedders in her senior year.

Emmitsburg was yet another sheltered world for her. And if it was at all possible, Saint Joseph's was even more stringent in its Catholicism than Notre Dame had been. That was because it wasn't just a college, it was a shrine to Mother Elizabeth Ann Seton, a teacher who started the college plus an order of sisters, and who would become the first American-born saint.

It was said that a little girl dying of leukemia in Baltimore had been saved by her parents' praying exclusively to Mother Seton, placing one of her relics near the sick child. That was one of the miracles attributed to her that led to Mother Seton's being beatified in Charlotte's sophomore

year. She was canonized two years later. At that time, the
school exhumed Seton's body and placed the remains in a
gold-leaf casket behind the main altar of the church.

Saint Joseph's grounds were holy. Busloads of pilgrims,
accumulating indulgences, came daily to visit Mother
Seton's homestead and her original classroom buildings. As
they passed by the library in which Charlotte and her classmates studied, they recited the rosary together in loud, joy-
ful voice.

The campus also had the Mother House, or regional
headquarters, for an order of nuns called the Daughters of
Charity. So, besides the twenty sisters administering the
shrine and the twenty sisters who taught in the college, nov-
ices and postulants roamed the hills in reclusive prayer. The
nuns were hard to miss—their habits had extravagant, tall
white crowns, as stiff and winged as Japanese paper sculp-
ture.

"God's geese," the girls used to jokingly call them. The
nun's heavy wooden rosaries also called attention to them—
students could hear the beads rattling as the sisters walked
in the halls and be forewarned to stop whatever pranks they
could be up to in such a proper place.

Even scientific courses retained a Catholic overtone. In
Nursing 203, for instance, an introduction to medical and
surgical nursing, Charlotte took the following notes during a
lecture: "We are expected to be excellent Catholic nurses. If
a patient becomes critically ill, call a priest, then a doctor.
Stay with the dying patient . . . say prayers for or with the
patient. If patient is non-Catholic or even Jewish try saying
the 'Our Father.' In an emergency, baptize anything that
looks like human tissue. . . . When the priest passes you in
the hall distributing Holy Communion, kneel; after he
passes, you can get up."

"Everything was a little more intense there because it was
a shrine," says Charlotte. "But I really believed that I was at
a very special, holy place and that made me feel very, very

special as well. And it was an exciting time because of Mother Seton's being beatified and then canonized. We all would pray at chapel for her becoming a saint. I would never have questioned that that girl in Baltimore had been saved through prayer to Mother Seton. I was just a good Catholic girl at a good Catholic school.

"It was an excellent nursing program, even with the religious doctrine. I also thought it was a really good school for me to attend because it allowed me to continue my slow, steady growth instead of thrusting me into something big that I couldn't cope with. There were only one hundred and four girls in my freshman class. It continued my childhood. Saint Joe's was a very safe place. I thought that was the best thing for me. Maybe it would have been better had I gone someplace that would have exposed me to more. But at the time I was very happy."

"Yeah, we were naive dumb bunnies, but that was acceptable in Emmitsburg," says Charlotte's friend Sally Sullivan, who studied nursing with her. "We joke about the rules, but I don't think there's any Joe's girl who doesn't tear up at Howard's 'Ave Maria,' the arrangement of that hymn we heard at convocations. We loved the place. Many of the sisters were very good to us, very protective. We also had wonderful friendships. It was so small, there was nothing for us to do but know each other. So we got to know our friends really well, like sisters. It truly was like a family."

Cloistered with other gentlewomen, Charlotte easily made friends and displayed the natural sense of fun that before she had generally saved for her family. She giggled and joked and quickly charmed classmates who took the time to draw her out. Several of them adopted her father's nickname for her, "Schatz," "treasure." The inscription under her senior year photo, composed by friends, reads: "She grasps Life's hand . . . a treasure chest of thoughts . . . praised stability . . . donned in mischief."

Of course, the mischief had to be pretty tame. Rules at

Saint Joe's were strict. Attendance at Sunday Mass and Thursday evening Benediction was mandatory. Rooms were checked to make sure students went to church. Caps and gowns, issued at freshman orientation, had to be worn to all chapel services, all four years.

"You had to go to Mass even if you were sick," remembers Nancy Bentley, another classmate of Charlotte's. "I tried to go to the infirmary one Sunday because I was so sick with the flu and they wouldn't let me."

Dress had to be demure and feminine. No tennis shoes, no pants worn on campus, even when students were on their way to ride horses, even when they were walking down dorm hallways to the bathroom. Slacks were allowed only in the privacy of their rooms. The standard dress was a kilt, matched with a crew-neck sweater, and loafers.

All meals were mandatory as well. Rooms had to be neat and orderly and were checked routinely. Mess brought demerits.

On weekdays, women had to be back on campus by 5 PM. The Student Center closed at 9 PM, and prayers were led by the hall proctors in the dorm each night immediately afterwards. For freshmen, lights out at 11 PM.

Not that they were missing much in town anyway, since Emmitsburg didn't even have a movie theater. Students weren't allowed to go into any of the town's few restaurants that served liquor without their parents. Drinking alcohol brought immediate expulsion. The only place they could really go to, then, was the drugstore, and that had to be in the company of another student. No solo trips off campus were allowed, even to buy aspirin.

When they did depart. Saint Joe's girls had to sign out and in. They were not allowed outside a 25-mile radius of the school's grounds without written permission from their parents. If they planned to go home for the weekend or to stay at the home of another student, they had to send postcards to their parents telling them when and how they were going to arrive. Housemothers would read and record those cards.

Single dating, one boy with one girl, was not permitted until senior year, and only if the couple was engaged. Boys were allowed only in the Student Union hall, never in the dorm lounges. There were a few mixers at Mount Saint Mary's, after which Saint Joe's students had a curfew of 11 PM. Sometimes boys would ride back to campus with girlfriends and snatch a quick embrace in front of the dorm. It had to be quick, though, since proctors and housemothers stood at the door waiting to flash the lights right at the appointed curfew hour. Friends could also be merciless, teasing those with dates, as they passed: "Child of Mary, you owe him nothing."

But chastity and the appearance of it was not a joke to the nuns. The body was the temple of the Lord. In *Youth Before God,* a collection of prayers and meditations popular with Saint Joe's girls, the Church deemed any kind of sexual pleasure outside marriage as being a "mortal sin against chastity."

"Subdue your passions and do not let yourself be carried off," it says. "Learn to give up things that are allowed now and then. . . . Do something that is hard and does not please you. A few times during the day overcome yourself in this way and you will soon sense how your will is being steeled."

The book includes an entire section on purity for girls, although it has no such directions for boys: "What is my attitude toward dress? Am I orderly and clean, or negligent? . . . do I dishonor the temple of God through vain and scandalous clothing? What is my attitude toward young men? Do I meet young men with polite modesty or with crude importunity and gaudiness? . . . Have I allowed myself to become bound to a young man of another faith so as to put myself in the danger of a mixed marriage? Is life all play for me, or am I preparing myself to be a helping, un-

derstanding companion on the way to God for my future
husband?"

Good Catholic women were to fight for purity and avoid
any kind of temptation or unseemly behavior. "If she ne-
glects this duty, then she will gamble away and lose that
beauty which she should treasure. She will be shallow and
superficial and in the end incapable of lasting and successful
love," continues *Youth Before God*.

The school administrators took such rhetoric to heart.
Some of Charlotte's nursing friends were once put on strict
social restriction—having to sign in at the dormitory hall's
front desk every hour when not on duty at the hospital—
when their hospital supervisor discovered them simply talking to three male interns in the clinic's waiting room right
after the clinic was closed.

But the girls retained their sense of humor about their
unisex predicament. Loaded on the "cattle car" buses, on
their way to Mount Saint Mary for a mixer, for instance,
they sang these songs, which Charlotte and her friends can
still belt out:

> Far below the hills of E'burg
> Everybody knows,
> There's a bunch of desperate spinsters,
> We're the girls from Joe's . . .
>
> The boys from Mount Saint Mary's
> They say are very sweet,
> But how the hell would we know,
> They're always on retreat
>
> Oh, I don't want no more of college life.
> Gee, Mom, I want to go home. . . .
>
> We drink Scotch with the Harvard men,
> Beer with the rest of them,

Milk with the Mountain men.
We like big, strong, umph,
Hairy-chested men,
But we ain't got them here.

Most of Charlotte's friends remained as ingenuous as she was. The most shocking aspect of their college careers before they began nursing was a teacher who actually—they fake gasps in telling the memory—smoked in class and wore high heels.

Their first glimpse of the outside world came when they made rounds as public health nurses in Hagerstown, driving a pink station wagon belonging to the health department and calling on families who needed such social services as immunizations for their babies.

"Everything was a shock to us in those days." jokes Sally Sullivan. "We were all pitifully shy. Even at the dances with the Mount, there were the with-it, really social girls and then there was us. The boys were on one side of the room and our gang was usually on the other."

Charlotte's roommate was also devout and wholesome. "Susan said grace before each meal and attended chapel almost every day," remembers Charlotte. "She was one of the valedictorians of our class. She was petite and incredibly neat. I felt like a slob next to her, because she was just so perfect. She'd take three days to write a letter to her boyfriend and it had beautiful handwriting and was poetically turned. Her drawers were unbelievably orderly.

"She was a perfectly lovely person, though. I know she helped inspire a little more devotion in me. Before I left for Rome she did a "spiritual bouquet" for me. She went to five Masses, five Holy Communions, ten visits to the Blessed Sacrament, said five rosaries, plus fifty ejaculations—short prayers. It meant that she offered the bouquet for me, to wash me of some of my sins and to protect me on this trip."

The trip to Rome was a school-sponsored pilgrimage for

the beatification of Mother Seton, March 17, 1963. Charlotte traveled in Italy for nine days. The summer after her
junior year, she would again travel to Europe, this time
visiting seven countries over seven weeks. This too was a
group tour, organized by a travel agency authorized by the
Church.

Her diary of this last trip in particular indicates how in
experienced and fearful of the world Charlotte was, how
guileless but prejudicial her culture could be.

June 29, 1964, aboard the MS *Aurelia:* "The Statue of
Liberty was beautiful—made me proud to be of the USA.
Joke of the day—some girl asked me if I were Jewish—after
a gasp I replied, 'Far from it.' "

August 5, in Paris: "We saw all the artists and found a
real lively place to drink and talk. Got home after a terrifying walk with three Negro men following us."

She was not a somber, reflective traveler. A viewing of a
Nazi concentration camp was as casually mentioned as what
she had to eat that night.

But the daily accounts also indicate how simple Charlotte
was, how affectionate, how easily she could be happy, how
quickly she became immersed in friends' lives. She wrote not
of the countless historic or artistic landmarks and sights, not
of the shopping, but of the people with whom she traveled—
the girl who fixed her hair, the boy who asked her to dance,
the illness of their tour guide's father.

July 20, Switzerland: "Stopped to swim in Lake Lucerne
in Uri. It was great and so refreshing . . . we came down
(after supper), went out and sang on a rock. Everyone was
so happy and gay. Hans, Parker, Gene, Dotti and we five
were all there . . . we laughed so hard. . . ."

"I didn't realize then what really made me happy," says
Charlotte. "I like people. I like having a lot of people
around. The country club and all was nice, but it wasn't
what made me happy. Give me a good relationship, some
unconditional love, that's all I really want. But then I

thought I was supposed to look for an ambitious man who could take care of me, like Daddy had."

Charlotte came upon a man much like Daddy five months later, in the second semester of her senior year, when she was finishing her nursing degree by working in Providence Hospital, in Washington, D.C.

Several of her other close friends were in the capital with Charlotte. Many of the restrictions of Saint Joe's were relaxed when the students lived off campus, so Charlotte and the other young women could actually experience some of Washington's nightlife firsthand. But they didn't go downtown or to Georgetown much, because their shifts on the hospital's wards were long.

Usually when they were off duty, the Saint Joe's nurses walked in a giggling brood to the Shrine of the Immaculate Conception for Mass, and then to eat in its cafeteria.

The Shrine just happened to be on the campus of Catholic University. That, of course, was part of the attraction for them. That also happened to be where John Fedders was in his second year in law school.

Early in February 1965, Charlotte spotted a lanky, handsome man across the cafeteria and lost her heart. She and the girls immediately dubbed him "the Jolly Green Giant" and set out to discover all they could about him. There was never any question about for whom the catch would be. Charlotte wanted to meet him and they were going to help her do so.

They noted the time of day he ate, and ate then as well. They followed him to the parking lot and learned that he drove a new Ford Falcon. They noted that he wore a new leather coat. They grilled a friendly waitress on what she knew about him.

On February 16, Charlotte wrote her parents: ". . . am after a guy at CU. Know nothing about him except he is at least 6'8" tall. (Looks like Paul Newman on stilts!) No, I'm not boy crazy—it's just a riot having someone to talk about." Two weeks later, her friends convinced her to send a silly note— "Have friends, will travel" —to John as he ate dinner, by way of the friendly waitress.

John crossed the cafeteria. "Charlotte saw him coming and got all aflutter," says Nancy Bentley. "The main thing I remember was his presence, big and hulking over the table."

John told them that he was a former basketball player at Marquette University and now was in CU law school. That, as Charlotte recalls, he wanted to have a dozen kids and that when he married he was going to take his bride on an elaborate honeymoon in the Bahamas. He was everything she wanted—a Catholic who wanted a family, a man who promised a comfortable life, a man with a dream for himself. And he was tall, dark, and handsome.

He asked them if they'd like to come to a party that evening that some of his law school buddies were throwing at a restaurant in the Holiday Inn next to CU's campus. Blushing, Charlotte managed to stammer out an acceptance.

"Charlotte was always bubbly, always laughing, always happy, but coming home after this—" begins Nancy Bentley. Sally Sullivan interrupts her. "Charlotte had always been a chatterer, but that night she was in the hallway twirling around, laughing, shouting. I think my mouth was hanging open; I just couldn't believe how Charlotte was acting. She was bursting with joy. He had talked to her and she was going to see him at this party. She had won the lottery of her life. She had met the man of her dreams. This was it.

"After that, Charlotte just wasn't normal. Everything in her life revolved around John."

5

"Dear Mommie and Daddy, have been dying to talk to you. So much has happened. Things are going super-well with John. He is just the finest fellow. I hope this lasts a while. Had a short date last Friday—just beer and talking. Saturday we went to a cocktail party at CU. It was a rush party for his graduate school fraternity, Phi Alpha Delta. . . . John was one of the co-chairmen so I was real proud to be his date. (He seemed proud to be mine too—that's what really counts!) . . . Do you know he even bought Jack Daniels black label for us to drink—he knew I considered it the BEST!! What a guy. Had a dinner date Sunday—only three hours, but it gave us both a little break. . . . I can't wait for you to meet him. Found out Saturday (one of his friends told me) that he was all-American b-ball at Marquette. How lucky am I. Now don't get upset. I'm being sensible and have not gone over the deep end so to speak but I'll say he is really GOOD and good for me!"

Charlotte wrote this letter twelve days after meeting John.

There was never any question in her mind that this was the man she wanted to marry, if only he would have her.

He seemed to want her. John had singled Charlotte out from her klatch of friends the night they went, on his invitation, to the law student's gathering. When the girls arrived, he held a lobby door open for them, then jokingly shut it on Charlotte as she tried to pass through. She and John laughed and started talking. His flip easy manner impressed her. So did his aplomb, and the popularity and respect he seemed to command from his compatriots.

Then John asked her out to see the movie *Zorba the Greek*. Even though she recalls that he fell asleep and slept through the entire film, she didn't care. She was so excited that he had called at all. They were together almost constantly after that.

John took her to the NCAA regional tournament at the University of Maryland, to a Gilbert and Sullivan light opera at Washington's Sylvan Theatre, and to more fraternity parties. Charlotte lovingly tucked all mementos into her bureau drawer, including a parking ticket he had received at Providence Hospital when he had come to pick her up, as if these slips of paper would validate the existence of a relationship that seemed so dreamlike to her.

Although John was never really possessive of her, he told Charlotte to save special outings for him. A flattering demand no other man had ever made of her. She spent less and less time with her girlfriends. "I only remember his getting really angry once while we were dating," she says. "It was over my seeing *My Fair Lady* with the girls. It was a big movie and he was annoyed that I hadn't waited to see it with him. I was taken aback because I didn't remember our having discussed going before. I felt very guilty because he acted so hurt. So I thought, 'Gosh, I'll never do anything like that again without asking him first.'

"We did go to see *Sound of Music* together after that and

the date was very romantic. He took my hand during the wedding scene."

Mostly, they dated around his studying—reading in a majestic Library of Congress, right next to the Supreme Court and the Capitol, followed by a steak-and-cheese sandwich at the Hot Shoppes on South Dakota Avenue. They also attended Mass every Sunday. John was as ardent a Catholic as Charlotte, mostly tutored as she had been in Catholic schools. She remembers that he often would carry a rosary in his pocket.

"Most of our dates were poor-student type things," says Charlotte. "He was putting himself through school. He worked as a proctor in the dorm he lived in, so he didn't have much spare money, even though his parents would basically send him 'book money' whenever he asked for it.

"Of course, I didn't care what we did, just as long as I was with him. When we first started seeing each other he would ask what I wanted to do and when I said I didn't care, he'd laugh, and once he said, 'This is too good to be true.' "

Charlotte had been originally attracted to John because of his height. It was unusual for her to meet anyone who towered over her. And indeed, they were a striking couple with their combined stature. Charlotte wouldn't notice until later, however, that, because he did stand a full foot higher than she, she couldn't just spontaneously reach over and kiss him. He would have to lean down for her lips to reach his cheek. She and her sisters remember that sometimes John just wouldn't accommodate such displays of affection.

Quickly her admiration for his physique was augmented by awe for his intellect. John was charming and witty, fast on the comeback. He was business editor for the law review, administrative editor of the law school newspaper, president of the student bar association, and an outstanding scholar.

Charlotte preened in April, two and a half months into their courtship, when he led his CU team to victory in a moot court competition with students from Fordham, Yale, and Cornell universities. The Sutherland Cup Appellate Court Competition was a substantial win for John, especially since a retired justice of the US Supreme Court was one of the judges. Charlotte presented him with a miniature wooden gavel as congratulations, despite the fact that she had been hurt when John neglected to introduce her to his parents that day. They had even been sitting directly in front of Charlotte in the audience, she says.

"John Fedders was everything Charlotte had been told to want in a man and probably thought she would never be able to get," says Nancy Long, Charlotte's Notre Dame friend who also studied nursing at Saint Joe's. "He was aggressive, bright, and a lawyer. She could go back to the Homeland crowd with him and say, 'I couldn't do this in high school, but look what I have now.' It gave her an image she had never had before. She fell madly in love as only a young person can and overlooked anything bad."

Charlotte swallowed her hurt when John didn't come to her graduation that May. Emmitsburg was only a two-hour drive from Washington, if that, but John was studying for his exams and she recalls that he couldn't be disturbed.

"I couldn't understand that," says Charlotte, "but I never said anything to him about it. I look back on it now and realize that was a telltale sign of how much he was willing to commit to me."

Of course, the following year, John didn't attend his own graduation ceremony from law school—even though he had been a leader of his class—because he was preparing for his law boards. Work simply came first. Charlotte learned to accept that. After all, her father was a workaholic.

"John studied all the time," she remembers. "He had incredible self-discipline. He never seemed nervous to me about his studies because he just worked all the time on them. He always seemed self-assured and cocky, although people he lived with told me how compulsive and high-strung he could be about his studies. But the truth is, once John put his mind to something, he could do anything."

He studied hard because he wanted a job with a Wall Street law firm, to be an undeniable success there, and to live on easy street, says Charlotte. "We didn't talk that much about his specific plans," she remembers. "But he definitely didn't plan to represent the poor. John never talked that much. I was the talker of the two. But I knew from the start how ambitious he was."

John traveled to Baltimore to meet Charlotte's parents shortly after her graduation from Saint Joe's. He also escorted her to her parents' elaborate twenty-fifth wedding anniversary celebration at Green Spring Inn two months later. John fit right in with the doctor's prosperous friends— this was a decade of incredible economic boom, and young men were applauded for high dreams. The O'Donnells, too, were impressed with the tall man and his tall aspirations.

Says Dotti, who was thirteen: "My only impression of Charlotte before this was about how social she must have been because of all the girlfriends she had in high school. She went away to school when I was only nine, so I don't remember much else. Then I met John. I knew that Charlotte absolutely had to be the best of all us sisters because this fellow wasn't going to have anything other than the very best, because he was so handsome."

A few months later, Dotti and Martha went to stay for a few days with Charlotte in Washington. John took the three O'Donnells out to dinner and the younger sisters developed their own crush on him. "We went to the Mayflower Hotel," remembers Dotti. "It was the first time I had ever had Caesar salad. He ordered aspic or something similar, which to me was so Continental. I just figured that this was it, that this was the way you were when you grew up."

Also that summer, Charlotte met his family. The visit went smoothly, except for his mother's accidentally calling her by the name of John's old girlfriend, says Charlotte. But the Fedders seemed to like the match.

With such approval from their families, Charlotte renewed her comitment to John. She found a nursing job at Georgetown University Hospital and arranged to work the night shift so that she could have her weekends free to be with him. She openly adored him.

Her friends felt differently about John.

"He treated her like dirt," says one. "[He said that] she was too fat. That he didn't like her hair. We'd hear him be very critical of her when he came to pick her up. And she'd be upset about it, but then she'd just do it. She'd lose the weight when he complained. She wasn't depressed about it, though; it was like John was remaking her. But she became more self-critical after that."

Charlotte thought so little of herself anyway that her own opinion came to mean almost nothing to her. Only John's approval really mattered and she gladly let him play Pygmalion to get it.

She was mortified once, however, when John asked her in front of some of his friends, "Charlotte, what happened to your mustache?" He had complained about her facial hair and Charlotte had taken it off with depilatory to please him. That indignity angered her. But for the most part, she just tolerated the criticism and followed his instrucions.

"One time he came to pick her up after work for dinner," remembers Nancy Long who shared a rowhouse with Charlotte when they worked at Georgetown, "and he was annoyed that Charlotte had perspired through her blouse. It was a very hot day. But he told her to change her clothes and she did without a word.

"He was critical about all our appearances. If my hair had been blown around by the wind, he'd comment on how messy it looked, or if he thought the dress I was wearing was ugly."

"John just didn't like us," says another Saint Joseph's

classmate. "We were all dumb according to him. He was very sarcastic to us. When we saw him in the lobby, it'd be 'Oh, you again.' But we never said anything about our not liking him to her because she was so excited about him. It wouldn't have made any difference anyway. I've never seen anyone so blinded by love.

"And on the surface, he seemed to have everything. He was a big man, athletic, very handsome, with great potential, a brilliant mind, a lawyer. Obviously, he was going to go far. On the outside, it looked perfect."

But their relationship didn't progress perfectly. In September, Charlotte remembers that John kissed her goodnight and told her he'd call the next morning. She didn't hear from him for almost two months.

For weeks she plaintively asked her roommates, "Did he call, did he call?" remembers Nancy Long. "She was just devastated. She did start to tell us a little bit then about some of John's criticism of her. But none of us told her that we hadn't liked him, because she was so depressed. We worried that it would just make her feel worse."

"We hadn't had a fight," says Charlotte. "Nothing. When he did call, eight weeks later, it was just 'Hi, Charlotte, how are you? This is John.' And I thought, 'John who?' I had never expected to hear from this man again. I had seen him a couple of times at parties, dating other girls. He had ignored me.

"It never occurred to me to call or walk up to him and say, 'Hey, what's going on?' I didn't have the confidence to do that. And, in 1965, a good girl knew that if she was dumped, she didn't fight it.

"I was just so relieved that he took me back that I didn't ask him to explain it. Later he told me that he felt he had to concentrate on his studies because it was his third year at law school, and, of course, I accepted it.

"My first reaction was to worry that I had gained weight

since he had seen me and that he would be displeased. But he told me for the first time either that first date back or shortly thereafter that he loved me. Of course, he also confused me by adding on to that, 'That's what you want me to say, isn't it?'

"But there was no gradual rebuilding at all. We were back together like gangbusters. He had first called around Thanksgiving and three weeks later he took me to the Barristers' Ball, the law school's big dance of the year. It was a big deal for him because he was president of the bar association. And he was introducing me as his lady."

December 11, 1965, the night of the black-tie ball, was very important to Charlotte. She had her hair frosted and swept up in a flaterring bouffant. She spent a large portion of her monthly paycheck on an extravagant evening gown with a velvet and beaded emerald bodice. She wore appropriate cocktail-length white gloves and had her shoes dyed emerald to match the dress.

"The girls I was living with made a big fuss over helping me dress," remembers Charlotte. "They were all so excited for me. For once, I felt really attractive."

But the evening's real importance for Charlotte came when she proved herself a valuable companion for John in a refined, formal gathering. At the Mayflower Hotel, she stood in the receiving line with John with the law school's dean, associate dean, and the rector of the university. She charmed them all. Even the dean's wife commented on Charlotte's tutored graciousness to John. In many ways, because of her association with the Homeland crowd and Notre Dame's stringent instruction in propriety, Charlottte was as much a catch for John as he was for her. Of course, she never saw it that way.

But the fact remained that John was a non-affluent boy, whose father had only finished high school. John had dreams of walking in higher circles, circles for which Charlotte was trained. He even joked to her about someday being governor of his home state. Socially, she would be an asset for him—cultivated, yet not threatening because she was naturally obedient and grateful to belong to him.

"That evening meant a great deal to me. One of the professors' wives actually told me I looked like Jackie Kennedy with my hairdo. All the feedback really buoyed my confidence that I could bring something to John. I think I passed a kind of test that night, whether eiher of us realized it or not. For years, the first thing that I hung on our Christmas tree was a simple red ball that we had gotten at the dance."

Charlotte felt close to John again, although he was beginning to talk seriously about moving to New York City following graduation. For Christmas, she gave him a black, lacquered rocking chair with a silver plaque on the back, inscribed with his full name and "Christmas 1965." "A la Jack kennedy," she says with a laugh. He gave her two Krementz pins, a gold circle with small rhinestones and pearls, and an ivory rose on a gold stem.

When she was home for the holidays, Charlotte dreamily danced in the kitchen when her mother put the Ray Conniff song "Santa, Make Me His Bride for Christmas" on their stereo. The tune had always been a favorite of the O'Donnell girls, but this Christmas Charlotte sang the words with a greater longing.

One month later, John told Charlotte they were going to be married.

"He had been saying, 'Oh, don't worry about my going to New York, you'll probably be there too,' " remembers Charlotte. "I had hung on little crumbs like that. Then one day he just walked in and told me the date in August that he had free for us to get married. Never asked, just told me. But I didn't care. I just thought it was all too good to be true. I didn't want scads of money, just a comfortable life with a house and lots of kids. Here was this man I was madly in love with, and I was going to get all this good stuff, too."

Charlotte called her mother and told her to start planning

the wedding. Within a month, she moved back home to help her parents organize the festivities. She took a job as a public health nurse in the county, earning an annual salary of $5,437, almost as much as a recently graduated lawyer could hope to start with. But most of her time was taken up with shopping, dress-fittings, showers, and parties.

That Easter, Charlotte traveled again to see John's family. It was her first glimpse of John as a community hero. Besides being an outstanding athlete in his high school, John had been a popular swim coach, taking a group of neophytes to victory at the state championships. He had even won an award as one of the state's most outstanding coaches. When John and Charlotte went shopping or to church, children he had coached ran to him.

"He really did seem like the Pied Piper then, he being so tall with all these kids hanging on him," says Charlotte. "I was so happy about what a wonderful father he was going to be."

During their drive to his parents, Charlotte recalls John singing along with the radio to the hit by Herman's Hermits, "Mrs. Brown, You've Got a Lovely Daughter," inserting O'Donnell for Brown. But their return to Towson was not as happy as their departure had been. John never seemed to like visiting the O'Donnells and Charlotte remembers their arguing about it. Besides the two months when John hadn't called Charlotte the previous fall, it was the first sign of trouble her parents saw.

"I think Charlotte had been doing all the driving," says her mother. "They just were not happy as they drove up. I was so excited to see them, because I had bought all these silly little presents and strung them all over the house with ribbons. She was so slow getting out of the car, I knew something wasn't right.

"Charlotte never knew this, but I saw a letter from him, opened already, on her dresser, and I read it. In that letter he wrote that he couldn't wait for them to be independent of us. I tell you, I thought I would die. I nearly died when she graduated from high school. But I closed it up and never said anything because I felt so guilty about having read her mail. I never even told Charles.

"John had never liked me but I just thought there was something wrong with me."

Although her friends never said anything to Charlotte about their concerns over John either, two of his friends did. "They told me that I didn't really know what I was getting into, that I was too nice for him," she remembers. "I was horrified. I just figured that it was sour grapes because John had beaten out one of the guys for the presidency of the student bar. The other I dismissed by thinking, 'You just don't know him as I do, you don't love him.' "

"I think Charlotte always felt that she could change John, that he would settle down, if she just loved him enough," says Nancy Long.

But Charlotte's dutiful place in John's life seemed hardly to be the gentle teacher. He was to be the catalyst. As were most brides of the era, she was to wait to respond to him. That spring, John wrote her a note after they had had a disagreement. He wrote rather than calling because, he said he couldn't afford a phone call. It's not clear whether he meant he couldn't afford the money or the time to call. He concluded with: "I love you, and don't you forget it—although I do have my nights of preferable separation."

Charlotte recalls, however, that John had been willing to disobey a priest for her. Earlier that year, they both felt that they had sinned when John touched Charlotte in what the Church decreed an improper manner. They each confessed to separate priests. Both clergymen told them the same thing: "Break up, you are obviously bad for each other."

"The priests said that we were leading each other into sin and therefore weren't right for each other," recalls Charlotte. "I remember feeling very bad about it. So did John. But we didn't stop seeing each other. We just tried to be good. John did say to me after that, though, that he had never sinned with his old girlfriend. I felt really awful, like I was corrupting this innocent man."

The priests Charlotte and John had seen were at Catholic University, so they proved no obstacle to the wedding to be held in the O'Donnells' parish in Towson. The young couple, however, did attend the pre-wedding sessions ordered by the Church. "A priest and a successfully married couple led the lectures," remembers Charlotte. "They talked about not going to bed angry and to not use birth control, and about mutual respect and communication. But I really didn't listen that carefully because John and I had never had a major argument before then. I just assumed either we wouldn't argue or that we'd be able to work things out easily."

The wedding day, August 13, 1966, dawned unusually clear and cool for the month, a reassuring blessing on the union about to take place. As Charlotte awoke and saw the sunshine, she said a swift prayer of thanks to the Blessed Mother. She had placed her statue of Mary on the windowsill so that she would bring good weather. Charlotte had also chosen blue bridesmaids' dresses because that was Mary's color, a gesture she hoped might add a small extra blessing to her marriage.

There was no time for lengthy prayers or meditation, though. The wedding was at high noon and there was still so much to do. She and her sisters were off to their mother's beauty parlor early to have their hair done. The bridesmaids would be arriving soon to dress at the O'Donnells' and pose for the photographer.

The night before, at the reception dinner, Charlotte had slipped John a note that read in part: "Tomorrow will bring the beginning of this love's fulfillment. I say beginning because I feel our love has only just commenced on the undoubtedly rugged road to perfection. Indeed, it will be difficult at times, but just loving each other will compensate for any and all hardships, as it will also complement our successes and joys."

Her thoughts this morning were hardly that solemn. She was atwitter with a maiden bride's imaginations. "My mother had come in to say good-night after we got home from the rehearsal dinner, to tell me about my wifely duties," says Charlotte. "She told me that it was my duty to accommodate my husband whenever he felt the urge, even if I was almost finished dressing for a big night out. And I, of course, thought, 'Gee, that sounds, like fun.' I was just very happy and very excited."

The rehearsal dinner, however, had not gone quite as smoothly as expected. "We were at the Tail of the Fox," remembers Charlotte's father, "which is a very nice private club. The guests were very nice people. One of the ladies walked up to John and said, 'Do you mind telling me how tall you really are?' And John says, 'I'm six-foot-ten; did you win your bet?' "

Charlotte had been a little hurt by John's choice of a wedding present for her. "I gave him fourteen-karat gold cufflinks and a tie pin. He gave me avocado-green alligator shoes and purse. I know they were expensive. I know he thought they were very nice. I guess it just showed our difference in cultures and standards I had wanted to give him something he could keep and use all his life as a reminder of the day. It was just a disappointment, especially having to open them in front of everyone. I never said I didn't like them, though, because I would have felt I was betraying him."

But this morning, nothing soured Charlotte's joy. She was about to enter a world that she had dreamed of all her life. Her only concern was that John had a slightly sore throat. She hadn't seen him to inquire after his health, however, because that was bad luck.

Charlotte's sister Susan, the next in line of the O'Donnell

girls, and Helen helped the bride don her ornate dress. The gown was white organza over taffeta, with an empire bodice embroidered with lace. The short sleeves were also lace, and a sleeveless coat of the same materials fell to the ground in a long train. Her veil headpiece was a web of pearls.

Her mother's dress was an elaborate pink affair, of stiff silk, with a jeweled bodice and matching short coat. The bridesmaids—Susan; John's sister; Nancy Shepard (Long); Charlotte's college roommate Sue Flanigan; and a high school classmate, Cyrilla Bollinger—wore floor-length dresses with matching headpieces of blue silk chrysanthemums.

Charlotte swept downstairs to have her portrait made. She was twenty-two years old. She was wearing contact lenses and had chiseled her weight down to 129 pounds. She smiled at the camera with unusual confidence and warmth.

The wedding at Towson's Immaculate Conception Church was formal and traditional. Charlotte's one innovation was the playing of "Here Comes the Bride" as she entered, a secular piece of music just allowed by Vatican II reforms the year before. She also asked the organist to play "O Lord, I Am Not Worthy."

The ceremony retained the reading of the epistle of Saint Paul that tied a wife to love, honor, and obey: ". . . the husband is head of the wife just as Christ is head of the Church . . . just as the Church submits to Christ, so should wives submit in everything to their husbands . . . each one of you should love his wife as he loves himself; and the wife should revere her husband."

The reception, too, was punctilious, a lavish sit-down dinner for two hundred in Baltimore's elegant Belvedere Hotel. The tables were covered with pink cloths, conveniently the same hue as Helen's dress, and were ringed by gold chairs. The three-course meal was served by waitresses in black dresses and stiff, bobbing white aprons and caps.

"Everything was just perfect," remembers Charlotte's sister Dotti. "The wedding was lovely, the band was great. The nicest of Baltimore were there in attendance."

While the guests danced and happily exchanged proper pleasantries, however, Charlotte says she got her first real taste of John's churlishness.

"There were two things that upset me that day. He was very annoyed when the wedding party discovered where he had hidden his car. He didn't want anybody to touch it. I hadn't told anybody where it was, but he was furious with me. He had me in tears right before we were supposed to march into the reception with 'Here Comes the Bride.'

"The other thing was he ground the wedding cake into my face after we cut it. People might think it's funny, but as I know now, it's a sign of power and control. It embarrassed me. The cake was all over me."

One of John's uncles filmed the cake-cutting. John and Charlotte kiddingly struggle over the knife before pushing the blade into the cake. They pick up two pieces. John places a linen napkin under his chin; she smiles at him adoringly. He faces the camera, grins, and holds up his finger in a "watch-this" gesture, then busses her on the lips.

John holds the cake to Charlotte's lips, hesitates as she starts to nibble daintily, then pushes it up into her nose, holding it there as the pastry crumbles. Charlotte steps back and turns away, bent over almost double. The film stops abruptly before another of John's uncles hurries to the bride to wipe her face with his handkerchief.

In the next photos, the garter-throwing also seems to embarrass Charlotte. She stands on a chair, with her leg on a table, her skirt hoisted modestly. John pushes the dress up her leg, she pushes it down. He turns away from her to play to the crowd, she reaches out for him and turns him back toward her. John grasps the garter right below her knee and tugs and tugs, as if it's stuck. She whispers something to him and finally he takes it and throws it.

Watching the films today, Charlotte grows quiet and sad.

"Everything my family prepared was so storybook and he just played around and clowned."

But the image of the ideal couple remained for wedding guests.

"That fall one of my teachers asked me to write an essay about what event in my life had affected me most," says Dotti. "I chose Charlotte's wedding. I wrote that her wedding had made the biggest difference in my life because I had never before seen 'the culmination of perfect love.'"

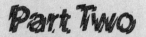

THE DUTIFUL WIFE

She'll be the first one to praise him, when he's going strong,
The last one to blame him when everything's wrong.
It's such a one-sided game that they play,
Ah, but women are funny that way.

"When a Woman Loves a Man"

Finally finished with the reception's rituals, Charlotte re-
treated to one of the hotel's private rooms to change. As she
pulled off her gown she discovered icing from the smashed
cake had trickled down her front and congealed into a
nasty, sweet plaster on her skin. She grimaced as she wiped
it off, but said nothing. She was a good sport, she could take
a joke as well as the next girl. Besides, the wedding ceremony had been beautiful, and she had more exciting things
to think about.

Charlotte still had no idea where John was taking her for
their honeymoon. All she knew was that they were spending
the first night in Washington, D.C., at the Sheraton-Park
Hotel on Connecticut Avenue. She had arranged that, and
the price was right—because they had had their reception at
the Belvedere, which was part of the Sheraton chain, the
night's stay was free.

After that, everything was unknown. Charlotte just knew
John had a big surprise planned. The Bahamas. It had to be
the Bahamas. He'd gone there for an Easter break during

school and loved it. The first time Charlotte had talked to him at the Shrine, a year and a half before, John had said that he was going to take his bride there. That on their wedding night he was going to play a record of the sexiest music he had ever heard. That he would make it all so romantic. Charlotte blushed at the thought and tittered nervously.

She yanked at her dress, a drop-waist linen shift, and then attacked her hair, stiff from the beautician's hair spray. She brushed, she twisted locks, she pouted. She had looked so fresh and lovely as a bride and now she just looked, well, wilted. But there was no time to fuss. She shoved her white pill-box hat on her head, put on her white gloves, and took one more critical look as she pinned on a corsage taken from her bouquet. She was ready.

When Charlotte met John, she was followed by an entourage of giggling girls in bright, pastel dresses, he by a gang of boisterous boys, crowing about what they had done to the groom's prized Ford Falcon.

The car. Charlotte had momentarily forgotten about the darn car. How bad was it? Why couldn't John believe that she didn't have anything to do with their decorating it? What was the big deal, anyway? Charlotte thought it'd be kinda fun to drive off, a fanfare of cans clattering behind them, advertising their happiness. She had waited all her life to be a Mrs. Somebody.

About twenty-five people gathered to toss rice and heart-shaped tissue cut-outs as they walked out of the hotel. John slowly inspected the car. It didn't look too bad, thought Charlotte. Only some shaving cream on the windshield and trunk and some rice and tissue inside. She remembers, however, that John started grumbling as soon as they drove off. The first order of business, he said, was to clean and vacuum the car.

Fifteen minutes later, just outside Baltimore, they stopped at a car wash.

That done, John seemed to relax a little, even though his sore throat continued to plague him. Charlotte slid across the car seat and slipped her arm through his, content.

Mr. and Mrs. John Fedders arrived at the Sheraton-Park in the late afternoon. He told her to take off her corsage before they went in. He didn't want to be conspicuous. Inside the lobby, Charlotte sat with the luggage, waiting. She kept her eyes cast demurely down as the bellhop took them upstairs and down the hall to their room. Her heart pounded as he reached the door.

The room was already occupied. So they trooped back to the lobby and John checked in all over again. By now everyone seemed to know they had just gotten married and Charlotte's face flamed red.

Finally safe in their room, Charlotte was mildly disappointed that John hadn't carried her over the threshold. That there didn't seem to be any champagne waiting.

John did present her, however, with two small boxes, one a wedding day gift, and the other a gift for her twenty-third birthday, which was the next day. He didn't want to wait until tomorrow to give them to her, he said.

"They were two gold charms for my charm bracelet," says Charlotte. "One was a scale of justice, and the other was a set of teeny wedding bands. I was really very touched by it. Those charms always meant a great deal to me."

The rest of the night, unfortunately, was not quite as wonderful as that moment. "John was sick. He slept and I had a bit of a problem. I found out a few days later from a doctor that I had a torn hymen. I was mortified later, when John told people and joked about it. I was just so embarrased that I had done this, our first encounter, so ungracefully. I had never felt too happy about my body anyway and this just made me feel worse about it. And guilty because it certainly wasn't his fault. It was my body that caused the problem.

"Then, in the middle of the night, one of his relatives called, just to annoy us. 'What are you doing?' he asked. He wanted to talk to John and I explained that he wasn't well and was asleep and the man says, 'Sure, he is.' It really embarrassed me."

Charlotte finally fell asleep, concentrating on imagining what the islands would look like.

The next morning, she and John woke early, starving. They ate in the hotel's coffee shop and attended noon Mass. After checking out, they got in the car and Charlotte waited. Now he'd tell her what fantasy trip he had arranged.

But John didn't. He just drove south. "Where should we go?" he finally asked. Charlotte figured he was joking and waited. He must be driving to the airport, she reassured herself. But he wasn't.

"John hadn't planned anything," remembers Charlotte. "We honestly just drove south, looking for someplace nice to stay. So I think I suggested going to Rocky Mount, in North Carolina, where my Aunt Cha-Cha lives, for the second night. We stayed in a dumpy motel. The nicest thing about that was I woke up the next day and found a huge picture and story about me on the front page of the society section, because my uncle had been so important in town. That made up for the fact that I had been buried in the back of the *Baltimore Sun*. We just weren't socially high enough to rank a big mention in Baltimore.

"Then John and I just sort of wound our way to North Carolina's Outer Banks, which were very rustic in those days, then to Virginia Beach, then back up to Williamsburg. We had a hard time getting decent rooms because we didn't have any kind of reservations and it was summer vacation time.

"I was crushed that John hadn't made any kind of plans at all. But I didn't say anything, because I didn't want him to think I was complaining. I also continued to have my physical problem, which wasn't very pleasant. It was terrible as honeymoons go, but it was mine and I told everyone it was wonderful."

Charlotte and John arrived back in Baltimore on August 21. The O'Donnells had gone to Ocean City, so the newlyweds were alone. They had much packing to do before leaving for New York City, where John had taken a job with the law firm Cadwalader, Wickersham, and Taft.

While they were at Virginia Beach, John had written a gracious thank-you to Charlotte's parents expressing his gratitude and praising the perfection of the wedding and reception: ". . . I want to say thank you for making a daughter so lovely . . . she and I are what our folks have given us. . . ."

But now John seemed to resent being back under the aegis of her family, says Charlotte. He also seemed to resent the fact that a doctor in Williamsburg had told her that she was hurt badly enough that she and John should abstain from sex for a week.

"We had a terrible fight," remembers Charlotte. "I told him I wanted to be with him, too, but the doctor had told me not to. Then John told me that he didn't like being married. That he was going to join the Army and that I would never see him again. I was frantic. He had me convinced that he was leaving me. I actually bolted all the doors —they had double cylinders—and held the key away from him. I couldn't believe his face, the hateful way he looked at me. It looked so distorted that I just stared at this person I didn't know.

"I promised him it'd be better. That I'd be what he wanted me to be. I'd be better. So we went upstairs to make love, despite what the doctor had said. He really set the tone for our marriage right there. He controlled me from that moment on, if he hadn't already. That kind of fear—of having come so close to his leaving me—I'd do anything to avoid it. It put me in line right away."

A few days later, her hurt over their fight dissolved in Charlotte's excitement about moving to New York City.

This was the real beginning of the life of Mr. and Mrs. John Fedders, she told herself as she drove north, following the U-Haul truck John was driving. Everything was going to be fine now. The honeymoon might have been less than first class, but their new home and his prospects certainly weren't.

A month before, Charlotte and John had leased a new, one-bedroom apartment at 75th Street and Second Avenue. She worried that they should have found something less expensive, but John wanted to live in Manhattan, an area befitting an associate in a prestigious Wall Street firm. Football hero Joe Namath lived nearby.

They arrived in the city on Labor Day weekend. Most of their furniture was delivered a few days later. It too was new and expensive—old hand-me-downs and bookshelves made with cinderblocks simply wouldn't do. The right image was crucial.

Shortly after announcing their engagement, Charlotte and John had ordered complete sets of living-room, dining-room, and bedroom furniture from C. H. Lears, a Baltimore store, owned by the father of one of Charlotte's Notre Dame classmates. The pieces were "Italian provincial" style—big, long, and tall to suit John's size, modern yet conservative, and very formal. Straight-backed and boxy, the furniture was probably more to John's tastes than to Charlotte's. But then again, most everything in their home was. Even their china had a masculinity about it—white plates rimmed with a thick, gold-leaf border, inset with tiny rectangles of indigo blue.

Buying three rooms of furniture was no small proposition financially. The total cost, says Charlotte: $7,000. An astounding sum in 1966 in any case, but especially for two people just out of school. John had had difficulty scraping together the $150 for Charlotte's modest engagement ring. So they borrowed the money from Charlotte's father and received credit from the furniture store. The payments on those loans would so siphon Charlotte and John's finances that she says she often had trouble buying their groceries. John's starting salary at Cadwalader, Wickersham, and Taft was about $8,000; her nursing salary $6,500.

But Charlotte tried not to worry as they moved in, enjoying the fuss over where things should be placed. No room for error in that either, though. Charlotte recalls that John wanted everything perfect from the onset. He carefully measured the distance from the ceiling to the nail for each picture he hung. Framing had to last a lifetime, too. The Williamsburg prints they received for a wedding present had to be encased in ornate gold frames, and done for the young couple by a ritzy frame shop on Third Avenue.

Those frames were one of several such only-the-best-will-do purchases. That Christmas, for instance, John told Charlotte to order Christmas cards imprinted with their names from a Hallmark store on Fifth Avenue. Soon, he ordered what would be the first of several tailor-made suits from Bernard Weatherill tailors. Part of John's reason for custommade clothes, of course, was his unusual height and lean physique. But the suits also had to have certain refined, Continental touches, such as real button holes in his coat sleeves, and button flies on his trousers; his custom-made shirts, French cuffs. He eventually wore suspenders, which he called "braces," as do Britons.

"I think John was insecure and thought having all these things would make him look better," say Charlotte. "I think he felt he had to prove himself. He entered Cadwalader at the same time Haven Roosevelt, one of FDR's grandsons, did. He was in a law firm with people from Harvard and Yale, and he was from the Midwest and Catholic University, with no family connections. So we had to have all the things that other people, like the Roosevelts, who were secure in their social status, overlooked. They didn't flash their money around. They lived in an older apartment with old furnishings. But we had to have this spiffy, spanking-clean apartment and all this furniture."

But Charlotte deferred to her husband and trusted him. John knew what he was doing, she was sure. Her father always had, and her mother trusted him. She dispelled her fears by concentrating on being proud of where John was working and what he was going to achieve.

That first month, John took her to see his office, and later they filmed the street where they lived and where John worked, in a home movie that reflects their small-town awe of their surroundings.

It starts from the roof of their apartment building. The camera sweeps the horizon, a swell of high rises. Then the viewer sees footage of the Irving Trust Building, John's office, and the plaque on the entrance, "One Wall Street." Again, there is a slow, panoramic creep of the camera up the length of the tall building, pausing momentarily at the spot where his office was, then up to the sky, in a telling metaphor of John's soaring ambitions.

His daily work experience was quite different from his wife's. While John took the subway downtown, to a sea of three-piece suits and well-guarded wallets, Charlotte took the train in the opposite direction, to East Harlem, where she had taken a job as a public health nurse. There, she worked in clinics and public schools, and made home visits. Most of her patients were poor, many on welfare; many spoke only Spanish. She had taken this job rather than a hospital position not out of social conscience but to ensure regular hours and free weekends. She wanted to be home to cook John's dinners and to be available on his free days.

Her territory was a decided shock to the sheltered Saint Joe's graduate, and Charlotte worried that she was "way over her head." But she did well in her position. She consistently received high marks in her progress reports and, by 1968, after two years in the field, her responsibilities included students enrolled in one parochial and three public schools, plus duties in a child health station and a chest and social hygiene clinic (i.e., tuberculosis and VD).

Right before Charlotte took maternity leave, her supervisor wrote this: "Mrs. Fedders has carried a heavy case load in the most difficult north end of the East Harlem district, which abounds in narcotic traffic and addiction. The multi-problem families with whom she works have frequently enormous medical and social pathology . . . her approach, always [is] sympathetic, understanding, never judgmental. She has been alert in detecting and referring the unmet needs of her patient and families . . . Mrs. Fedders is soft-spoken, dignified and composed. . . . She is an excellent public health nurse, courteous, patient, and uses sound judgment. . . . Her intelligence and interest in the job, in people, and in specific cases she is working with led to more responsible assignments as a trouble-shooter on the field. . . . She should be encouraged to compete in the promotional examination for supervisor of nurses."

But despite her own professional growth and accomplishments, Charlotte still saw John as the center of their world, his job as being the only one that mattered, his happiness with her as the only real talisman of her worth. She worked only because they needed the money. As soon as she had a baby she was going to quit for good.

Because her job was completely secondary in her mind, Charlotte loathed to disturb John with work-related problems. When she had difficulty transferring her nursing license from D.C. to the state of New York, something she had to do before she could start her job, Charlotte drove up to Albany and back, a round-trip drive of more than six hours, in one day, by herself.

Within a few weeks of starting her rounds, Charlotte was slugged in the face by an irritable pregnant woman she was visiting in Harlem. Her supervisor called the police, and Charlotte's lip swelled into an ugly knot. She hoped for sympathy from John when he came home. The whole incident had unnerved her. The woman had called her "a white bitch" before she struck and Charlotte hadn't even said anything to her yet. But John didn't baby his wife at all that she remembers.

"He didn't really show any concern about it," remembers Charlotte. "It was more just 'Well, you're okay,' and then he encouraged me to go back to work the next day. It was probably the best attitude for him to have because it kept me from being scared and sent me back on my way. But I was a little hurt that he didn't seem more worried about me."

Even though she worked full days for a full salary, Charlotte remained doggedly traditional. John was the head of the household; she would turn her paycheck over to John. If she needed money, she asked him for it. He didn't provide her with a weekly allowance. He kept the checkbook. She pushed herself to keep a spotless apartment as if she was home all the time, playing the perfect housewife. She alone did all the cleaning, even though it was John who set the standard for it.

Each Sunday night, for instance, she remembers that he held what he jokingly called a "white glove" inspection, making sure Charlotte had the apartment in top shape. Occasionally he would run his fingers along the tops of doors and windows.

Besides doing all the cleaning and shopping, she moved the car every day, as the city required, made his breakfast of two eggs over-easy, cooked every meal, did the wash, ironed his shirts, and packed his suitcase if he went off on business.

When Nancy Long and her husband visited Charlotte and John, Long was amazed to see that Charlotte's schedule seemed so dependent on his. "In the morning, she asked us not to go into the bathroom before John did, because he was so compulsive about his routine. We waited in the living room while he showered. John had the whole routine timed." Charlotte knew that when she heard John drop his newspaper, it was a good time for her to start his eggs and toast.

When Charlotte and John visited Long and her husband several months later, Long recalls that Charlotte slept on the floor of their living room so that John could stretch out on the fold-out double bed. Although her hostess disapproved, Charlotte was proud that she could "tough it out" to make John comfortable.

"We left their apartment in Cleveland around midnight to drive home," remembers Charlotte of that visit. "I drove for six hours in the dark, in an incredible fog, on the Pennsylvania Turnpike, while John slept. He didn't offer to drive until dawn. He would occasionally wake up and say, 'God, you're such a strong woman, you're so wonderful,' and go back to sleep. Of course, I was dying I was so tired, but I wasn't about to disappoint him and pull over to ask for help. I was so proud when he said that to me.

"I never moved the car seat up to adjust to the length of my legs. I kept it at his setting, and was proud of that too. That Saint Patrick's Day we went to a Marquette basketball game in the National Invitational Tournament at Madison Square Garden; we didn't have enough money for the cab ride home. So I walked the thirty blocks back in my high heels, and kept up with him, even with those long legs of his. It made me feel good about myself that I could keep up with him."

And John did reward Charlotte with generous gestures, much as Dr. O'Donnell had lavished gifts and trips on his girls. In the fall of 1967, for instance, he took Charlotte on a buying spree to her old favorite, Peck & Peck, in preparation for a Christmas visit to his parents. Of course, she didn't buy clothes on her own, because he controlled all their finances. But Charlotte saw this and the other shopping expeditions they went on in New York City as being very grand affairs.

"We went in on a Saturday and I tried on things for him

and he said I like this and this and this, and that's what I got. He bought me three lovely dresses, at full price. It made me feel wonderful because we were on show at that store. His paying that kind of attention to me was incredibly flattering."

Charlotte was also flattered by John's suggesting she try certain styles of the day. He gave her scarves, for instance, because he liked the way women slicked their hair back and tied it in ponytails with them. Charlotte struggled to grow out of her fine hair so she could wear the style, even though she didn't like it much. She lived for the times she murmured, "Oh, look at that woman, she's so beautiful," and John would respond, "You're prettier than all of them."

And there were simple, happy afternoons, just walking through the city, window-shopping in boutiques and art exhibits, or sauntering through Central Park, holding hands, dreaming.

"Those were very romantic moments," says Charlotte.

To repay John for his love, his confidence-building attention, his bringing her to such an exciting place, Charlotte worked hard to become not only a competent but a gracious hostess, a polite American 1960s version of a European nobleman's courtesan. The perfect helpmate to the rising attorney.

Their dinner parties were mostly business, recalls Charlotte. John usually chose the guests. They were typically legal associates and often the Roosevelts. She prepared meals that included "meat and potatoes," no short-changing casseroles, no matter how tight their budget, served on their good china, with silver settings and candlelight.

Serving the guests was also entirely her responsibility. John would loudly announce, so-and-so needs water, Charlotte, but he never left his seat to fetch it himself.

"The dinners were always sit-down, so that meant I could have only six total, because we had to have the full service," says Charlotte. "When we went to other people's homes, I saw them mixing their china sets, but we couldn't. And these had to be full meals. I used to have to use Kennedy half-dollars given to us as a wedding present to buy groceries for us, but we always had the money to host a big dinner, to put on a show. And I always put on a good show for him when we entertained.

"People must have thought we were rich. We had things people ahead of him in the firm didn't have. But he wanted that, especially since the first people we were really friendly with were the Roosevelts. John was always very competitive and our friendship with them gave him a taste for the good life.

"We used to do a lot with them. They would take us to Hyde Park, to the childhood home of Haven's grandmother Eleanor, to pay golf. We went to sports events with them. They'd also take us to Bunny's family home at Salter's Point in Massachusetts, on Buzzards Bay, near Martha's Vineyard. That was her family's summer home; their winter home was in Bermuda. It was right on the Sound, and there was a small golf course there too."

Quite a social circle. And although Charlotte was in another "poor cousin" relationship, similar to the one she had had with her Baltimore friends, she no longer felt quite as inferior to the Homeland contingent. How many of them knew a Roosevelt? How many of them had a husband succeeding on Wall Street in his mid-twenties? Someone whose career was built totally on his capabilities and not on any family connections?

Charlotte and John's climb was becoming an intoxicatingly fast one. One that infected her family as well. "I don't know how many times I heard my father say that he bet one of his lawyer friends wished that he had John Fedders as his son-in-law," she says.

John worked hard but didn't keep ridiculously late hours. He was generally home by 7 PM and would take time away from work for a month's vacation, things he would sacrifice later in his career. He seemed to be a natural. "Of all the firm's associates, he was the best," says Charlotte. "He told me that."

John even found his legal niche relatively early. Although he had planned to specialize in litigation, the Wall Street fever took hold and he switched to securities and corporate law. He never really discussed his changing professional interest with Charlotte, though. She just saw him circling tender offers in the morning paper as he ate breakfast.

When Charlotte's parents visited the newlyweds, John took his father-in-law for a tour of his office. Dr. O'Donnell remembers that when they passed the largest corner suites, the cushioned bastions of the partners, John smiled slowly and said, "Now, there's power corner."

Dr. O'Donnell says he disapproved of John's awe. Perhaps his son-in-law's obvious ambitions recalled a melody the doctor himself had hummed in youth and then outgrown. Perhaps it was too earnest an expression of a lust most were too sophisticated to warble outright.

But it was the song of the age. America was the richest country in the world and getting richer all the time. Anything was possible. Americans, after all, were even landing on the moon.

One of Martha O'Donnell's best memories of her brother-in-law, in fact, had to do with the Apollo ll astronauts. She came to New York City's ticker-tape parade for the returning crew in the summer of 1969. John took her and Dotti downtown and told them where to stand and wait, playing the concerned older brother. He'd be back to join them before the parade started.

"It was one of those golden moments with John," says Martha. "It was the first time I had ever ridden the subway during rush hour and I remember being so impressed with

John. He didn't even have to reach up to put his hand in those rings on the ceiling, he was so tall. He knew exactly where to go and what do to to get the best view of the parade.

"Even in that crush of people, he stood out."

7

John and Charlotte seemed to be a flawless portrait of the model, thriving, all-American couple, a portrait to be envied for its seamless perfection. Yet, that hard-cultivated persona was like the pictures Georges Seurat painted in the late-nineteenth century. Seurat meticulously lathered together dots of color to create images of polite Parisian gatherings and serene landscapes. The closer one moves to the canvas, however, the more the individual dots become evident and the smooth image distorts. Sometimes it dissipates entirely in a rainbow of paint smudges.

John's life seemed ideal, effortless perhaps. Yet to maintain that image, he seemed to need complete control over it, including his wife. Charlotte was naturally obliging and happy to comply to his imposed order. But she wasn't as disciplined as her husband. Sometimes she forgot his instructions. Sometimes she didn't understand them. Sometimes she was just plain stupid, he said.

Like forgetting to unplug the iron when she left the apartment to fetch more of John's laundry. He had told her to pull that plug, that turning it off wasn't enough. It'd just slipped her mind. But when she seemingly countermanded him with such forgetfulness, Charlotte recalls that John told her she was "openingly defying" him.

She made mental lists of things he didn't like, trying not to repeat the same mistakes. Once he had gotten angry when she took her winter coat off during Mass, even though she had on a Sunday dress underneath. Charlotte hadn't understood his reasoning. But John seemed so irritated, as he hissed at her to put it back on, that from then on she tried to always wear thinner dresses so that she could keep the coat on throughout the service without becoming overheated.

When Charlotte told John she needed a check, often he opened her purse to put it in her wallet. If her purse was messy, he told her to clean it up. He didn't like coffee on her breath, so she tried never to drink it around him. She also recalls that he didn't like her weighing over 135 pounds, so she started dieting whenever the scales' needle crept upward. He didn't like her hair frosted, so she didn't do it frequently. He didn't like her wearing much makeup, so generally all she wore was lipstick.

The list of "don'ts" seemed to get longer and longer and sometimes Charlotte just couldn't keep things straight. And the criticism was so hard to take.

"It was black-and-white with John," says Charlotte. "One day he'd tell me I was beautiful and the next day I was letting myself go. He'd say, 'Your hair's a wreck.' So I'd cut it or perm it and then that was all wrong too. I would cry when he'd say these things and that would disgust him. Crying was for babies. The criticism of my appearance really hurt, especially after I discovered that he was still carrying a photograph of his old girlfriend in his wallet." She remembers that most of their arguments, however, were about money. Because of the furniture loans and their high rent, paying the bills of their day-to-day living expenses was almost impossible.

"Yet, we'd have money for these binges, like the framing, the clothes, and the dinner parties," says Charlotte. "Whenever I tried to talk to him about it, we fought. Maybe it threatened him. Maybe he thought I was questioning his judgment. So he'd say something sarcastic and then I'd get upset and say something he'd consider argumentative or combative and it'd escalate from there. He hardly ever raised his voice. But he could be very brutal, very firm, very authoritative. I'd usually run away, crying, and go throw myself on the bed.

"He never followed me or came to see if I was all right. I never stayed away from him, though. Once, he threw me down on the bed and it frightened me, so I tried to never withhold sex from him."

About a year after they married, after a particularly explosive argument about their finances—Charlotte thinks it might have been caused by her opening her own checking account—John locked her out of their apartment. She spent the night with a friend from Catholic University's law school, who was also living in town. It was the first person she had really confided in about her disappointment over the honeymoon, their stretched pocketbooks, John's criticism of her. The friend listened sympathetically.

John didn't call her at work the next day to see if she was all right, she says. So Charlotte checked into the Barbizon Hotel for Women, afraid to go to the apartment, afraid to leave, not knowing what to do, all alone in New York City. Finally, she called John and he told her to come home. In Charlotte's mind, John was taking her back. "Thank God," she thought. They quickly reconciled and Charlotte closed the checking account that she suspected had caused the trouble.

Several months later, when she and John were visiting married friends in Maryland, the wife told Charlotte that she knew about the night she had stayed at the friend's house. Was there anything she could do to help?

"She did try to reach out to me and help me and I didn't respond," says Charlotte, "because I was so embarrassed. She was this beautiful blonde, a cheerleader-type woman, perky and happy and married to a seeming sweetheart of a husband. Here I was, sitting in this perfect little suburban home, which belonged to the perfect little suburban wife, and I was mortified that our mutual friend had told her that John and I fought. Mortified that our life was not as perfect as theirs seemed to be and ours was supposed to be. So I changed the subject."

Besides, everything was better with John now. That charming, witty winner-of-a-guy was back. Like a drug addict, Charlotte would tolerate the deterioration of almost everything else in her life for the rush she felt when John was good to her. "When things were bad with John they were very, very bad," she says, "but when they were good they were perfect."

Despite the occasional wrenching arguments, Charlotte remembers the first years of her marriage as happy. But she also remembers, vividly, the first time John hit her.

"It was in the early spring of 1968. I was sitting in a side chair next to the dining table. I think it was a Saturday morning. We had been talking for a while. All I remember is that this conversation seemed to be going well. That we were really conversing, sharing ideas. We were not fighting, we were not being sarcastic or nasty. I swear we were just talking.

"But I think it was the first time I disagreed with him and was sticking to my guns. I was arguing my point calmly, but I was holding to it.

"I got his right hand to the left side of my face," says Charlotte quietly, as, almost in a trance, she sweeps her right hand up across her body and sharply turns her face away from it. She pauses. "That's how I always got it." She repeats the gesture. "He is right-handed.

"It was one good sock to the left side of my ear. Then I heard this ringing sound. I found out later that he had broken my eardrum. I was completely shocked. I can remember thinking, 'I wasn't even yelling.' I would have thought I deserved it had I been yelling.

"I had been slapped in the face only once before in my life. My mother slapped me when I was about fourteen. I was being flip, so I knew I deserved it. She was the authority and I was talking back to her. I had the same feeling when John slapped me. I kept wondering what I had done wrong, like a child who had been spanked. I thought, 'I've been a naughty girl.' You see, I never considered myself an equal with him, so he was the authority figure disciplining the child, just as my mother had done that one time.

"I think he left and went to work. I sat and cried, a really sad cry, at the table. Then I just shut down. I felt sick. I couldn't eat. I'm sure I slept on the couch that night.

"My ear kept ringing, and I couldn't hear well, so I knew I had to see a doctor. I called the hospital to ask for a recommendation, because I didn't know anyone. I went to a doctor on East Sixty-eighth Street, in a neighborhood of old brownstones. It was an old, dark building, with a dark lobby. His office had older equipment. I knew it wasn't that bad but I was so upset and the office seemed so dark it felt as if I was going to a back alley for an abortion.

"I was ashamed to be going to a doctor because my husband had hit me. I sat in that examining room in a dental-type chair for ten minutes going back and forth, 'Should I tell him how it happened or not?' It seemed like an hour went by.

"Of course, I didn't tell him. I fought hard not to show any emotion and I lied. Said that I had blown my nose and suddenly heard this ringing. But I was mortified. I was convinced that he could look into my ear and know that it had been caused by a slap to the head. And I just knew he'd think, 'I wonder what she did to deserve this.' Because I didn't know that this ever happened between people who loved each other. I had never even seen my parents argue. My intelligence kept telling me that I had done nothing wrong, but my heart kept saying I must have. Why else would he have done it?"

The FBI estimates that today in this country a woman is battered every eighteen seconds; that every day, four women are beaten to death by their husbands or boyfriends; that more than 30 percent of female homicides are committed by their mates; and that battering predates one in four suicide attempts by females.

In fact, battering is the single major cause of injury to women, more significant than auto accidents, rapes, or muggings. According to data compiled by the Minnesota Department of Corrections, 20 percent of visits by women to emergency medical services are because of injuries inflicted by men they love. A total of one million women each year are believed to seek medical help after being hit. And in almost 24 percent of violent families, the wife is attacked when pregnant, says the National Coalition Against Domestic Violence.

Yet, only one out of twenty-five cases of abuse is recognized and treated as such by the medical professionals seeing them. The women are bandaged, billed, and sent home, without their doctors recommending the couple seek counseling or maybe without their even realizing what awaits their patients at home. Police studies show that once a man has attacked his woman, a taboo is broken. It is easier for him to strike her again. Her staying after that first attack is an unspoken acquiescence that can be fodder for his dominance. Although she believes each assault is the last, statistics indicate that the violence will only escalate over time.

These, of course, are recent studies. In 1968, no one talked about domestic violence. It was a private matter. And even if you had asked people what they thought about a man who hit his wife, you probably would have been told that the husband, as head of the household, had the right to quell a hysterical, shrewish woman. Nearly ten years later, during the feminist movement's prime, a Louis Harris poll revealed that one out of five Americans, including women, still approved of a man slapping his wife.

Or the people you quizzed might have repeated a joke to you. The comedian Jackie Gleason was inundated with laughter and approval on the television series *The Honeymooners,* when he shook his fist and threatened his wife: "To the moon, Alice. One more time and, pow, right in the kisser." ("Atta boy, Ralphie," applauded his henpecked friend Norton.) Charlotte remembers John's joking at cocktail parties that the first thing a man ought to do in his marriage is sock his wife to show her who's boss. People laughed, perhaps only tolerantly, then Charlotte followed suit, even though her stomach churned every time John said it.

Or you might have gotten this response: "Oh, that only happens in hot-blooded immigrant families or in ghettos." Or "She must like it; why else would she stay?"

All stereotypes and social attitudes that helped shove women back into a cage of silence and shame.

Charlotte couldn't imagine any other husband hitting his spouse. She concluded that she must be a horrible wife, indeed. How could she admit that to anyone, especially since the only real goal of her life was to be a good wife?

The doctor put a thin sheath on her eardrum to help heal Charlotte's physical ailment. Then Mrs. Fedders went home to fix dinner for her husband.

She says that she and John never talked about their fight or about her injury. He never offered an apology that she recalls. She never asked for one, afraid he would tell her what horrible deficiency in her personality had forced him to hit her. She just tried to forget it ever happened.

But shortly thereafter, perhaps trying to escape the tension caused by the slap and their avoidance of talking about it, Charlotte fled home to her parents in Towson. She stayed two days. During that time, she told her father what had happened.

"To break an eardrum," says Charlotte's father, "a slap has to be good and hard because air is what ruptures the eardrum. Nothing went down the ear canal to puncture it. The slap forced enough air down the canal to rupture the drum."

As a medical examiner, Dr. O'Donnell had seen a lot of ugly scenes. This, however, did shock him. "We were genteel folk," he says. "You can disagree but you don't get violent. I called his father and told him to talk to his son. That this wasn't what we raised our daughter for and that this marriage was headed for disaster."

John's father did call him. And then his mother called Charlotte. She recalls that her mother-in-law said, "Johnny's crying and he says that you left him." A true fact. A clever twisting of the sequence of events by John that engendered Charlotte's guilt. Suddenly she saw John as the victim of her insensitivity.

Her father didn't buy it. He says now emphatically: "I told Charlotte to divorce him, that he'd never change. She got upset with me."

"My father told me to get out while I still could," says Charlotte, "before I had children. But I just couldn't leave John. I loved him and I was convinced God had sent him to me as an accident, that I wasn't good enough for him. And I was convinced I couldn't live without a man and that John Fedders was my only chance. My father told me that of course I could, and that I probably wouldn't have to.

"I was only twenty-four at the time. I could have started over. But I thought the ultimate disgrace was a failed marriage, especially coming so soon after being married. Nobody was more shunned than a divorced woman. It wasn't just a scandal, though—the Church told me divorce was a sin. I could just scream now that I was that insecure."

Charlotte went back to New York City, back to John. She didn't communicate with her parents for several months, a silence that particularly hurt her father when he had a hernia operation and still didn't hear from his daughter. But Charlotte just couldn't talk with them. She was too embarrassed, and she believed that they were too disappointed in her. Denial was becoming one of Charlotte's main ways of coping with her life. If she could avoid people who knew about the flaws in her marriage, she could almost forget they existed.

And Charlotte was pregnant. John was ecstatic. She was sure everything would be fine now.

They had been saving up money to go to the 1968 Olympics at Mexico City, the honeymoon they really hadn't been able to afford. But now, with the baby coming, they happily diverted money to another use. It was time to buy a house.

House-hunting, however, seemed to cause a lot of tension between John and Charlotte. In late August, when Charlotte was almost four months pregnant, John hit her again.

"He hadn't threatened to hit me after he broke my eardrum," remembers Charlotte. "He never threatened it. I honestly don't believe any of the attacks were premeditated. Once it happens to you, though, you are afraid. You know it's there. And his being so big—he's a foot taller than me and weighs around two hundred thirty pounds—was very intimidating.

"But things seemed to be all right. He didn't seem to like how I looked pregnant, but we still had relations. And he was very happy about the baby. I thought everything was fine.

"There was tension over the fact that it was getting close to when we had to move out of the apartment and we still hadn't bought a house. I think we were arguing about something like what kind of street the house should be on. It wasn't anything big. It hardly ever was. The intensity of the argument, what you were talking about, didn't matter. There were plenty of big arguments that didn't erupt into violence. It depended on his mood.

"We had found a lovely little house in New Jersey. It was perfect. But it was on a busy street and I didn't want my child playing near so much traffic. We had always had that problem with my little sisters on York Road. So again, I was sticking to my guns.

"I was on the sofa. I remember because he towered over me. I was also just getting over tonsilitis, so I was probably lying down.

"He was very angry. He loomed over me and hit me in the abdomen, three, maybe five times, hard. I bent over, trying to protect my tummy. They were powerful blows. It felt like taking a heavy fall. It's not like someone is stabbing you so that it's sharp pain. It's pounding, like the pain you feel when you fall into a heavy object and bruise. It seemed like it went on forever, although the whole thing probably only lasted thirty seconds, maybe a minute. How long can a blow take?

"I tried to push him away, which only seemed to make him madder. He yelled that he didn't care if he killed me or the baby.

"I don't remember how it stopped. If I managed to run away or if he walked away. The next thing I remember clearly is sitting in the doctor's office.

"I was afraid for my baby. A baby was something I had wanted all my life, so I went to the doctor and told him what happened. I didn't see my own doctor; I saw one of his associates, who could take me the next day.

"Telling him was as bad as I thought it would be. He gave me a complete examination to make sure the baby was unharmed. It was humiliating. I thought that I had 'openly defied' John, so that I deserved being hit. I was already making excuses for John. He had been tense and I was nag-

ging him. We had found a perfect little house and I was
being stubborn. I had been sick and unable to take care of
the apartment the way I was supposed to and he was justifi-
ably angry.

"The doctor didn't say that what John had done was
wrong. He did tell me to get out of the situation. It wasn't
what I wanted to hear. I was pregnant. I was convinced I
couldn't take care of myself anyway. How could I take care
of a baby too, on my own? I guess I wanted to hear that it
would never happen again. Reassurance. Something.

"I found out in 1985 that all the doctor put on my record
was: 'Husband trouble.' But I didn't know that then. I assumed it said, 'Examined woman because her husband beat
her.' I was so embarrassed the next month when I went in to
see my doctor for my regular monthly appointment. I
wasn't going to bring up the last visit. But when he didn't
say anything I figured that he didn't want to discuss it, that
he thought I deserved it. It also reinforced the idea that this
wasn't something you should talk about. I never told another doctor until 1976."

Charlotte wasn't going to tell her family either. They had
already told her to leave John. Going back to him was the
first time she had really disobeyed her parents. She thought
they probably thought her a fool for staying with him. How
could she admit to them that John had hit her again? And
when she was carrying his child?

"After a while," says Charlotte, "I just stopped telling my
family. Because John and I'd get right back together, and
they couldn't understand. And it made it so uncomfortable
for them, knowing. So it became my own horrible secret."

Riding home on the bus from the doctor's office, Charlotte felt more alone than she ever had in her life. She was
helpless. To whom could she turn? When Charlotte got
home she said the rosary, as she frequently did in times of
stress, keeping her mind and her fingers busy. Then she
flipped through her *Women Before God* meditations, looking

for something to offer solace, something that fit her situation.

Of course, there was none for a wife fearful of her husband physically harming her. Instead, there were prayers such as this one, "For a Happy Married Life," included in *Mothers' Manual* by A. Francis Coomes, S.J.:

> Lord, bless and preserve my cherished husband, whom you have given to me. Let his life be long and blessed, comfortable and holy; let me ever be a blessing and a comfort to him, a sharer in all his sorrows, a consolation in all the accidents and trials of life. Make me forever lovable in his eyes and forever dear to him. . . . Keep me from all ungentleness; make me humble, yet strong and helpful . . .

Then Charlotte closed with a plea of her own. She recalls murmuring something such as: "Hail, Mary, full of grace, you are so wise. You are so loving. You were a good wife. Help me to be more like you. I don't seem to be able to understand my husband. Help me to understand him so that I can be a better person, a better woman, a better wife."

8

In the last week of September 1968, Charlotte and John moved into their new home, a cream-colored, six-room Tudor cottage surrounded by dogwoods, in Westchester County's Pelham Manor, a suburb just outside New York City. John's commute to Wall Street would take about fifty minutes. Charlotte would drive him to the last subway stop on the Pelham Bay line, in the Bronx, which bordered the county. She continued to work only through the end of December. The baby was expected to arrive in February.

The neighborhood was a homogeneous, established one, populated with husbands employed in Manhattan and their well-educated wives who stayed home with well-scrubbed babies and joined the Junior League. Like countless other suburbs of the age, Pelham was a verdant, female ghetto during the day, a pretty hatchery for the upwardly mobile.

It was also a cloister with which Charlotte was familiar and comfortable. She would happily retreat into the world of Pablum and housework, hearing nothing but the coo of her baby for hours at a time, occasionally chatting briefly with other mothers pushing children in strollers, her world shrinking to the circumference of her house and the man she lived with.

Their street, Clay Avenue, was more modest than most of the affluent byways of Pelham, but it was sheltered, shady, and quiet. Tall trees and thick, well-trimmed hedges lined the streets and delineated individual yards. In the spring, settled and content, Charlotte would watch for flowers to shoot from bulbs planted by the previous owner, a widow who had recently died.

The first few days they were in the house, in fact, John and Charlotte shared the space with the widow's furniture, awaiting the estate auction her executors were going to hold that Saturday. They crammed all their possessions into the bedroom and posted a sign telling people coming to inspect the furniture that it was off limits. But even when she was trying to nap, exhausted from the move, Charlotte had to keep shooing out strangers.

"But we actually had a lot of fun the day of the auction," says Charlotte. "We bought a table and cabinet and a couple of other things for very little."

They couldn't buy too much, however, because their money was basically spent. Drained by the payments on the furniture purchased in Baltimore, Charlotte and John didn't have much cash saved. They had needed two loans to pay for the $29,500 house—a loan for the down payment as well as the mortgage. John was making about $15,000, and despite the fact Charlotte's paycheck would shortly stop, the banks were more than willing to take a chance on the young lawyer.

Charlotte had been surprised intially that John wanted an older house that needed a lot of work; he had been so adamant two years earlier about finding a new, clean apartment building in the city. The kitchen on Clay Avenue, for instance, had a filthy, old linoleum floor and an almost unworkable sink. But they had found the house through one of

the law firm's partners, who had purchased a similar house
in the area and renovated it, and John trusted the advice of
his superior. Driving to see the house for the first time,
Charlotte remembers John forbidding her to say anything
against it.

A few weeks after they moved in, John's parents came to
help paint and clean.

"By the time they left a week later," remembers Charlotte, "there wasn't anything that didn't look brand-new except the kitchen, the basement, and the spare bedroom. We
worked dawn to dusk, every day they were here. We painted
everything, including the closets. It was spotless.

"His mother was very conscious about appearance. She
didn't like us to take a snapshot of her if she hadn't just had
her hair done. Her house was always extremely clean. She
had ant traps in practically every corner. I remember she
was worried once that neighbors might think she had a
problem at her home when the exterminators were going to
the house next door and parked in front of her house. I
think her neatness probably had to do with the concept of
cleanliness being next to godliness.

"John's father had his own business, installing and repair-
ing industrial refrigerators. He would be dirty when he came
home. They had a separate shower built downstairs in their
basement, and he would use the garage entrance, go downstairs, and shower before he came upstairs.

"Everything had to be very orderly as well. She bought
groceries on sale to save money and then marked almost
everything, cans, soap, even Kleenex boxes, with magic
markers or nail polish as to when they were bought and at
what price.

"I remember there was some controversy and tension between John and his mother when they came to help us about
what was going to be done first. I didn't have anything to
say about it, so I stayed out of it. I never questioned her,
even the time right after we were married, when John and I

went to visit them and she put us in separate rooms. We were married, but I slept with John's sister. John didn't challenge it either.

"She seemed to have complete control over everybody. She purchased and laid out all his father's clothes. She kept all his books. When she came to stay with us, often to help take care of me right after I had had one of the babies, she was the boss. She didn't let the boys open the refrigerator without asking her first. She thought it was terrible that I would let the children open the door and stand there for a few minutes trying to decide what they wanted. I think their not asking for permission was an act of disrespect for adults in her mind.

"No one crossed her. She wasn't nasty or vindictive; she just had this terrible Catholic saint martyrdom about her when she was upset. She'd say to my kids, 'If you love [me] —you won't do that.'

"She did everything by the Catholic rules. She went to church as much as possible. Every time she got into the car, even to go to the grocery store, she'd say, 'Jesus, Mary, Joseph, we pray, be with us on our way.'

"She seemed to have total control of her emotions and a strong belief that self-discipline could accomplish great things.

"I think John picked up a lot of that. I know he was an altar boy, as a daily-type thing, for several years. He was very disciplined about doing his homework and I'm sure that he rarely did anything wrong. So I doubt she really had to punish him much.

"She had several unsuccessful pregnancies in John's early childhood and gave birth to at least one baby who died. So sometimes she was, understandably, preoccupied with those tragedies. But she was very, very proud of John and his accomplishments. She even did his laundry for him all through college. He'd mail it home to her.

"But even though he loved her, I think John had felt

dominated by her, growing up, so that he wanted the total control now."

Despite tensions over renovating the house, these months were happy and peaceful for the young couple as they awaited the coming of their baby.

John wanted his first child to be a boy, and he was certain that it was, says Charlotte. Certain enough to cover the pink walls of the baby's bedroom with blue paint. Before beginning work in earnest he had taken the paintbrush and written the name he and Charlotte had chosen across the wall in big letters.

Charlotte remembers that John wasn't the type to be fascinated by a pregnant body, wanting to listen to the child's heartbeat or kicks. He made a lot of jokes about pregnant women being fat. In the early months of her pregnancy, Charlotte had run into the bathroom after they had made love to put on a nightgown so he couldn't see her rounding tummy. John told Charlotte that they couldn't afford to buy her a Big Mac, a new McDonald's hamburger, one of the few real cravings she had during those nine months. But John did attend Lamaze classes with Charlotte.

"He was very good about that," remembers Charlotte. "I remember him turning pale only once, when we saw a film sort of from the doctor's view of a birth. He came to every class. We were going to Elizabeth Bing, one of the pioneers in Lamaze, because the Roosevelts had gone to her. That's how we got interested in it."

Fortunately, Charlotte's first pregnancy was a relatively easy one. Fortunate in that John didn't seem to tolerate his wife being ill. When John caught a stomach virus, Charlotte says he demanded that she spoon-feed him soup. If she contracted the flu and was sick to her stomach, however, she had to fend for herself. But with this pregnancy, his seeming indifference didn't matter much. Charlotte was healthy and resilient. The day before she gave birth, in fact, Charlotte

walked almost a mile in snow with John to the house of one
of his partners.

"It was one of the major snowstorms that New York ever
had," remembers Charlotte. "The highways weren't even
open. One of the firm's partners lived nearby and John had
helped shovel out this man's car. We had walked over and
back to do it. I felt fine.

"When my water broke the next morning, we called that
partner. Our car was in our garage and the snow was piled
up God knows how high. John hadn't shoveled us out. We
weren't in too big of a hurry, though, because I wasn't having any contractions yet, so I knew it would be a while
before I was really in labor. I drank a little hot tea and fixed
John's breakfast. The usual thing, two eggs over-easy, bacon
or sausage, and toast.

"The partner picked us up but we could only make it as
far as the Bronx subway stop. Just as the train was ap-
proaching, some guy tried to snatch a lady's purse and John
went running after him. The partner stayed with me until
John got back a few minutes later.

"We got on the subway and then had to take a bus to get
to the hospital from the station. Luke was born at 11:30 PM,
February 12. John was there coaching me. He was very
emotional and held my hand and wiped my brow. The
births of my children were some of John's and my happiest
days together."

Within a few hours of having Luke, Charlotte baptized
him herself, holding her newborn close and dabbing his fore-
head with water from a glass sitting on her nightstand, saying: "I baptize thee in the name of the Father, and the Son,
and the Holy Ghost." It was a moment of special bonding
between mother and son and was an act John seemed to be
proud of as well. Charlotte baptized all her children this
way and John seemed pleased by it.

Two weeks after Luke was born was the official ceremony
at John and Charlotte's church in Pelham. Charlotte hosted

a party afterward, preparing a meal for about twenty guests. They had the ceremony so soon after Luke's birth because John wanted an uncle to be the godfather and that was the only time he could come to New York for it. That was fine by Charlotte; she was tired but jubilant.

"The food was lovely for that baptism party," remembers Charlotte's friend Nancy Long, who drove down from New Haven, Connecticut, to attend. "There was a fire in the fireplace. It really was a lovely affair. She had done it all herself. John was so proud of Luke. He had his son."

The only bad moment came later that day, when John and his sister had an argument. Charlotte listened with concern and confusion; she and her siblings had rarely fought. But she also listened with an almost desperate interest. It was the first time she had heard John argue with someone else. Charlotte noted how his sister's rising anger cooled John, how he got quieter as she became more emotional, his answers becoming shorter and curt. She resolved to try not to make the same mistakes herself.

Right now, anyway, most of her time was taken up with Luke. Care of the baby fell almost entirely to Charlotte, she says. John never changed Luke's diaper except for the day before Luke's baptismal ceremony, when Charlotte left to have her hair done. She doesn't recall his ever getting up in the middle of the night to quiet or feed Luke.

But John did like to bounce the baby and was elated when Luke stood in his crib as early as six months old, evidence that his son might grow into an athlete. John could be rough with the baby, but obviously, thought Charlotte, he loved his son.

The home movie of Luke's first Christmas almost a year later shows John lying on the floor, flat on his back in front of a Christmas tree stacked high with toys. He holds Luke above him, throws him breath-gaspingly high, catches him, throws him again, and turns him over, letting the baby slide down his belly to the floor. Luke laughs and flashes dimples and climbs up for more. John patiently lets his son kick and fall over him, rolling and laughing, then hugs him close and rocks him for a minute. It was the kind of scene that sustained Charlotte for months.

In March 1969, a little over a month after Luke was born, John presented Charlotte with a black Labrador puppy. She really didn't want it, she knew nothing about dogs, and there was no backyard for it. But it seemed to complete the image John wanted to project. John and Charlotte named the dog Cassius, playing off the name of their street, "Clay." For the following Christmas, December 1970, she and John had a formal portrait taken in the living room, with Luke and Cassius. Charlotte was always amused by the photo, since Cassius was never allowed in the living room except for that day.

November fifteenth, Charlotte and John hosted Cadwalader, Wickersham, and Taft's annual party. "John came home and told me that we were going to have the 'privilege' of hosting the firm's party for seventy people.

"I was panicked. I had done little parties but never anything like this. The other people who had done it were partners, and they had huge homes and domestic help. I definitely remember that we were the only associates to ever have anything this size, something for the whole firm.

"Of course, we had to have the kitchen redone because of this party. So, two days before all these people were coming, everything from the kitchen was in the dining room. It was a mess. I couldn't have done it without my sister Martha. I had to do all the cooking and cleaning. She helped. John went and got the ice and liquor basically. But it turned out to be a beautiful evening. My mother had given me all her recipes for a cocktail buffet. I fixed meatballs, chicken wings, dips, steak tartare, pastries, shrimp molds. I don't think anyone went home hungry.

"Those events were usually high times for us. We'd pull it

off and people were impressed. John would be very proud and up, up, up. He'd hug me and tell me how great I was, and I'd be singing in the kitchen as I cleaned up. He'd go to bed, leaving me to clean, but I didn't care. I had so much energy then it didn't matter, and I was happy that he was so happy. Entertaining was something I could do, knowing it would please him rather than doing it out of fear, or to avoid making him angry. So they were good experiences for me."

That night, Charlotte managed to gracefully juggle all her roles, playing hostess to dozens and taking care of her baby, without missing a discernible beat. Her self-confidence was perhaps at the highest it would ever be in her married life.

Says her sister Martha: "Luke was crying because John kept coming into his bedroom and flipping on the light to introduce him to people. Charlotte went up there but Luke still kept crying. She realized right away, in all this hubbub, that the trouble was that she had her contacts in and Luke was used to seeing her with glasses. So she just put her glasses on overtop her contacts and sang to him and Luke fell asleep immediately."

"I basically was living this charmed life then," says Charlotte. "I was taking care of only one lovely little baby. John seemed happy. We even took a few trips together by ourselves. My parents seemed to be happier with us. They gave us a washing machine for Christmas the first year we were in the house and John was honestly so touched by it that he cried.

"Those were our most innocent days." Charlotte doesn't remember any physical abuse during the three years she and John lived in Pelham. But she faced new problems with John— "black moods" and silences that could stretch on for days. She had learned that during an argument the more distraught she became the more likely John was to clam up and shut her out entirely, at best becoming brusque and patronizing, at worst glowering at her without saying a word.

But these moods were different, more unnerving, because they seemed to come out of nowhere and to last forever. She remembers that small transgressions could trigger them, but nothing she did seemed to pull John out of them.

Two especially difficult times occurred around Thanksgiving of 1969 and Luke's first birthday in February 1970.

With John's permission, Charlotte promised to spend Thanksgiving with her parents. She says that John made no attempt to leave with her that morning. Instead, he lay in front of the television set, refusing to answer her questions. She finally left him there, driving down to Towson and back in one day with Luke in tow, to keep John from getting angrier.

Again, with John's prior approval, Charlotte had made arrangements to celebrate Luke's first birthday at her parents' home in Maryland. John seemed withdrawn the day they were to leave and told her to drive ahead; he would join her there, he had things to do at work. She and her parents delayed the party a day, hoping John would show up. He never arrived.

The home movie of the party captures somber smiles on the faces of Charlotte's family. Luke is sleepy when they give him his cake, in a noticeably lackluster presentation. Charlotte remembers that she finally woke him from a nap to eat the cake when it became clear John wasn't coming. Not exactly the celebration she had hoped for her firstborn's first birthday.

"Those were the first real black moods I remember after we got married," says Charlotte. "Looking back on it I realized that his not calling me for those eight weeks when we were dating was a withdrawal period like this one. Right before we were supposed to go down to my parents', John had been getting quieter. I blamed myself later that I had made it worse by pushing to go, by going ahead without him, even though he had approved of the trip before. But I could always figure out why it was my fault. Real easy. I would think, 'I shouldn't have gone home. I should have kept my mouth shut. I shouldn't have gotten upset.'

"The physical stuff was bad enough, but I think the silences were worse. They were psychological torture. You could never predict what would send him into one of these silences. Or how to get him out of them.

"These silences were the ultimate control. He must have known not talking to me, not responding, would make me crazy. You can't imagine what it's like to walk into a room where your husband is, your husband, and to get absolutely no response. None. For days. Maybe weeks. Or just responses like: 'What's wrong?' I'd ask. 'Nothing's wrong. I'm fine.' 'But you're not acting normal.' 'I'm acting perfectly normal.' 'Why won't you kiss me, then?' 'You want a kiss? Here,' and he'd kiss the air.

"There was nothing I could do to make him come out of it. He came out of it when he was ready, not before. I would get more and more emotional, trying to get a response, and he would get more and more silent. Self-control was very important to him, it was important in the Catholic Church, and I think he viewed my getting upset, losing control, as being very wrong, a sin. He would look at me with disgust. Or if he answered, it was terse and icy. 'Look in the mirror,' he'd say. 'There's our problem.' "

John's rejection of her would so frustrate Charlotte that sometimes, out of self-loathing, she would actually slap her own face.

"The first time I did that was in New York City," she says. "We had been arguing about something and he was lying in the bed ignoring me. I tried to seduce him. Making love had always seemed to settle arguments between us, to make things better. The culture at the time told us that sex was the way to make men happy, that that was the main thing they wanted. So I tried everything. I even begged him to make love to me, and he rejected me. I was humiliated and hysterical. Finally I said, 'Maybe you're queer.'

"The way he turned and looked at me terrified me. I was sitting in the rocker I had given him, by the bedroom window, and I slapped myself in the face, several times, hard. 'I'm so stupid,' I said, whack, 'I'm so ugly,' whack, 'I'm so fat,' whack. He watched me do it.

"By Pelham, I would do what he told me to. I'd look in the mirror, at the cause of all our problems, and say, 'I hate myself,' over and over again as I slapped. His response was 'You see, you're crazy. That proves my point.' "

To try to prevent arguments and his silences, Charlotte became obsessed with not repeating mistakes. For instance, somewhere along the line when she was packing his bag for a business trip, she forgot an item he needed and had been reprimanded. Consequently, she hung a list of everything he needed in his closet and referred to it each time she packed after that.

"It was almost like a game—'Well, he won't catch me doing that again.' I was very sensitive. For me to put up that list, he had probably said something like 'You forgot my razor, don't do that again,' and I would be crushed by that criticism and get too upset.

"I've often thought that had I not been so afraid to make a mistake and so anxious to please at the very beginning of our marriage and had had enough confidence just to tell him a couple of times that he was being ridiculous, that maybe things would have been different. If I had realized that making a mistake was no big deal and treated it as such, maybe he would have learned to accept that I'm human, he's human. I think my fear almost justified his anger to himself. Because I was so apologetic, my goof really was a big deal after all and he was right to be mad."

Reconciliations, when they came, generally happened quickly, and revolved around making love. There was little

talking beforehand. But a honeymoon period, during which
John was attentive and loving, always followed. For Charlotte sex was an unspoken acceptance and praise of her, and
she subconsciously defined it as expression of what John
really felt about her.

Though other aspects of their relationship fell into painful
cycles, she says their sex life remained healthy, and perhaps
was the most normal, most naturally loving, part of their
relationship. Charlotte was not the first to try to be content
in an otherwise mediocre marriage because of the gratifying
communication provided by love-making. She came to rely
on it to establish a temporarily healing yet ultimately false
intimacy between them.

"I can't explain how these reconciliations happened. I
would look for little signs to tell me that he was coming out
of it. He would answer a question that day. Or actually give
me a command instead of being silent. Somehow, we'd end
up in bed and—boom—things would be back to normal,
immediately. There was no gradual, tentative building. Back
to normal.

"I guess it is surprising that our sex life was normal and
giving. But it was. There were never complaints on either
side. It wasn't routine. He wasn't domineering or aggressive.
Sometimes he tickled me hard. But he could be gentle. It
was spontaneous and very loving. I guess that's why we
always turned to it when nothing else seemed to work between us."

Charlotte wasn't the only one to feel the sting of John's
occasional aloofness, however. Slowly, her family was expe-
riencing his sarcasm and his moods for themselves.

"I felt that John never approved of me," says Dotti, who
was in high school during Charlotte and John's time in Pelham. "And he rarely spoke to me. When he did, it generally
wasn't very nice. One time, when they were visiting us in
Towson, I was in my parents' room watching television and

talking on the phone and John came in, I guess to use my parents' bathroom. I was sitting cross-legged on the bed. As he walked by, he said, 'You ought to sit like a lady—that's indecent.'

"But I thought John was so cool, that his humor was so cool. He was sharp as a tack. He'd set you up for the kill, to pull the rug out from under you. One time we were coming back from church, and John said to Mimi [Charlotte's middle sister], who didn't have the best voice, 'What did you do with the money?' She thought he was talking about the collection money and said, 'What money?' And he answers, 'The money for singing lessons.'

"If you said something that was really obvious, his reply was 'No shit, Red Ryder,' or if you said that you didn't like a band or a politician, he'd say, 'Yeah? Well, they always spoke well of you.' There was no letup in the teasing. If I had a boyfriend and he heard me talking about him to my parents, he'd interrupt with 'Who you talking about, Bart the turkey?' He could be merciless and once he found a tender point, that was it; he kept going until someone else saved you by changing the conversation.

"When I was fifteen or so, I felt like I was coming out with some relatively intelligent remarks, and he flattened me. But I just figured that that was the way men were, what did I know. I figured they were a father or they were John."

Martha was John's favorite of Charlotte's sisters, perhaps because she looked like Charlotte and had a similar, light sense of humor. But that preference didn't save Martha from his roughness. Once he badly hurt her arm, wrestling with her in the O'Donnells' home.

Of all the O'Donnell clan, Martha saw the most of John and Charlotte when they were in Pelham, because she attended Manhattanville, a prestigious all-girls Catholic college in the hamlet of Purchase, about thirty minutes north of Pelham.

"I was aware that I was the favored sister," remembers

Martha. "John would always say to me, 'if they knock off Charlotte, you're the replacement' kind of thing. I had a terrible crush on him. But even with his liking me, I didn't see that much of them together. When Charlotte and I talked on the phone, it was only during the day, when John wasn't around. If I was there for dinner when he came home, he'd usually just say, 'Hi Moffa,' and go upstairs and eat in their little den in front of the television, and we'd eat downstairs. Charlotte would always buy four lamb chops and give one to me, one to Luke, and two to John. She'd eat something else.

"Usually, she'd ask me over to dinner when he was out of town. She really was my security blanket during college, but I tried not to intrude. I didn't know any specifics in those days, but I knew that if I did intrude, Charlotte would pay a hefty price as far as his taking on an attitude.

"I was so innocent in those days, so inexperienced, so uncomfortable with men that I didn't realize how strange all this was until I got out of college. I've often thought how lucky I was that I didn't fall in love with someone while I was in college, because I probably would have ended up in a similar situation; Charlotte and I are so similar."

Charlotte recalls that John just didn't allow many people into their lives. Perhaps he wanted to be the sole influence on his wife. If he permitted any of Charlotte's friends in their home, he could make them feel so uncomfortable they'd leave. Nancy Long says she preferred to visit her old school chum in his absence, sometimes willing to drive from New Haven and back in a day to avoid John.

Even if he didn't somehow make their guests uncomfortable with his kidding, sardonic cracks, or vulgarities that shocked Charlotte's Catholic girlfriends, he'd often make them feel unwelcome by falling asleep on the couch as they talked. People generally excused it as evidence that he was tired and working too hard.

"It was just something people knew about John," remem-

bers Charlotte. "A few days before Luke was born we had
gone to dinner at another associate's house and John had
fallen asleep there. I had to stay and talk with these people I
barely knew until he woke up. I guess that really was a sign
of being self-centered."

He also seemed to expect people to wait for him. Once,
when John and Charlotte visited her parents for Thanksgiving, Helen says that he refused to come to the table when
she announced dinner was ready because he was still watching a football game, splayed out on the floor of the O'Donnells' den. Helen remembers that she managed to hold the
meal until the game was over.

"Charlotte and I were only nine-to-five friends," remembers Joy Ricci, a Pelham neighbor who was the first and the
closest friend Charlotte remembers making after she married. "My son would play with Luke all day, and she and I
went to the zoo and shopping together regularly, but at five
o'clock Charlotte disappeared into the house to prepare for
John's homecoming. She seemed very pressured by him.
The house was always perfect.

"It didn't hurt my feelings that she didn't ever suggest
our doing something with our husbands, because I enjoyed
her so much. She's the type of person you like very easily.
The day after I moved in, Charlotte appeared on my door-
step with this beautiful little boy and this casserole for me. It
was like something out of *Family Circle* magazine, but she
was for real. She's a very gentle, sweet woman, with a great
sense of humor, even though she was always surprised when
I laughed at her jokes. She was very generous with her time.
She would make special events like Halloween so much fun,
by making costumes for the kids.

"She made excuses for John all the time, saying he
worked very late. I knew he was on the fast track and that
we weren't really going to be a help to him [professionally or
socially], therefore we were expendable. Charlotte never
said that to me, but I could tell that was his attitude because

of the people she told me John wanted her to become friendly with. He almost insisted that she join the [Pelham women's] club.

"I rarely saw him or talked to him. Maybe we waved when he was raking leaves. One evening—this was highly unusual—she and John arrived at our door after dinner. Maybe they had been out for a walk—it was early evening. One of my children had spilled something on the kitchen floor, so I had the mop out. And John says to Charlotte, 'See, she has a mop in her hand,' almost chastising her."

Charlotte hypothesizes that John didn't like Joy Ricci's possible effect on her. Ricci was one of a rare breed in those days, a career woman, who still free-lanced while she cared for her children. She introduced Charlotte to shopping at discount stores and told her that she should be able to buy things for herself without asking John's approval, that she should purchase things occasionally to make herself feel good, not solely to make John look good at a special event. Once Ricci bought Charlotte a little Christmas angel, presenting it to her and saying, 'I know that you never buy anything for yourself, so I wanted to give this to you.' Her comment surprised Charlotte.

Ricci also insisted on giving her money for baby-sitting with her children, because she often asked Charlotte to watch them when she left the house on business. Besides easing her own conscience about imposing on Charlotte so frequently, Ricci thought her friend should have a little pocket money for herself, since she rarely had more than a few dollars in her wallet. When Charlotte told John about the arrangement, she says he wasn't pleased.

"It's funny," Charlotte says now, "John didn't mind my watching her kids. He just didn't like my taking money for it."

Because she, too, was a product of stringent, all-girls Catholic training, Ricci knew some of the reasons Charlotte seemed to passively accept so many things. "Charlotte was very religious. I didn't buy into the philosophy as much as she did, the attitude that if someone smacks you, you turn the other cheek. And if something is going wrong, you offer it up as a penance for your sins. It's your lot in life. You don't do anything to stop it, you just survive it, believing firmly this too shall pass."

Like many of Charlotte's friends who now speak about her past with regret, Ricci worries that she wasn't enough of a support. "I think Charlotte was as frank with me as she was with anybody, and that wasn't very frank. Occasionally she would hint at something about John and then back off it immediately. Women just didn't talk about those kinds of things in those days. We were the last of a generation that stood by its men no matter what."

In late 1971, even though they were much younger than most of their neighbors, John and Charlotte were well on their way to becoming established in the affluent community. They had joined the Pelham Country Club, and Charlotte was being wooed by the wives of Cadwalader partners to join the Manor Club, the local women's group, which held its meetings and luncheons in an old Tudor mansion nearby. John and Charlotte had already picked out their dream home, a large, stone Colonial on the Esplanade, near the home of one of the firm's partners.

"To get into the country club we needed about three sponsors. But it wasn't that big of a deal," says Charlotte. "It was pretty small. It had swimming, golf, and tennis, and a small clubhouse. We were only Junior B members because of our age, but it was still going to be expensive for us. The annual dues were $350, plus $50 for the wife. Swimming fees were $100, and golf was $575 for the year. We also had a food minimum of $300 per annum.

"I hated the idea of joining that women's club. The name

alone was so stuffy. A lot of the members were into garden shows and that type of thing, which was totally foreign to me. Three partners of the firm lived near us, and their wives took me to a meeting. They were all quite well-to-do. I just couldn't have kept up with them. But John was already acting like we had money that we didn't. He was impatient. He wanted everything right then.

"I was miserable about that women's club, but it didn't matter. I was on my way to becoming a member."

Charlotte was saved from joining, however, when, in November, John unexpectedly announced that he had accepted a position to be executive vice-president with Gulf Life Holding Company. They were moving to Dallas.

"The whole thing was very sudden," remembers Joy Ricci. "One day Charlotte told me that they were moving to Texas and the next day, almost, they were gone."

"It did come as a complete surprise," says Charlotte. "I was more stunned than upset. I wouldn't have been that surprised if he had told me we were going to his home state for him to run for political office. He was still talking about doing that. But I had never heard him complain that he didn't like Cadwalader, so leaving the firm for business completely surprised me."

John, in fact, was doing well with his firm. He seemed to be one of the favorites. Going to the annual meetings of regional bar associations, for instance, was a perk within Cadwalader, Wickersham, and Taft, recalls Charlotte. He was sent in both 1970 and 1971 and she accompanied him. And in 1971 in New Hampshire, when his firm was assigned the task of picking up legal dignitaries at the airport for the meeting, John had the distinct honor of driving Warren Burger, then the chief justice of the United States Supreme Court. That was very exciting, she says.

"He had friends in the firm," says Charlotte. "Once a month he'd go to play poker with three other lawyers, and we wives would come along. I was very happy with these women. I really thought that this was where we were going to be forever.

"Looking back on it, I think leaving New York was one of the biggest mistakes we ever made, because John did seem satisfied and happy with his firm. He was never happy in his work again, from what he told me, until he joined the SEC, ten years later.

"But then it seemed to be a great idea. John had two more years before he was made partner, and the job in Dallas promised so much more money immediately that he thought it was just too good an opportunity to miss.

"He just told me that we were going, he didn't ask. But I didn't mind. It was a challenge, and we were young and he seemed so excited. At that point I always thought that more money would make John happy. It's what he said he wanted and it was a definite sign of success. So I was willing to follow him anywhere. We were going to Dallas to be rich. He was making $22,500 annually plus a $3,000 bonus at Cadwalader. Gulf offered him a $50,000 salary."

John relocated to Dallas almost immediately, leaving Charlotte to pack up their possessions. Charlotte visited Texas to look for a new home. They narrowed their choices to two large houses before she returned to New York. The difference in price was about $20,000. Charlotte preferred the smaller, less expensive one. It had only one less bedroom, and she liked its layout. It seemed much airier to her than the other one.

The smaller size also made more sense to her. Following Luke's birth, Charlotte was having trouble conceiving again, and after a series of tests the doctors informed them that Luke, then almost three years old, was certain to be their only child.

John had seemed to agree with her reasoning, and Charlotte returned to New York making mental notes as to where she'd place the furniture in her new home. But after she left, John purchased the larger house.

The house John chose was a prototypical, spruced-up, and suburbanized Texan ranch. Its nine rooms sprawled out along one floor, wide and flat like the landscape. An ostentatious half-circle driveway cut to the front entrance from the wide street, and the spacious yard was bare and sunbleached. It and the surrounding houses seemed to be purposeful islands. Charlotte would rarely see any of her neighbors, since the garages were in the back of the homes and the owners were busy, private people.

It was a big, flashy home, perfect for an attorney who had just struck oil, and seemed to suit him better than the understated Tudor homes of the East Coast. John paid $83,900 for the house, a quantum leap in the value of their residence almost equal to his new salary. The mortgage was $66,700 and their monthly payments $716.

"This house was in a little bit better neighborhood than the other," remembers Charlotte. "But it was way too formal for me. It had lots of ornate, gold-flocked wallpaper, vaulted ceilings, a marble fireplace, a master bedroom which opened out into the covered patio and had two dressing rooms, and a huge sunken tub in the bathroom. I'm just not the sunken-tub type.

"Luke immediately got lost in it when we moved in. I remember him standing in the hallway, crying in his toddlerese, 'Mommie, where you are?' We didn't even have enough furniture for it. All we had to put in the living room were two chairs and a table. But John seemed to like it. He liked big things."

Again, as in New York, John wanted the house to be showcase-perfect immediately, recalls Charlotte. "We spent $1,337 for draperies all lined with white to look the same from the street," she says. "He always had to have curtains up in every room right away. We also spent $1,500 on a sprinkler system in the yard, $750 for a fence, $90 on a dog run for Cassius, and $3,542 for shrubbery, grass, and trees. It pinched us. It made it harder for us to pay for Luke's

Montessori school, which I thought was the priority. John and I had always agreed that a good education was very important. In fact, he was the one who introduced me to the Montessori method of schooling. But private schools cost money.

"It would have been a lot easier on us buying that other house. We wouldn't have had so many expenses furnishing it and surely a $20,000 or so difference in the mortgage would have given us more money each month. But we stretched as far as we could. This neighborhood also had a public pool, but we were already looking at Dallas's most prestigious country club.

"But I always knew that I could live with what John was comfortable with, not vice versa."

Charlotte recalls that John took to Dallas, a prairie town just starting to flex and grow into one of the Southwest's major commercial centers. It was a town whose people happily crowed about its achievements and new stature. He worked in the LTV Tower, one of the city's tallest buildings.

John also quickly adopted Texans' zest for healthy, brawny bodies and became an avid runner, telling Charlotte that he wanted to improve his time each day. Gulf Life paid for his membership at the Cooper Clinic, a prestigious gym where aerobic exercises were invented. John would come home at 4:30 or 5 PM each day and then head over to the clinic's track.

Perhaps because he was so physical and agile himself, John liked Charlotte to be fit also, even though athletics were never her forte. She hurt her knee playing tennis a month after they moved to Dallas. Even though she was on crutches for several weeks, John insisted that she go out and pick up after the dog each day.

And when John roughhoused with Luke, he could inadvertently hurt the child. That spring he was swinging Luke around and dropped him. The fall knocked out a front tooth. Accidents like that happen during childhood, especially with a little boy as game and rambunctious as Luke. But John's way of playing with his son often frightened Charlotte.

The summer before, when they had vacationed with Charlotte's family at Ocean City, the O'Donnells say they had had to bite back criticizing their son-in-law for the way he would pick up Luke. A home film captures John, so tall, leaning down to lift Luke from a hole he had dug in the sand. John yanks the two-and-a-half-year-old up by his hands and, quick, hauls Luke way up over his head before plopping him back on the sand.

"Babies aren't as fragile as some people think," says Charlotte's father, the doctor, remembering John and Luke on the beach. "But the fact remains that one of the things that helps a baby grow up calm is the way he's held. They can lose their feeling of security when they're thrown around."

That scene in Charlotte's home movie is followed by another, very different, picture of John—sitting on the beach, at the water's edge, curled protectively around his son, holding him loosely and gently, pointing out something far down the coastline. Luke laughs and smiles at his father during this filmed play.

And yet, despite his obvious ability to be tender, John demanded that his son be tough, say Charlotte and her family.

"Once, when Luke was about eighteen months old, Charlotte and John visited us," remembers Dr. O'Donnell. "This little fellow was out in back of our house, standing on a brick wall about eighteen inches high, jumping off. I was sitting on the stoop watching him. He would jump off and laugh and climb back up and jump off again. One time he fell and banged his head on the concrete. I reached down to get him and his father pushed my hand away and said, 'Let him learn to do it right or take the consequences.' He thought letting a child bump its head, that's how you toughen them up. That's a macho man thing."

Charlotte hated when John held her back from rushing to one of their children when they were hurt. But she did what he wanted. She remembers that John seemed committed to a tough-man style of parenting. None of his sons were going to be sissies. America still frowned on little boys who cried.

In fact, Charlotte doesn't recall really disapproving of anything John did with Luke until that year in Dallas. "Really, John was a good father until Luke starting thinking for himself and challenging John. The first time I really remember not agreeing with something he did was when Luke said a bad word for the first time. John used the words 'shit' and 'damn' all the time. John didn't 'use the bathroom,' for instance, he 'took a shit.' If he thought something someone had said was stupid, he called them 'a dumb shit.' I don't know how many times he called me that. It's the way he talked.

"Luke said either that or 'damn,' and John made him repeat it and then slapped him. I agreed with John that I didn't want Luke using it, but I didn't agree with the way he handled it. I can remember seeing that Luke didn't want to repeat it. John lulled him into a false sense of security by saying something like 'I'm not going to do anything, I just want to make sure I heard you.' And as soon as Luke said it, John slapped him."

Looking back on it, Charlotte says she is grateful that her firstborn, the child John spent much more time with, was as plucky as Luke was, instead of quiet and shy. At this age, Luke seemed able to handle his father's demands. And his father was pleased with him because he was so naturally coordinated. Luke could ride a tricycle before he was three. He also seemed to have inherited his mother's capacity for being a good sport.

When Helen and the doctor visited their daughter and grandson in Dallas during the fall of 1972, Helen remembers how Luke could stubbornly stand up to his father. "John wanted to see some sports event on television. Luke was trying to watch cartoons and kept turning the channel. John picked up Luke bodily and threw him across the room into the couch. Luke got right back up and turned the set to the cartoons." Charlotte and Helen laugh at the memory. They can't remember if John laughed or not.

John wasn't laughing much during that visit anyway, says Charlotte. Something had sent him into a silence that stretched on for several weeks, even during the O'Donnells' visit. It was the first time Charlotte's parents had witnessed John's simply not speaking to their daughter.

"I would try to joke with them about it," remembers Charlotte. "If he'd throw a command at me, I'd say, 'See, Mommie, it's getting better.' At that point, I didn't realize that not talking for several days, even weeks, was really weird. It did embarrass me, though, because it was so strange and awkward for them. We took them out to dinner, and John talked to them, but wouldn't talk to me at all."

"There was such an air of fear in that house," remembers Charlotte's mother. "I stayed for three days. They were the longest three days."

But this time Helen didn't advise her daughter to leave John. Despite her doctor's prognosis, Charlotte was pregnant. Helen tried to reassure her by telling her that John probably just didn't like the looks of a pregnant woman's body, even though he wanted the child. Things would get better when the baby came, she said, as she hugged Charlotte good-bye at the airport.

And Charlotte believed it. John really wanted a second child. In fact, he had initiated the paperwork for adopting a baby in March. But Charlotte had gotten pregnant right around the time they had filed their application with a Dallas adoption agency. Just as he had been certain Luke was going to be a boy, John was positive their second was going to be a girl. They were going to name her Maggie Hagan. It

was one of the few times John was wrong, jokes Charlotte.
Mark was born November 18, 1972.

The year had passed quickly and for the most part un-
eventfully. Charlotte basically spent her time shuttling Luke
back and forth to school, often driving John to work as well,
and taking care of the house. She and John were starting to
put down some tentative roots. They attended the parish of
Saint Rita, the saint of lost causes, and John was even starting to serve as a lector.

Charlotte remembers only one long silence, when her parents were there. She was even learning to stick up a little for
herself. For her twenty-ninth birthday, she pierced her ears
even though John had told her not to. The only reason she
had courage to do it, she says, was because her aunt had
sent her the money for it. The day she had her ears pierced,
Charlotte tried to pull her hair down over her ears so that
her husband wouldn't notice, but Luke chirped out the
news. John was annoyed, says Charlotte, but she survived.

During the silence that she remembers, Charlotte tried a
new way of communicating with John. When he ignored her
or turned vindictive, Charlotte had trouble remaining calm.
She knew she made it worse by pleading with him, crying,
or yelling. So she wrote him a letter on a legal pad, rationally explaining that she thought he was being unreasonable. It had seemed to help. A few days later John started to
talk more freely with her.

But she was also learning to fight back verbally during
their arguments, something she didn't do much in New
York, and which she says she still isn't proud of. Slowly, she
was beginning to assimilate some of the language she heard
John using regularly into her own vernacular.

And during February, when tension between them was
high—they had been in Dallas only two months, his parents
had been visiting for Luke's birthday, she had just hurt her

knee, money was tight—John said something critical to her, recalls Charlotte, and she threw a package of sheets at him.

"Of course, I missed him," she says. "And this was my luck; he moved and it knocked over a vase, which broke. I'm pretty sure he gave me a slap then, but I knew I deserved it for having thrown something at him.

"I remember scouring the papers, trying to find someplace to fix that vase. I went to a place in downtown Dallas and had a car accident. I ran into someone. There was hardly any damage, but the worst thing was having to call John and tell him. I was in tears, and said, 'Well, you better get the divorce papers out right now.'

"But this was one of the times John came through for me. He handled it. And he handled the insurance claim. I wouldn't have known how to handle it myself in those days. The only thing I didn't tell him was where I had been going when I had the accident."

Although John enjoyed his new salary and privileges with Gulf Life—whenever he traveled for the company, for instance, he flew by private jet—his and Charlotte's tenure in Dallas lasted only a year. She remembers that John was uncomfortable with his employer. When he was approached at the end of 1972 by Arnold & Porter, a well-known law firm in Washington, D.C., he jumped at the opportunity.

Three weeks after Mark was born, Charlotte was hosting a formal dinner for Dennis Lyons, the partner from Arnold & Porter who wanted to hire John.

"It was a terrible experience," she recalls about that evening. "I had had to go to Neiman-Marcus and buy myself a full-length skirt and try to stuff myself into it, right after having a baby. John told me to fix a hot seafood salad with lobster. As I was handing out hors d'oeuvres that had some kind of seafood in them, Dennis declined. I realized then that he didn't eat seafood. I did manage to make a joke.

'Would you like a hot dog?' I asked. After all that preparation, I had to send John out for a steak.

"I was exhausted. I was having a slow recovery from the birth. I had to leave in the middle of the meal to nurse the baby. He was only about twenty days old and he was just beginning to develop an awful cough. That night, after Dennis and his son left, the cough developed into some awful virus.

"John never accepted any weakness from me. I had had to ask my sister Martha to come down after the baby was born because I knew that John wouldn't be able to handle cooking a meal for Luke or for me when I was laid up that first week back from the hospital.

"I didn't think to ask John why he didn't just take Dennis out for dinner. Or just have him by for dessert and coffee. Instead, I was good old Char. I went into it with great vigor. I always did. I guess that's part of what kept me in all this trouble."

The move to Washington, especially coming so quickly on the heels of the transfer to Dallas, did surprise Charlotte a little. She can't recall that John ever told her that he had started inquiring about other jobs.

"I think that was part of his compartmentalization," she says. "He prided himself on keeping his work and his home separate. I think he might have thought it was a weakness to complain about work. That your family shouldn't know about the hardships at your job. He'd come home in a bad mood, but he wouldn't say why. I just learned that I shouldn't interfere."

Charlotte simply threw herself into preparing for the move back East. Again, John moved ahead of his family, right after Christmas, leaving Charlotte to pack and, this time, to sell the house. She had trouble finding buyers, partly because the house was just beyond the line for Dallas's best public school district. It was hard work trying to juggle that and the care of a newborn and a four-year-old.

Finally, in March 1973, she and the children moved on to Washington, even though the house wouldn't sell until July.

Charlotte was excited about moving back to Washington. She liked the city and would be close to her family again. She had been lonely and uncomfortable with the fast-living, sun-worshipping, money-hungry circles of Dallas. And Arnold & Porter was a law firm of renown. Surely John would be challenged and happy working there, she thought.

Little did Charlotte know that the pressures of the nation's capital would only make the troubles between her and John worse.

Part Three

BUILDING A WASHINGTON FAMILY

You who are wives, be submissive to your husbands, this is your duty in the Lord. Husbands, love your wives. Avoid any bitterness towards them. You children, obey your parents in everything as the acceptable way in the Lord. And fathers, do not nag your children, lest they lose heart.

Letter of Paul to the Colossians, 3:12-21, read each year in the Catholic Church's celebration of the Holy Family

10

In 1974, the reporter Sally Quinn, then the queen of the *Washington Post*'s "Style" section, wrote of the city: "Prominence in Washington has little to do with traditional social credentials or wealth. . . . Washington is about the only city in the world where the word 'nouveau' is laudatory, where the least known people often have the greatest chance of making it."

Quinn wrote this in a profile savaging one of the city's most well-known social climbers. She used the story as a springboard to lampoon the how-tos of Washington's social circuit. But her analysis was apt beyond the city's parties.

Washington is unique in that it is a functioning microcosm of democracy, a place where a nobody who's smart and works hard, really hard, can actually make it big. The city is filled with ambitious people from someplace else, with children of manure-poor farmers, who made it to Ivy League colleges on the power of their brains, and have everyday hopes their parents never even dreamed. It's a haven for intellectual Jay Gatsbys.

That's because Washington is the only city purposefully built in modern times to be a country's political capital. There's no manufacturing to speak of, so there are no factory lords and the imposed social strata that come with them. National elections keep the population turning over, so longevity doesn't count for much either. It's not a trading center, an artistic center, or a commercial center. Politics was the reason for its genesis, and politics is the linchpin of the entire whirligig of Washington. But only the linchpin.

Today, only a fifth of the civilian workers in the District are employed by the federal government. The majority of Washingtonians work in industries that are natural leeches —in both definitions of the word, parasite and physician— on policy-makers. People are needed to interpret the laws and regulations being made, to write about them, to pressure and sway those making them, and to explain the complicated issues tangled up in those laws. Interest groups, policy analysts, economists, lobbyists, think tanks, foreign experts all have homes here, as well as politicians, diplomats, and bureaucrats.

The major currencies in the nation's capital, then, are knowledge and influence. Witness the fact that one of the most commonly asked questions during cocktail parties in the city is not "Where are you from?" or "Who is your family?" but "What do you do?"

It is a city that is heaven-tailored for someone like John Fedders, a comer from nowhere in particular, a man who had pulled himself up by his law books. Of course, it is seen as the promised land also by thousands of others just as smart, just as aggressive, just as ambitious as John. Washington has the highest proportion of college-educated residents and of lawyers per person of any United States city. The latter fact prompted the comedian Mark Russell to once quip that "Washington without lawyers would be like Rome without priests."

So, Washington is an open-doored coliseum full of promises for the intellectually stout, but a highly competitive one, pitting equals against each other. Just to stay in the game requires the stamina of a gladiator, since above-average job performance is standard. The strategic advantage needed to win laurels often comes only with befriending the right people. That makes for a lot of insecurity and stress, especially since some people try to get ahead by fawning to superiors and backbiting peers in a calculated, Darwinian campaign.

Arnold & Porter, the law firm employing John, was a formidable arena. It is one the city's most venerated firms, because of its age, size, Fortune 500 clientele, and the fact that it is indigenous to the city, not merely a branch office of a New York firm. Arnold & Porter was started after World War II by some members of President Roosevelt's administration. FDR's New Deal programs and the restrictions implemented by Congress and the White House during the war had spawned a whole new body of federal regulatory law, and an unprecedented need for Washington-based lawyers who understood how to challenge it.

As high-ranking veterans of FDR's programs and of government service, the firm's founders were especially well-qualified to do just that. They included: Thurmond Arnold, one-time chief of the Justice Department's antitrust division and then a judge on the US Court of Appeals; Abe Fortas, undersecretary of Interior; and Paul A. Porter, chairman of the Federal Communications Commission and then director of the wartime Office of Price Administration. The firm grew quickly. Its attorneys defended civil liberties by representing individuals fingered by Joe McCarthy's anti-Communism campaign, and also developed an extremely lucrative practice defending the needs and interests of big business. By the time John joined the firm, at the end of 1972, Arnold & Porter had quite a reputation for succesfully representing corporate clients in trouble with federal agencies and commissions, for assigning a lot of employees to a single case, for the long hours its 150-plus lawyers put in,

for hiring only the best young attorneys, and for the difficulty the associates had in making partner over their well-
qualified colleagues. Charlotte used to joke that the phrase
"the prestigious law firm of" was actually part of Arnold &
Porter's name, since it almost always was referred to as such
when mentioned in the press.

Charlotte noticed changes in John's work habits immediately. She remembers that before, in Dallas, John had left
for work around 8 AM. In Washington, he set his alarm for
5:55 AM and usually left by 7, often not returning until 7:30
PM. He started staying at the office several nights a week and
on weekends, and also brought work home.

Just as John's work habits grew more regimented, his
morning routine became more regulated, his demands of
Charlotte more dictatorial. To Charlotte, it seemed John
feared that anything being out of place, any deviation in
practices at home would distract him from work and hamper his concentration.

"I noticed the change in his work habits grew instantly.
He spent less time at home, less time with the kids. It was
work, work, work. Everything got worse between us here
because of pressure on him and his need to have a non-
problematical and orderly family.

"There's just something about Washington that's even
more cut-throat than New York City. For John anyway.
Maybe it's because he didn't stand out as much here. I think
he had always been the star everyplace else. Here, he felt
like one of the pack. Arnold & Porter is filled with very
smart lawyers. I think he felt that he'd have to do something
really outstanding to be noticed the way he wanted to be
noticed.

"I think all the rules at home had to do with completely
controlling his environment so he could focus on his work.
Since some of our sons have learning disabilities and they
are hereditary, maybe he had some—a lot of brilliant people

do—and his obsessive neatness and order were unconscious ways of compensating for them."

Perhaps John was subconsciously distancing himself from his family and the disconcerting demands they could make. In her best-selling book *Women Who Love Too Much,* the family therapist Robin Norwood suggests that some men who felt as children that their emotional needs weren't always met grow up to concentrate on their jobs or hobbies, whereas women of similar circumstances become obsessed with relationships. Such men, according to Norwood, often become "workaholics" as a way of avoiding the emotional intimacy they fear. Norwood also states that rigidity about housework "can preclude contact and intimacy, because the emphasis is not on relating, but on following the rules."

Charlotte remembers that she had a lot of rules to follow, such as the ceremonial feeding and dressing of John each morning. The routine was as meticulous and ritualistic as a squire would have had when arming his knight for a joust.

"I don't know how I started helping him dress," she says. "It just happened one morning when he was in a hurry and it stuck. The routine never deviated. He got out of bed. Took off his pajamas. Brushed his teeth and shaved. Then he would stand in the shower for two minutes or so, cut off the water, and soap up completely. Then he'd turn on the water and stand for a long time. I knew I had enough time, when I heard the water come back on, to get up, put out a fresh towel—it had to be a fresh towel every morning—go downstairs, get the paper, and start his breakfast. After he dried himself, he took the towel and wiped the counter, the floor, and left it in the sink.

"Breakfast was either eggs, cereal, or frozen waffles, which I would butter, cut up, and put syrup on for him. I didn't cut up his eggs, because he liked to eat the white first, then the yellow in one chunk.

"I laid out his clothes, including all his underwear. He told me what suit he wanted to wear. I would hook up his suspenders, tie his bow tie for him if he was wearing one, wash his glasses and hand them to him, put his wallet in his coat. Then I'd either help him put his coat on or, in the summer, carry it on a hanger down to the car for him.

"I kept doing all this for him even when he was in one of his moods and not speaking to me, because I didn't want to rock the boat. If we had an argument and I held back from these routines, or was caught up with something with one of the kids, he told me that I was being really selfish. Sometimes I'd have to stop nursing the baby to help dress him. Sometimes I'd forgo taking a shower for a day or two because there just wasn't time for me.

"Eventually, as more babies came, I was too overwhelmed to wash and iron all his shirts for him. But I never told him that. I found a laundry that used pull-off tags instead of stamping the shirts and would do them in one day. I would bring them home, rip off the little tags, and hang them on hangers in the basement and bring them up a few at a time."

There were household systems as well.

"When the mail came, I put it all on his desk. Even if it was a magazine for me, I'd put it on his desk first, and he would distribute it later. If a letter came to me, I'd open it and read it, but then I'd put it on his desk. He often rubbed the stamps I had put on letters to make sure they were really stuck on. Almost every envelope that left here had to have a piece of tape on the flap. Once a week, all the magazines were thrown out. The only ones I remember his saving were *Fortune, Architectural Digest,* and any of his law reviews. If I wanted to save something, I had to put a note on it.

"There was no privacy or freedom of choice. The radio was always on WTOP, an all-news station. We really only used the stereo when he wanted it on, but sometimes he'd let me choose the records. When things were good with us, I'd sit in John's study with him at night and we'd read. He'd get up and turn the light off when he thought it was time to go to bed. I finally learned to say, 'I'm in the middle of a sentence, could you leave the lights on, please.' But I'd always follow him to bed within a few minutes.

"When he was coming home, he would call me as he was leaving work so I would know to start dinner. We always had to have meat, not macaroni and cheese, even when we were short on cash. Once I gave him a peanut-butter-and-jelly sandwich for lunch and he was annoyed.

"Then I'd make sure the house was straight. If I washed curtains, I made sure to get them down and back up in one day. All the beds had to be made.

"I'd have the kids dressed. He didn't like it if the baby was just in diapers. The TV was off. He'd drive up, honk the horn. I'd open the garage door automatically from inside. All the kids were spit and polished, at least in demeanor. It was almost like *The Sound of Music,* lining up for inspection kind of thing.

"I don't remember that day-to-day, knot-in-your-gut, how-is-he-going-to-be-tonight fear until we got here. It was a terrible way to live."

Much of that tension revolved around Charlotte's fear that she wouldn't have the house neat enough for John. It was his castle, a non-refutable talisman of his success, and he wanted it orderly and perfect, all the time, she says.

Right after accepting Arnold & Porter's offer, John had come to Washington to look for a house. He went to Potomac, a nearby Maryland suburb, which once had been the haunt of landed horse breeders and fox hunters. Because of Washington's population boom and the affluence of the times, farms were being subdivided for the upwardly mobile, with plantation-sized mansions sitting on half-acre lots. Many of the houses had their own swimming pools, tennis courts, and telltale burglar alarms. Most of the residents belonged to a country club. With such opulent development, Potomac was fast becoming *the* place for the city's newly

rich. In fact, today Potomac has the metropolitan area's
highest concentration of households earning an average of
$100,000 a year.

It seemed to be John Fedders's kind of place.

Of course, they couldn't quite afford one of Potomac's
more lavish spreads. But John did find a suitably large, im-
pressive, cream brick Colonial in an established neighborhood, McAuley Park, which had been carved out of lands
once belonging to the Sisters of Mercy. The house was the
last one built on Carmelita Drive, a street named for one of
the order's important members, and was across from a mo-
nastic retreat. The street was on the back perimeter of the
development, facing woods and the monastery's grounds,
isolated and quiet. At Christmas, Charlotte would see the
star atop the Spanish Mission–style chapel, gleaming som-
berly through the bare trees.

To reach McAuley Park from the city took about thirty-
five minutes. John drove down the long, winding River
Road, past the austere gates of the Congressional Country
Club, one of the city's premier establishments and the past
site of the Kemper and PGA gold tournaments, and turned
onto Bradley Boulevard, a two-lane road left over from
Potomac's rural era. After turning left at Our Lady of
Mercy Church, he was in his neighborhood, an area studded
with Monopoly hotel–like houses, big brick boxes obviously
completed at one go. There were no unsightly additions to
suggest the owner might not have been rich enough to afford
a sun room when he purchased the house. Many of the
homes, including John and Charlotte's, sat atop knolls,
scaled-down, suburbanized châteaus.

Dollhouse-size mailboxes lined the curbs. The lawns were
manicured. No unruly wildflowers or rose bushes, no impa-
tiens growing in colored waves, spilling onto the flagstone
walkways. Instead, there was a predominance of low-grow-
ing, spiky flowers, marigolds or red salvias, marching in
straight, orderly flowerbeds. The only real touch of flamboy-

ance was an occasional purple crape myrtle bush. The major landscaping device of the neighborhood was thick evergreen shrubs, clipped flat into sharp cubes and geometric shapes, creating dozens of mini-Versailleses. During the summer the smell of freshly mown grass constantly hung sweet in the air.

It was a formal, well-groomed subdivision, one without any hints of idleness or bohemian whim. A striking metaphor for its polished residents, who were savvy enough to be chameleons in a conservative town. A buttoned-down, proper, "I'm-going-to-fit-in-because-this-is-what-I've-always-wanted" kind of neighborhood for the upper-middle class who still dreamed of bigger things.

Charlotte didn't see the house until after the signing of the closing papers. She gasped when she did. What was John thinking of? The house was even bigger than the one in Dallas, with five large bedrooms, including a master bedroom with a huge dressing room off it, a living room, family room, kitchen with a breakfast nook, and dining room, plus a full basement. She was still convinced that their second son was a gift from God, that she wouldn't be having any more children. What would they do with the space?

"I was stunned by the size," she says. "I don't know why he wanted something so big. It was larger than most of the homes of partners at Arnold & Porter, who were several years ahead of John. But while it made me self-conscious, I think John was really pleased that he had a bigger home."

But at the time, Charlotte said nothing. They did seem to have enough money for it. The house cost $116,500, and, even though they wouldn't sell the Dallas house for several more months, John had received a lucrative contract settlement—about $75,000 total—from Gulf Life when he left. His salary at Arnold & Porter was even better than what he had received in Dallas. They could easily handle the $70,000 mortgage, as long as they were careful about their other expenses.

But Charlotte says she and John quickly spent more than $20,000 on decorating the house. When Charlotte arrived in March, John told her that he wanted the house furnished quickly. He just never felt settled until everything was in its place, remembers Charlotte. She was to contact the decorator who had done the home of the neighborhood's builder, who lived down the street. John wanted it as grand as theirs.

"At first, I thought it would be fun," says Charlotte, "because I had never 'decorated' a home before. But we had to do it so fast it was very intimidating. By October, eight months later, this house was pretty much the way it is now. And it was so expensive. We had to buy several pieces for the family room—a couch, a bench, and a chair. The rug in the family room cost about $2,000, and that was more than ten years ago. It was about two inches thick, an all-wool shag. I had a smaller, less expensive one picked out, but John said we had to have this one. The curtains in there were beautiful. During the day you could see through them and at night you could see trees etched into the material.

"In the living room, we had to have this gold, hand-cut, custom-dyed rug. The couch was re-covered and the back cushions resculpted, and we refinished a tabletop. We wall-papered the living room and the hallway. The hallway paper just happened to be the same as that in the builder's dining room. The dining-room furniture we left alone except for recovering the chairs with blue velvet, to match the specially made curtain rod. We put wall-to-wall carpeting in all five bedrooms and the upstairs hall. And curtains in all the rooms. In our bedroom, we had a bedspread made, to match our new curtains."

With the new house and its fancy, new furnishings came more household rules, including that no one in the family would wear shoes indoors because it would wear down the carpets.

It was hard teaching a toddler to walk in stockinged feet and to constantly stop Luke each time he ran into the house to tell him to take off his shoes. But Charlotte did it. She'd even tell her guests that John didn't wear shoes in the house, subtly hinting for them to remove theirs as well. Most complied without a word.

"We knew what John was like," says one Saint Joseph's friend, who had teased Charlotte about the size of the house the first time she came by, asking, "Is there a servants' quarter I should use to enter?" They visited in the kitchen, since Charlotte didn't want to disturb the living room.

"Things were new and perfect, and they had to stay that way because we no longer had the money to replace anything," says Charlotte. "This was a shrine to him, not a home. Whenever he brought people here, he wanted it clean enough that he could take them on a tour and open up everything, including the closets, to show them. And he did throw everything open like that, even after we'd been here awhile.

"We weren't allowed to have a fire in the fireplace because he thought the room would smell of smoke, although every time we had guests, there was a burning log. We couldn't open the windows. He was worried about dirt from the street blowing in and bugs, even though we had screens. Every other month or so we had to totally clean out the garage and hose it down, even during the winter. He'd cut the kids' toenails only outside on the patio, so that none of the shavings would get in the house. He had the same fetish about the car. I wasn't allowed to file a nail, even if I broke it right then, in the car, and I had to keep my feet on its floormats.

"All the furniture had to be in the same indentations in the carpet. I was never allowed to move anything from the place the decorator put it, even though I thought it was a little too formal. We didn't have family pictures up downstairs because he preferred paintings and prints.

"When he came home, he liked to see the vacuum marks in the carpet all going the same way. If there were footprints from one of the children, he was irritated. Not violent or anything, but annoyed. And he would tell me that I didn't control them enough."

Nancy Long remembers one of her Saturday visits to Charlotte's Potomac home: "I went to visit her with my two children and they ran into the family room and she called after them, 'Oh, don't do that, I just vacuumed in there.' She was joking about it, but clearly she was nervous. They played instead in the garage. John came home for lunch and came roaring into the kitchen, yelling because the boys hadn't put the garage back in order. I thought my boys were going to die of fright, John's so huge."

"Eventually," says Charlotte, "we just stopped using the living room and the family room because little things out of place would make him angry. The dining room was never touched except for special dinners or entertaining guests. If he was late getting home and the boys were asleep, he'd often flip on their lights to check on them. If their rooms were a mess, he'd complain to me, so I was reluctant to let them play there. So they pretty much played in the basement. My neighbors later told me that they always knew when we were away because that was the only time they'd see lights upstairs during the evening. We'd set timers for them to go off, but when we were there, we were never upstairs.

"I'd let them play only in the backyard, not the front, because John was so proud and particular about it. He wanted it perfectly green, and orderly. I wasn't allowed to plant any flowers because the blossoms would die and look ugly. He ordered his own fertilizers, as well as hiring Chem-Lawn and another maintenance firm to spray the bushes. God, the grass. Cutting the grass made us all miserable. He used to write down on his calendar each time it was cut, and it had to be perfect. If it wasn't, we ended up cutting it twice in one day to make him happy.

"He didn't like my putting a swing set up for the kids in

the backyard, so it had to go all the way in the back, where no one would see it. I would go out and rake up any dribbles of sand from the sandbox before he came home.

"I know it all sounds crazy. These weren't direct orders, but we knew what bothered him. We did anything to avoid trouble."

Charlotte wasn't yet thirty years old when they moved into their Potomac showplace in 1973. John was thirty-one. They were both much younger than their neighbors, who tended to have children in junior high or high school. McAuley Park residents were mostly diplomats, ex-congressmen, doctors, and lawyers, and for most it was the second home they had purchased in Washington. Charlotte remembers that often when people came to the door they would hesitantly ask her if her mother was at home.

Although she could sometimes be bashful about having so much more than most of her contemporaries, Charlotte could also have moments of boastfulness about their house. She was very proud of everything her husband had accomplished and accumulated so early in his career. She had never dreamed that she'd be loved by so outstanding, so handsome a man, and her wonder at that sustained her even as she watched him grow more obsessive about their home. Besides, it was a beautiful house; John was right about that.

Shortly after all the decoration was completed, Charlotte, prodded by her mother, invited a dozen of her Notre Dame friends to a luncheon at Carmelita Drive. Now she had a home as big as their childhood homes in Homeland. John seemed pleased that Charlotte wanted to show off a bit, especially since her mother wanted to pay for the food and flowers. Helen offered because, after all, this was partly her triumph as well.

The Homeland delegation arrived and "oohed" appreciatively. Yes, indeed, their friend Charlotte, funny, gawky Charlotte, had made quite a catch. But Charlotte didn't enjoy the afternoon as much as she had thought she would. "Revenge is not sweet, if you call that revenge. It was just real phony, the whole thing. Yes, we had made it, and I wanted to show them that. But I guess I knew in my heart that our outward image was really a facade, so the event just seemed flat to me."

11

During their first year in Washington, Charlotte started feeling overwhelmed by the pressures of her new life. Part of the trouble she had adjusting to Potomac came from the fact she had spent several months on her own in Dallas after John had moved to Washington and had become accustomed to some independence. Suddenly she had more rules to deal with, in addition to completing a major decorating project and caring for a four-year-old and a baby.

John was tense as well, not only with his work but with the fact that the decorating seemed to be taking so long, says Charlotte. She recalls that even a vacation to Disney World turned stressful for her. In July, they traveled to Florida with Luke and another couple, old friends of John's from Marquette University, and their little girls and baby-sitter. They stayed in a new townhouse on Lake Buena Vista, at no cost, through a connection of Gulf Life. Disney World was only about two years old, still new and exciting. But it was hot, and even though the house was lovely, eight people were a few too many. Charlotte was also very upset when one of the little girls ate the Ex-Lax she had bought for herself and became very sick.

One day late that summer, when Charlotte was talking on the phone to her sister Mimi, she broke down and sobbed. She just wasn't feeling right, she said. She was so depressed and she should have been happy. She had thought moving to Washington would be the tonic for John's seeming dissatisfaction with her. But he seemed more rigid, she said. Her sister suggested that Charlotte see a psychiatrist she knew of in Silver Spring, another Maryland suburb of the city.

At first, Charlotte hesitated. Didn't going to a psychiatrist mean you really were crazy? Was John right about her after all? The one psychiatrist she had talked to—a man her father had taken her to in Baltimore for one session after her eardrum was ruptured—had simply told her that both she and John were immature, reinforcing her belief that things were her fault. If only she'd grow up, maybe things would be right. What if this man told her the same thing?

But Charlotte was desperate enough to swallow her pride and insecurity and to go see him.

She nervously drove the twenty minutes around the Capital Beltway to his office. It was not a productive experience. Charlotte sat in a chair, next to a table with a blindingly bright lamp and a box of Kleenex. The doctor seemed to sit miles away, across a large room, hidden in a net of pungent pipe smoke.

The first hour was taken up entirely by questions about her past: How old are you? Tell me about your father, your mother, your sisters. When did you get married? How many children do you have? On and on. She didn't understand. She wasn't a biology lab frog in need of dissecting. Wasn't he going to tell her anything about what was wrong right now? Wasn't he going to give her something to hang on to, some advice as to how to survive the week?

By the next meeting things were better with John, so Charlotte started cloaking the harshest aspects of her situa-

The O'Donnell family at New York City's Latin Quarter nightclub.
From left to right: Martha, Mimi, Charlotte, Charles and his wife,
Helen, Susan, and Dotti.

The perfect Catholic girl.
Charlotte as a lower school
student at Notre Dame.

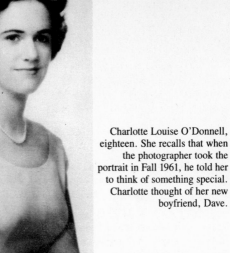

Charlotte Louise O'Donnell, eighteen. She recalls that when the photographer took the portrait in Fall 1961, he told her to think of something special. Charlotte thought of her new boyfriend, Dave.

John Michael Fedders, a high school senior.

John clowned around during their wedding reception, an elaborate sit-down dinner for two hundred at Baltimore's Belvedere Hotel.

John would embarrass Charlotte by rubbing a piece of wedding cake in her face.

John and Charlotte's first home, purchased in 1968 in New York's Pelham Manor.

Charlotte, John, and Luke with Cassius, 1970 Christmas portrait.

Charlotte and Luke at the
Pelham Country Club pool,
1971.

The Fedderses' dream home in Potomac, Maryland, a prestigious suburb
of Washington, D.C., where John was a partner with the Arnold
& Porter law firm.

Charlotte with John Michael in August 1976. Less than a year after this photo was taken, John Michael would die of spinal meningitis.

In 1981, John Fedders was chosen over forty-nine applicants to become the chief of enforcement for the Securities and Exchange Commission. He was thirty-nine years old. Charlotte took this photograph in San Francisco.

John was the first person chosen to be the SEC's "top cop" who was not promoted to the job from inside the agency. His selection was announced at a press conference, which Charlotte attended.

The Fedders family in Rehoboth Beach, Delaware, right after John had been selected for the SEC position.

In April 1987, Charlotte (center) testified in front of a House Education and Labor Select Subcommittee. The subcommittee was holding budget hearings to review the need and effectiveness of the Child Abuse Prevention and Treatment Act and the Family Violence Prevention and Services Act.

tion, wanting to protect her husband, not wanting to sound like a cry baby. She suspended her visits when she and John took another trip, in mid-September. This one she felt was, indeed, recuperative.

They went to Europe for sixteen days with one of John's former Cadwalader clients. Their travels included Germany, Poland, Yugoslavia, Hungary, Switzerland, and Spain, with stops in Frankfurt, Warsaw, Vienna, Budapest, Zurich, and Madrid. The vacation seemed to ease some of the stress. Away from work and financial and child-care burdens, they enjoyed each other's company. This trip was one of the rare instances when John and Charlotte traveled without the children and without visiting family or attending a Marquette basketball game, she says. On one of their last nights in Madrid, Charlotte recorded in their travelogue, "It's really nice to have John alone. We can really laugh, joke, and have fun together, alone. Not bad after seven years!"

Charlotte was very excited as their Pan Am plane left Dulles Airport, heading for Germany. She hadn't been overseas or on such a grand tour since her junior year in college, nine years before. The flight was pleasant. They were lucky enough to have an empty seat next to them on the plane, and after dinner John fell asleep stretched the length of three seats, his head in Charlotte's lap. She sat up the entire flight, content that she was being a comfort to him, watching the movie *Oklahoma Crude* and the sun rise over the Atlantic.

The couple with whom they traveled ran an importing company. They knew many diplomats and business leaders in the Eastern bloc countries the four visited. Charlotte and John were able to tag along on several dinners with trade ministers and well-placed American foreign service officers, treats they would not have had if traveling on their own, treats Charlotte knew she never would have had without being John's wife. Her gratitude to and pride in him swelled.

Their shared diary of the trip reflected how widely they

could differ in their abilities to relax and take note of the world around them. Charlotte's passages were filled with descriptions of sights, even the prostitutes they saw on the street, the couples they met, the lifestyle and poor plumbing of the countries, and the foods, especially sweets. John's notes were mainly tallies of costs, even though Charlotte recalls that their traveling companions were paying for almost everything other than John's and her meals and gift purchases. His final entry was a precise listing of all their expenditures, including everything from a ladies'-room fee in Frankfurt, to tips to doormen, to hot dogs purchased from street vendors, to the final taxi fare home, from Dulles to Potomac.

Clearing customs in New York had taken a while, and running across Kennedy Airport to catch their connecting flight to Washington was exhausting. They were carrying two large suitcases, a flight bag, boxes with porcelains and liquor, and a painting they had purchased in Warsaw that needed extra care in handling because it wasn't completely dry. But despite the cumbersome load and their hurry, Charlotte remembers that John didn't want to pay a porter to help them. He yelled at her when she couldn't keep up in their dash. On the plane to Dulles, she wrote: "It has been a fantastic trip although right now I ache and hurt so much physically and emotionally and every way. I wonder why all trips end in such turmoil. But the entire sixteen days were a thrill that will never be equalled."

The trip was a source of wonderful memories and stories for a long time, including one, however, that Charlotte was a little uncomfortable with because she felt it was a hyperbole. One night on an old estate in Poland they had been served a cold dinner, liberally washed down with vodka, and finished with hot scrambled eggs. Charlotte says that as John told the story, they had slurped down raw eggs.

Many people embellish anecdotes and Charlotte didn't mind the exaggeration except when John turned to her for confirmation, saying, "I swear this is the truth, isn't that right, Char?" She felt like it was a test, and says that it happened with stories about workmen and household crises. But Charlotte says that she corroborated his stories because that kept him happy. Besides, she felt it was part of her duty as a good, supportive wife. She hated to question him or to make any kind of mistake that might anger John.

When she did make what she feared might be a mistake, Charlotte would spend more time telling John *why* she did something than *what* she did, trying to ward off his irritation; going on and on. She realized, however, that her nervous babble could be infuriating in itself. She knew that not knowing when to be quiet could make matters worse. But she just couldn't stop herself.

Sometimes, when Charlotte defended herself by expansively explaining the reasoning behind her actions, John would say that she just couldn't take criticism. That's what her father had always said to her. In fact, John told her that, before their wedding, the doctor had pulled him aside and forewarned him about her inability to take criticism.

"I remember feeling very betrayed by my father if he had indeed told John that," says Charlotte. "But it also convinced me that maybe I was too stubborn, maybe I couldn't take criticism."

There was a lot of worrying her that Charlotte could have told that psychiatrist in Silver Spring. But she didn't. She just couldn't. She didn't trust him. He never said anything, just sat there puffing his pipe, occasionally asking one-sentence questions.

In December, she told him that she wasn't coming back to see him. She had seen him for only a few sessions anyway.

She didn't need him, she said, because she was pregnant. She was sure everything was going to be all right now. A new baby always made the marriage better. She also joyfully stopped believing the doctors' theories about their inability to conceive.

* * *

John and Charlotte's third son, Matthew, was born in
July 1974. John agreed to hire a cleaning lady to come once
a week to help Charlotte with the house.

That year would also be an eventful one as John started
image building. Charlotte recalls that he announced that
they were going to join the Congressional Country Club, the
posh, spacious club he passed on River Road. He asked two
of his socially prominent clients who were members to sponsor them.

John also purchased seventy acres of undeveloped land
across the Potomac River in Virginia's Loudoun County,
for $83,000. He said it would be a good investment for the
boys' college fund, but Charlotte says John also liked the
fact that the county was known for its blue-blooded gentry
and that some people would assume the tract was a lavish
horse-breeding estate.

"The land was something that really strapped us, because
we paid around $12,000 a year for it. It was supposedly for
the kids; still, it would have made so much more sense to
have made smaller investments slowly. He liked the sound
of it, though, and kept referring to it as the farm in Virginia,
like it was hunt country or something. There wasn't any
building on it. It was just acreage."

Whereas John called the land an investment, membership
in Congressional added status as well as recreational opportunities for the family. Country clubs are American phe-
nomena, a democracy's rather undemocratic stab at a European, landed-gentry lifestyle. Many on the East Coast were
started as fox-hunting associations. During its first years, in
fact, Congressional kept extensive stables and forty hounds
for its members. It and the other clubs like it retain that air
of refined, to-the-manor-born fun. They are bastions of
weekend recreation and of polite intermingling with social
peers, safe from ne'er-do-wells and other undesirables.
Membership means you belong to a tier of society that may

not have lineage crawling back for generations, but one that has money, success, and community prominence.

Washington has more than a dozen country clubs from which John and Charlotte could have chosen. About half of those, including Congressional, had a membership roster that would prove helpful to an attorney with high aspirations. Congressional was started in 1924 by then-Secretary of Commerce Herbert Hoover and over a dozen US senators and representatives; hence, the name. Original members also included a smattering of sons from some of Maryland's oldest families, such as E. Brooke Lee, rich industrialists, and national dignitaries: presidents Calvin Coolidge, Woodrow Wilson, and William Taft, plus J. D. Rockefeller, William Randolph Hearst, William Carnegie, and William Scripps, to name a few.

Today, not that many members of Congress belong. They are on the golf courses constantly, however, as guests of lobbyists and corporate executives who can afford the hefty dues, and who befriend them by playing on their love of the sport. Congressional isn't Chevy Chase, the area's oldest, perhaps most blue-blooded, and most exclusive club, but it was close enough to nicely round out John's curriculum vitae, by God, its posh grounds a fitting backdrop for entertaining clients or meeting new ones.

Congressional is entered through a long, straight, tree-lined driveway. A driver waits at the stone entrance to park cars. The clubhouse is a very large, aristocratic, Mediterranean-style whitewashed villa, with an ornate, red tile roof. Housed in the huge labyrinth downstairs is a co-ed mixed grill; a men's grill, cloistered behind closed wooden doors; bowling lanes; plus a small indoor pool. The halls are lined with photographs of the club's illustrious founders and of the various national golf tournaments held there.

Upstairs, on the ground floor, is a large cocktail lounge and an equally large dining room. Both are formal and filled with light from floor-to-ceiling French doors and windows.

The dining room's pervading flavor is medieval, with chairs with wide, cushioned seats and backs atop swirled wooden legs.

The main attraction of this floor, however, is the lavish ballroom, with a two-story-high ceiling and with monastery-like windows cut into the second floor where people can stand and watch the dancing below. The wooden floor glistens. The ceiling's beams are painted in somber tones and pristine lines, small tapestries hang on the walls, tremendous chandeliers drip delicately cut glass, and two tall marble fireplaces stand on either side of the room. Across from the ballroom's entrance tall, wide archways, festooned with gold drapes, lead to a long, sunny sitting room. That room opens through a wall of French doors onto a wide terrace, offering an exquisite view of the golf course and the four pools below.

It is easy to imagine the meeting of Juliet and her Romeo during a courtly dance in such a ballroom. All in all, Congressional is an elegant, romantic environment, seemingly custom-made to shut out the real world and any of its ugliness. In other words, not a place to bare one's soul and find sympathy since many people might willingly make slight ideological and financial compromises to belong in such an aggrandizing setting.

"I really didn't want to join Congressional because it was so expensive," says Charlotte. "I think the initiation fee was around $4,000, even then, in 1974. There were monthly dues, and eventually we had to use up an $800 yearly food minimum. All I really wanted was a club with a pool. John certainly wasn't an avid golfer, which is what Congressional is really famous for. We were just as close to the smaller Bethesda Country Club.

"But John wanted to join Congressional and was very proud of the fact that we got in so fast. We were summer members and then went to one cocktail party, where members could inspect us. I was very nervous for that but very soon after it we were in. John used to brag that even Vince Lombardi, the former coach of the Washington Redskins football team, had to wait six months to get in, insinuating that we got in just as fast."

Financially, John and Charlotte were spread about as thinly as they could be, she recalls. But December 1974, John made partner at Arnold & Porter. He was thirty-three.

By April 1975, four months later, Charlotte was pregnant again.

"Those first years here I was totally subservient," says Charlotte. "I was barefoot and pregnant, literally. I had three little ones and was expecting a fourth. I didn't seriously question any of these financially burdensome things John wanted to do. I didn't think at all except when I was dressed up and sent out to be a social asset at parties. When we went out, John would go over all the names and tell me whom to talk to and what not to say. I could make a good impression. But I was basically just a little housewife. Under 'profession' on our IRS forms, John would put 'none' for me. He didn't even say 'homemaker.' "

Charlotte doesn't remember John striking her those first three years in Washington, but she does remember the time in October 1974 when John came home from an Arnold & Porter basketball game against another law firm with a broken hand. John told her and Luke that one of the opponent's players had nudged him roughly and hurt him. They recall that John said it had angered him enough that he retaliated, hitting the offender and thus breaking his hand. "He was cocky about it," says Charlotte.

"He wasn't exactly proud of it, but he joked about it. It went along with his attitude that boys will be boys and to play with the boys you gotta be tough."

Her family remembers one Christmas during those years that Charlotte looked as if she had been struck, that her left eye appeared bruised and swollen and that her glasses were broken. "There were quite a few bruises from shoves and such that I just don't remember specifically, but my family remembers seeing," says Charlotte.

Martha, Mimi, and Helen gathered in the O'Donnells' pantry during their holiday meal and asked each other in concerned whispers: "Where do you suppose she got that bruise?"

"We all knew," says Martha, "but none of us was willing to confront her about it. She had said something like she had walked into a door. What were we supposed to do, say, 'You're lying'? Back then, none of us would tell anybody anything anyway. In the early seventies, you didn't rock the boat. And you figured that if that person really wanted to tell you they would. Part of it was respect for privacy.

"That was a pattern in our family. We just avoided unpleasantness. Our mother always used to say, 'I don't allow my girls to fight.' And we didn't. Anger was impolite, unacceptable behavior. So we wouldn't have brought up the subject of a bruised eye to Charlotte. We didn't know how to express our own emotions much less try to find out about hers."

12

While Washington gleefully celebrated the bicentennial, glorifying all the promises of the American way, Charlotte and John's difficult yet seemingly stable marriage burst into violence again.

The year before, 1975, despite his making partner, was full of pressure at work for John, remembers Charlotte. He told her that he was eager to become a percentage partner, the next and final rung in Arnold & Porter's salary ladder, which meant profit sharing. He worked even harder to prove himself and to stand out from his colleagues, specializing in white-collar crime and internal corporate investigations of questionable payments and money management. It was an opportune choice of specialties, because more and more companies were responding to the public's demand for corporate openness after Watergate.

But his responsibilities meant more and more out-of-town travel and ultimately more stress. They probably also brought a lot of strain since he was, in essence, often serving as a kind of judge, weighing the testimony of his clients' employees and deciding whether they were truthful. John rarely talked to his wife about his work, she says—perhaps because he felt that she wouldn't understand the complexities of corporate law, perhaps because she didn't know how to ask about his cases, perhaps because the house was full of active, tiny children when he came home at night, exhausted. He just didn't tell her much about it, so Charlotte never really knew who his clients were, or with whom he felt he competed at Arnold & Porter. At that point, she had never even met his secretary face to face. The few times she met him downtown during the week, John would join her someplace other than his office.

Of course, her major concerns were those of her children. Perhaps John began to feel like an outsider in his own home, since his and Charlotte's day-to-day worlds were almost entirely separate. Their mutual circles of interests were quickly shrinking.

Maybe John began to resent Charlotte. He had claimed the kingship of being the sole provider for his family, and now he was faced with its overwhelming responsibilities—four needy people, completely dependent on him for their daily bread. Perhaps if he had opened up to Charlotte and shared more of his professional life with her, she wouldn't have seemed so cloying to him, their relationship so one-way, his burdens so overpowering.

Charlotte says that he was not pleased that she was expecting again, and tension mounted as her pregnancy with their fourth child dragged on beyond the predicted due date.

"I wasn't thrilled either about having yet another baby, since it was happening so soon," says Charlotte. "There was only an eighteen months' difference between Matthew and John Michael. John Michael wasn't born until the end of January 1976, three weeks late. When you're pregnant with your fourth baby, every extra day seems a week long.

"In early March, there were some other children here playing with my boys, and I pulled my back and started having trouble breathing. It was one of the few times I called John at his office for help. At first, he wouldn't come. By the time he did get home, I could hardly breathe. I was hyperventilating. I asked him to get help. The rescue squad came. Neighbors were here trying to help. When most of these people finally left the house, and he figured out that I was going to be okay, he started being really abusive verbally, yelling at me about his being late for a practice game of a school basketball team he was coaching. He also yelled at me about the casserole I had been fixing for the boys' supper. It was a macaroni thing. It wasn't the greatest. But he said that the neighbors would wonder about what kind of mother I was, serving my children such 'shit.' Then he left. That incident started a siege that didn't stop until June.

"My sister Dotti and her husband were coming in from overseas that night, and they stayed and helped me. That was about the worst twenty-four hours of my life. Later that week, I packed up the kids and stayed with a neighbor across the street for two days. I never did that unless I was afraid of him hurting me physically. I stood at their window and watched him come and go for those two days. He never tried to find us.

"When I came back, he wasn't talking. He barely spoke to me for three months. I moved out of our bedroom. John never seemed to have any trouble sleeping, which made me feel that, since he seemed so guilt-free, I probably was the guilty party. He also even slept mad when he was angry at me. He'd lie flat and rigid, staring up at the ceiling with this gulf between us. I couldn't bear the thought that even subconsciously, in his sleep, he hated me. But even though I had left our bedroom, each morning I went in and made his bed. And I continued to do his laundry. John didn't even come to John Michael's baptism March twenty-sixth. That was humiliating.

"I was starting to lose control. I was driving car pools for two different schools at 8:30 and 11 AM and 3 PM every weekday. I had a seven-year-old, three-year-old, almost-two-year-old, and a newborn. I had to take them all with me whenever I went to the grocery store or on an errand. It took two grocery carts just for the kids. John didn't help me with any of these chores. He hardly talked at all and barely touched John Michael then, his own namesake. That was the biggest hurt. Nothing I said or did got through to him."

Finally, too distraught and scared to stay at home one night, Charlotte went to the home of her friend Sandy Oseroff, around dinner time. She arrived with all her children in tow. It was the first time her friend, a friend she had made when she first moved to Potomac, heard of the serious troubles between her and John.

"I can remember John Michael sitting in his little infant seat on the counter," says Sandy Oseroff. "We were having spaghetti when she arrived. She was very upset about the fact John wouldn't touch that baby. It was the first time she told me about real trouble. I remember once before seeing Charlotte with a bruise, but she had said that she had bumped into a door and I believed it because she always flits around like the wind, with all those kids. I didn't even think to question her. It wouldn't have even occurred to me that he might strike her. I mean, this was John and Charlotte, a successful young attorney and a sweet, good mom." Charlotte contacted a lawyer right around the time of John Michael's baptism. A sympathetic neighbor had recommended him. Charlotte wanted to know what her rights were. She recalls that when John did speak to her these days he threatened that he was going to sell the house and then she'd have to go live in a cheap apartment in Silver Spring.

The lawyer was "an old-timey Catholic," as Charlotte describes him. She told him she didn't want a divorce. She just wanted to know how she could make things better. He suggested that she needed something other than legal advice and gave her the name of a pastor he thought would prove helpful to her to call.

The priest turned out to be very helpful. "He didn't tell me that I was a battered wife or anything," says Charlotte, "but he did suggest that we needed marriage counseling. And either the priest or the lawyer suggested another psychiatrist, whom I started seeing. This psychiatrist was very nice. It was a much better experience than the one I had in 1973. I sat right across his desk from him in a cheery room and he was a reassuring, gentle, fatherly-figure type. I started going to him about once a week. I paid for it with our insurance so I wouldn't have to tell John until the time was right.

"I could talk to this psychiatrist about almost everything. He was into finding out all about my history too, and what in my past screwed me up, but at least I liked him and I could tell he liked me. That made me feel good. He seemed genuinely interested in me, and he seemed to continue liking me even when I told him about some of the awful things that happened between John and me. Of course, I never told him about slapping myself. I came as clean with him as I probably was able to in those days.

"I did tell him about the beating. That psychiatrist was the first person to say to me that John's physical treatment of me was 'inappropriate behavior.' Of course, he didn't say that it was unacceptable, or that I was abused. Now I know that then only a few specialists were just starting to write about the battered wife syndrome. It wasn't something people wrote or talked about at all. Because I was still so insecure, I didn't realize that, no matter what I did, no one deserves to be hit. So I figured that there was still something 'inappropriate' about me that was eliciting this 'inappropriate' response from John.

"That feeling was probably accentuated by the fact the psychiatrist's emphasis was not on the marriage but on trying to make me happier with me. Once we had done that, we'd see about the marriage, he said. So I set out to make myself better, too, mainly by going on a diet because I knew John hated me fat and unattractive.

"I continued to try to talk to John about going to see the marriage counselor the priest had recommended. That was pretty brave of me. John told me that he didn't want to see this counselor because he was a former priest. In other words, I guess in John's opinion, this man hadn't lived up to his religious vows and he had never been married, so what would he know.

"Another factor in all this trouble was that John's sister was getting married on Memorial Day weekend. She wanted us both in the wedding. John told his parents that he wasn't going if I was going. When I tried to reason with him about it, he told me that *I* was messing up his sister's wedding. My psychiatrist told me that John was 'transferring,' accusing me of things he actually was doing himself. But I still had to get him to that wedding somehow. I had his parents call the priest, because he had been so helpful. He told them to tell John that they expected both of us there, period. So that's what they did.

"In May, the marriage counselor called John and got him to agree to a meeting with him and me, to take place about a week before we were supposed to leave for the wedding. Of course, John wasn't talking to me, so I still didn't know if he was going or not. I went to the appointment with the counselor but John never showed up."

Even though John had failed to come, Charlotte owed the counselor for the session. The bill was about $80. She took a check from the checkbook in John's closet and left information about the amount and to whom it was written on top of the desk.

"I was in the bathroom," remembers Charlotte, "sitting on a closed toilet, bathing two of the boys in the tub. John came home, went upstairs, and saw my note. He came into the bathroom and started beating me with his fists and pulling on my hair. I turned away to protect myself, and he beat me on my back. I managed to get out and ran into Luke's room, because I didn't think that he'd hit me in front of Luke. But he ran after me. I can remember crouching in the corner. He beat my neck and shoulder and back. Then he chased me into our bedroom. He yelled at one point, 'I don't give a shit if I kill you.'

"It was one of the worst beatings John ever gave me. And I hadn't done anything but written a check. I hadn't even talked to him that night before the attack. It really frightened me. I went to see my internist because I realized that I might need evidence at some point if John did decide to divorce me. I never thought that *I* might need the evidence in order to divorce him. The doctor measured all the bruises. But the only thing I can remember him saying was 'This is very immature.' Nothing else. It must have been uncomfortable for him. He belonged to Congressional Country Club as well and John and I saw him and his wife socially. But I was probably ready to hear the truth this time."

Right after the beating, Charlotte fled up the street to her neighbor and friend Denise Gogarty.

"Charlotte appeared at my door, holding the baby," remembers Gogarty. "Then the other boys came in from the car. She was crying. She was hurting. I saw the bruise starting on her shoulder. She was afraid to go home and I was afraid for her too. My mother was visiting here and I didn't have room for all of them. So I called the police. They told me that they wouldn't come unless she was willing to press charges. I turned to Charlotte and she shook her head and said, 'No.' She didn't want to charge him. And I couldn't even keep them on the phone after she said no.

"Charlotte had told me before that John had broken her eardrum. We were sitting in the park at Cabin John, and the kids were playing on the swings. We were talking about something and she said that she'd be afraid to tell John that. And I asked why and she told me that he had hit her. I was astounded. The idea of someone I knew being hit was so foreign to me.

"I knew about the daily routine of the dressing and the house, too. I wondered why she loved him so much, although I understood why she was intimidated. Even when he was being polite, he was always baiting you in conversation. I also found it very difficult to talk to him when he was standing. It was a little bit easier when he was sitting.

"Charlotte was such a capable person. She could handle anything, without having to plan it. If something broke she fixed it. If the kids hurt themselves, she took them to the hospital, no problem. She handled everything easily, except for John."

As Charlotte drove to the airport with her children, she still didn't know if John was planning to come to the wedding. "I didn't know if he would get on the plane. Just before boarding, he showed up at the terminal. He didn't talk to me during the whole rehearsal dinner, wedding, or wedding reception. It did embarrass me. It also embarrassed me because the bridesmaids' dresses were sleeveless and I still had a very ugly bruise on my arm from the beating over the check. I remember having to turn the left side of my body away from the camera for the wedding party pictures.

"It really confused me, because he had a great time with all the guests. I figured since he seemed so happy with everyone else, that obviously all this trouble came from some terrible flaw in me. It had to be my fault. Luke fell during the reception and had to have some stitches. The husband of one of the bridesmaids drove me to the hospital."

Because her in-laws had been so immersed in this travail, Charlotte tried to talk to his mother about John and his treatment of her. Her response, as Charlotte remembers, was: "Well, honey, I think you better get some help so that you learn how to deal with Johnny."

"Which, of course, simply reinforced the idea that the root of all this was me," says Charlotte.

Somehow, in the motel, Charlotte and John reconciled. "We got back together with the usual romp in bed, nothing more concrete than that. But this time there were all sorts of promises. He promised that he'd never hit me again, that he'd do anything, anything to make it up to me. I made him promise me, as I held him in my arms, that I could keep seeing the psychiatrist. And he agreed.

"I went back to Washington feeling really proud of myself. I had managed to go and handle being at that wedding. It was the first time I had been able to play the role of the happy couple while knowing that things were really awful between us. That was a major accomplishment for me. I couldn't have done that a year before. I had pulled myself together. I had lost weight and looked good. And I had won my husband back.

"I had so much more self-assurance; even the psychiatrist asked how my husband liked the new me. I was pleased that I was pleasing my doctor, too, that he thought there was a new me. I thought things were going to be great from then on."

For a while they were. When John left for a business trip to London, Paris, and Brussels in June, Charlotte lovingly tucked little notes into his shirt pockets and jackets when she packed his suitcase. He gratefully acknowledged them in one of the nine postcards he wrote on his travels, cards rich with details on his doings, which he signed with "I miss you all."

When he was home, he was affectionate. "I could always judge how a day was going to go with John according to how he woke up," says Charlotte. "If he stretched and reached across and hugged me, then he was in a good mood and things were going to be great. Those were the days when he'd do the giant hug, when the whole family would just gather up in a bunch and do one big squeeze on the count of three."

But by August, Charlotte and John's relationship was already strained, she says. For a day's retreat from the tension in the house, Charlotte took the boys to Catoctin State Park in Thurmont, Maryland, near Camp David and near her alma mater, Saint Joseph's College.

"I never took the kids away by myself like that unless John was in one of his moods or silences. It was an escape for me. I went back to the mountains, back to an area where I had been so happy. I took the boys to see where I had gone to school and then took them to the little beach at a lake near Thurmont. It was a lovely day, even with my having to manage a seven-year-old and three children under four by myself. The boys and I always had a good time on those kinds of outings. I tried to make John's moods into relaxed times for them as almost a way of self-preservation for me. I knew that I could do that outing because I wouldn't have to explain everything I had done that day, because John was just plain ignoring my existence."

Although John had promised Charlotte that she could continue her therapy, he began complaining about the cost. Perhaps he didn't have confidence in psychotherapy, perhaps he was threatened by his wife's fledgling confidence. Perhaps he didn't like someone else influencing her. Perhaps he thought she should have the self-discipline to help herself, or at least control herself. In any case, his comments about her sessions could border on ridicule, recalls Charlotte.

"He'd sort of sneer at me: 'What did you do at your shrink today?' " she says.

In the early fall, Charlotte decided to stop seeing her doctor. Withstanding John's complaints did her more harm than the sessions did her good, she says. She was losing the energy to fight him about it.

When she told the psychiatrist she was stopping, however, she didn't admit the real reasons for it. "I padded it," she remembers. "I told him that things were working out so well, and I was so happy. I didn't say anything about the money, because I knew he'd see that as a hint that John might be pressuring me and I wanted the doctor to still like me. He left it very open about my coming back to see him. But I never did.

"It's hard to explain how depressed you feel when you realize that things haven't really changed when you thought they were going well. I was so sure that we were making progress and then John would be moody or silent and we were back to square one. It would make me crazy and so desperate. I would think, 'I've worked so hard. Good God, what do I have to do now?' "

The feeling Charlotte described is one that keeps many abused wives in their situation. Each time their husbands apologize and they float through a honeymoon period their hopes are rekindled. "This time will be different. He's so repentant that this time I can really trust him," they think. But after the reconciliations fade, time and time again, the women become more and more hopeless and depressed, making decisive action—such as leaving—almost impossible for them.

The weapons for control, then, don't have to be physical, says Dr. Susan Forward. She writes in *Men Who Hate Women and the Women Who Love Them:* "Abuse is defined as any behavior that is designed to control and subjugate another human being through the use of fear, humiliation, and verbal or physical assaults. . . . [It is] the systematic persecution of one partner by another . . . they wear down their partners through unrelenting criticism and fault-finding. This type of psychological abuse is particularly insidious because it is often disguised as a way of teaching the woman how to be a better person."

After having their spirit broken cyclically like this for years—whether it is purposeful or not on the part of their spouses—abused women, as defined by Forward, are worn down enough psychologically to be malleable and obedient. They become incapable of the self-confidence needed for changing their lives, and learn to hate themselves.

"I used to bang my open palm against the kitchen cabinets in complete frustration, hard enough to bend my ring," says Charlotte. "I also used to hide in the closet during that horrible, horrible year of 1976. It was terrible, a human being huddled in a closet like a prisoner of war. I wasn't hiding from him because he was yelling at me, or because he had threatened me. I'd usually hide when he wasn't responding at all. Looking at me with hate or looking straight through me, saying nothing. I just couldn't stand the emotional rejection anymore. I'd go in the baby's room and cower in the dark, curled up in a fetal position. It was like a tranquilizer, because it was a void. It was quiet, and I couldn't see him. But most importantly, it was dark enough that I couldn't see myself."

13

Some of the pressures on the burgeoning family eased in 1977, when John's yearly income at Arnold & Porter rocketed to around $137,000. Charlotte recalls that their increased bank account relieved much of the tension between them. They starting planning more family outings. During basketball season, for instance, the family traveled to Blacksburg, Virginia, for a Marquette game, and the boys had the thrill of sitting on the team's bench with John. Charlotte stayed in the bleachers with the baby, watching her husband and children with pride.

Charlotte says that they were given such wonderful seats because John was an active alumnus of his college, a steady contributor—starting in 1978, he would give $1,000 to Marquette annually. That April, John was one of three people chosen for the 1977 alumni service award.

That spring, the family also planned summer vacations to Maryland's Ocean City, Charlotte's old haunt, and to Florida's Disney World. It seemed to be a time of rebuilding after the explosive year before. Late that spring, Charlotte even told her sister Martha that things were going so well that she was afraid something bad would happen.

On July 3, their seventeen-month-old baby, John Michael, died of spinal meningitis.

The tragedy was even more wrenching for Charlotte because a few days before John Michael became ill, she and John had slipped into another tense time, and she later blamed herself for being too preoccupied with their troubles. She remembers that John had become moody and terse, speaking irregularly to Charlotte or throwing snide comments.

"We were at a neighborhood picnic when John Michael was still alive," says Denise Gogarty, "and we were talking about teenagers and sex. And John said something to everybody about the liberties that Charlotte had allowed him before they were married that she shouldn't have. It shocked me to my core that he would say something like that in front of all these people. The inference was that it had been bad and that it wasn't his fault, it was hers. Charlotte's response was an embarrassed laugh, and so was everybody else's. What could you say?"

"There are times I think had I not been so obsessed with trying to make things better with John," Charlotte says, "that I would have realized how sick this child was sooner. Or I would have had the strength to be more forceful with the doctor and the hospital.

"John had been coming and going without a word for about a week. In those days, he used to go to the men's grill at Congressional to eat dinner. He didn't tell me that's where he went. He never told me anything. I used to drive over to Congressional and look for his car. I would be relieved when I found it and just drive back home and wait. Occasionally I would go in to look for him and if he happened to pass by me, he would actually stare right through me and say nothing, even if I was going in the entrance as he was coming out.

"Two evenings before my baby would die, July first, I was sitting out front with the boys watching them play at the bottom of our hill. It was a Friday night. John came home, went upstairs, and changed his clothes and then got back into the car and drove off. He didn't even wave or nod at his kids. I sat there like a prisoner watching my captor walk away and thought to myself, 'I just wish he would die.' I had a hard time forgiving myself for that, too. I thought for a long time that God had heard me and punished me by killing my child.

"I put John Michael to sleep that night. He had a fever, but the next morning he woke up and was fine. No fever, nothing. That was the day I started packing John's suitcase for him, saying, 'This can't go on' type of things. Sometimes that would have gotten me a slap or anger; this time it snapped him out of it.

"We made up that morning and went to Congressional to swim. While we were there John Michael got hot and lethargic. I took him home and put him to bed. He had a high fever so I called the doctor. It's funny the things you have the hardest time forgetting. One of the things I feel worst about is following the doctor's orders and putting this child, who was twenty-four hours away from dying, through the trauma of immersing him in a cool tub of water to lower his temperature. He was screaming hysterically. But it worked; the fever came down and he slept.

"But the next morning John Michael wasn't better. I took him to the doctor's and that's when they discovered that his neck was rigid. I went to the hospital. At first they thought he had pneumonia. Eventually they found that he had bacterial meningitis, the kind of meningitis that kills. But I still didn't think he could die. Modern medicine was so wonderful, there was no way a doctor would let my baby die.

"By the time they were doing the spinal tap, John had come. I had had to call the neighbors to get him, because he was outside cutting the grass. He thought I had just gone to the doctor's office.

"We had to sign papers allowing them to give John Michael medication that might cause deafness. They had put him into intensive care. We thought the deafness was the worst that could happen. There was no indication of how serious his condition really was, so John went home.

"Things got bad very quickly. I called John and told him he better get back to the hospital. He asked me if I thought we were going to lose him and a few seconds later John Michael turned to look at me and said, 'Mommy.' Then the numbers on the monitor started going down, 90, 89, 88. I turned to the nurse and asked, 'What does that mean?' He was in cardiac arrest.

"They got me out of there so fast. John got there very quickly and went in while they worked on him. They tried to save my baby for more than an hour. My faith utterly failed me. There was a priest there trying to get me to say the rosary, and I thought, 'How can I pray to a God who's letting my baby die?'

"I went in and held him. I had to. John was with me. John was very good to me then. He handled the funeral arrangements for me. When we got home, I saw John Michael's little red sneakers and that's when I became hysterical. So John told the children what happened and did it very well. He was a great comfort to me. If anything, I feel that I didn't do enough for him.

"I didn't want the children to see their brother in a coffin, so we didn't have a viewing. John agreed with that. He's buried in his OshKosh overalls and he's holding his *Sesame Street* Ernie doll. He's also wearing a Miraculous Medal I had worn for years. I couldn't give up his sneakers; I still have them."

John Michael is buried in Saint Gabriel's, a small Catholic cemetery tucked into a Potomac neighborhood, where, ironically, John had found the only other house they had considered purchasing upon leaving Dallas. The baby's flat, white tombstone reads: "Having become perfect in a short while, he reached the fullness of a long career." It was a verse from the Bible's Book of Wisdom, read at the funeral mass for children. Charlotte requested they play "O Lord, I Am Not Worthy" at the service.

On the day of the funeral, July 5, hundreds of people crowded into John and Charlotte's church, Our Lady of Mercy, and followed the hearse to the cemetery. Through her tears, Charlotte recognized relatives and school friends she hadn't seen for years, interspersed with many of John's work associates. At the graveside, after the ceremony was concluded, John chose to lead a song unusual for a Catholic ceremony: "We Shall Overcome."

Afterwards, many of the crowd went back to Carmelite Drive. Their friends brought so much food with them that Charlotte says she just didn't have the heart to ask them to leave, as John would have preferred her to.

"I went upstairs and found John lying on the floor in his dressing room, attached to our bedroom. He was crying. He said, 'God has sacrificed our baby to save our marriage. It's to shake us up and make us realize our marriage is worth saving and to make us work harder.' "

Charlotte recalls that she and John pulled together well during their child's death and its aftermath. She loved him more for his strength and attentiveness during this time. The only thing they disagreed on was the gravestone. According to Charlotte, he preferred to have only a headstone, rather than the full-length stone.

"I just had to have something special covering the entire grave," says Charlotte. "I stuck to my guns on it. John was in Alaska when we had to make the final decision. I told him that was the last expense we'd have for this child. And then he accused me of being cruel. Maybe I was. But we had the money for it and I really wanted John Michael to have a tribute for all the happiness he had given us.

"I don't think anything is harder than burying a child. John grieved a great deal about it, even though he didn't talk about it much. Different people handle things differently. We read *The Bereaved Parent* that summer. They say the divorce rate after the death of a child is incredibly high. And John claims that that's when the marriage started going bad. I can't help but resent his saying that, because that's not the reason our marriage failed. I think the turning point for us had been the year before, when there had been so much violence. How can you ever really recover from that? And I know that after John Michael's death, we both worked harder on our marriage for a while."

John and Charlotte had always been regular churchgoers, and despite her momentary loss of faith when their baby died, they continued to go weekly. She prayed especially hard the day the Mass included a special tribute to the Holy Family and all families went as a group to the altar for a special yearly blessing.

Each Sunday, John attended Mass whether he was with his family or alone, says Charlotte. If he was out of town, he asked if she and the boys went. John had always held on to the self-control taught by the Church as his way of coping, she says, and he clung to it now as he doggedly tried "to go back to normal."

"John never missed going to church," says Charlotte. "Even when we were having terrible fights and he was staying away from home, I'd see him drive past the house up to the monastery's chapel for Mass. Those were the times that I'd spend hours by the window, waiting and watching, not knowing where he was.

"He'd always receive Communion, even when things were bad, which I had difficulty with. I believe that you have to be in some kind of peace with yourself before you receive the sacraments. If you believe, as I do, and Catholics are supposed to, that the sacrament is truly the body of Christ, then a soul in turmoil is no place for the Host. When we were in one of these bad periods, I would go to church with him but not go up for Communion. Even if he had just been yelling at me or the boys, he went, There were even times that we went to church happy and left upset. John dragged Luke out of church by his collar a couple of times. He would get very angry with the boys if they misbehaved. Of course, this was not for screaming 'I hate God' or something; it was for giving a brother the elbow or giggling.

"John told me that he never went to confession from the birth of Luke until after our divorce trial. Confession is not a very pleasant thing, especially for someone like John, because he would have had to admit that he had weaknesses. Confession is a strong part of the Catholic Church, so it is surprising that he didn't go. But I think he felt he had not done anything wrong. He's too ethical and too smart to do anything wrong at work, and I don't think he realized that the beating was wrong, so in his mind he probably didn't have anything to confess.

"But what was important to him was the self-control taught by the Church. He believed totally in it. If he set his mind to something, by God, he could do it. It was almost scary. He really could achieve anything, no matter the pain. I think that's why he was so good at work. And even though his quietness about John Michael hurt me a little bit, because I needed to talk about it more, I think that his self-control is what got him through the death."

Despite the tragedy, the family went on its prearranged vacations. Charlotte and John thought it would be better for the children. Their stay in Disney World was particularly pleasant, since an executive of one of John's more important clients, Coca-Cola, had arranged for them to rent a lavish room at the popular Contemporary Hotel. Without his influence, John and Charlotte probably would have had difficulty getting any reservations within Disney World. Charlotte remembers the room (overlooking the lake) as being one of the nicest the family ever had while traveling.

In September, Charlotte and John also traveled to California, for a wedding of a business associate. They stopped for a night in Las Vegas with some of the other guests for some betting fun. Sometime on that trip, Charlotte became pregnant, and the joy of having another chance with another child carried the couple for many months.

On Mother's Day, 1978, John gave Charlotte what she thinks was the most thoughtful present she ever received from him, a top-flight camera in acknowledgment of what a good mother she was. In his card he wrote: "You're the greatest. I love and appreciate you more each day." From then on, whenever they attended Marquette basketball games, John arranged for Charlotte to have a photographer's pass so she could sit on the floor, next to professionals from publication such as *Time* and *Sports Illustrated.*

"It was wonderful," says Charlotte. "It was one of those exciting status things that only John could have gotten, because he was so friendly with the assistant coach then. I really learned a great deal about photography during those games. It was a really nice thing for him to do for me."

Jekyll and Hyde. It's the best way Charlotte can think to describe the two personalities she saw of John: one generous, admirable, and affectionate, so easy to love; the other harsh, manipulative, and belittling. The kind man could dissolve into the oppressor so suddenly, and leave Charlotte just bewildered. Had he been just all bad, she could have left him, she says. But the memory of the shining knight kept her lingering in the nightmare forest, waiting, watching. Where did the man she fell in love with go?

A mere month after that heartwarming Mother's Day, for instance, she and John had dinner with several friends. Charlotte would go into labor later that night, several days early. Both Denise Gogarty and another friend, Nick Deoudes, remember Charlotte being in tears over John's comments about her during the evening, and that he reached over and roughly squeezed her belly, teasing her about her weight.

Within a few hours John would be holding her hand in the delivery room, so attentive. Then he questioned Charlotte, she says, for asking for an epidermal painkiller when the contractions became too much to bear. She felt that he was criticizing her when she needed his support.

And so it always was, back and forth, back and forth. Was she dancing with Dr. Jekyll or Mr. Hyde?

Then Andrew Marquette came and everything was wonderful. She smiled gratefuly into the eyes of Dr. Jekyll. The baby came on Father's Day, and seemed to be an answer to prayers.

About two months later, the family flew to Wisconsin to spend a week at a lake in Hiles. They shared a large cabin with one of John's college friends and his family. They had a lovely time, fishing, hiking, and just talking. Charlotte hadn't known the couple that well before and she was interested to see that the college friend's wife didn't fetch and carry for him. She recalls that John commented that he thought she was selfish because of it.

One night, the couple told Charlotte they wanted to play a record for her. They said, laughing, "This really describes your and John's relationship." It was a country song performed by Tompall Glaser called "Put Another Log on the Fire" and the verses go like this:

Put another log on the fire.
Cook me up some bacon and some beans.
And go out to the car and change the tire.
Wash my socks and sew my old blue jeans.

Come on baby,
You can fill my pipe,
And then go fetch my slippers,

And boil me up another pot of tea.
Then put another log on the fire, babe,
And come and tell me why you're leaving me.

Now, don't I let you wash the car on Sunday?
And don't I warn you when you're gettin' fat?
Ain't I gonna take you fishin' with me someday?
Well, a man can't love a woman more than that.

Ain't I always nice to your kid sister?
Don't I take her driving every night?
So sit here at my feet, 'cause I like you when you're
sweet.
And you know it ain't feminine to fight.

Charlotte laughed, although she was surprised that their
friends had picked up on how much she catered to John.
She was also surprised that John laughed good-naturedly
and thought it a fine joke indeed. "If he can laugh at it, why
can't he ease up a bit?" she wondered.

The night before their twelfth anniversary, while they
were in Wisconsin, Charlotte wrote in a diary she kept hap-
hazardly through several years. She started relating the
boys' fishing expedition, and then somehow, alone in her
reveries, all her childlike insecurities spilled out: "We are in
Wisconsin now. The boys think it is heaven—it is lovely—
cool breezes, large lake and everyone is relaxed. John is so
calm now, seems happy. I really love him. How I wish we
did this more often. Every year. It would be a renewal. . . .
When am I going to feel successful? I still have poor handwriting, still pick at my nail cuticles, I still freak out on
homemade, chocolate chip cookies . . . I really am a weak-
ling. Sometimes I think if I could only feel more useful I'd
have a better self image and better figure. I'd love to lose
another ten pounds and keep it off. Once you feel fat, you
always feel fat. . . . Hair is a wreck. I guess I just wish I
was a natural beauty. I hate glasses, flabby chins, and being

36. John says I'm unhappy. I love my kids. I really do enjoy being a housewife. I'm simple enough to enjoy driving my boys to school and other activities. I am impatient especially with John. . . . He says I have a good life. Why aren't I good enough for him to want to take out alone or go away with to something other than a basketball game? . . . Maybe too much has happened. Too much meanness—too much taking each other for granted. If only he could understand that I need a man to want to be with me. . . . Sometimes I think I'd like to live alone with the boys, but I can't imagine life without John. I just wish I was more important to him."

But all in all, the trip was a regenerative one, says Charlotte. Unfortunately, the healing didn't last for long.

John was becoming more and more restless at Arnold & Porter. Sometime during the middle of Jimmy Carter's administration, he was considered for a government post, says Charlotte. He didn't get the job, but suddenly the partnership and the lucrative salary, the goals of so many years, didn't seem to be enough.

Long ago, John had considered going into politics on the grass roots level. But now a Washington fever seemed to possess him—a desire so many have in the capital, to seep into the corridors of power without having to answer to a constituency; to snare a prestigious job high up in the bureaucracy, close enough to real politicians to ride on their jet stream, without having to sweat through an election themselves.

Twice during the Carter administration, Charlotte and John attended black-tie dinners hosted by the Democratic National Committee, as guests of the father of a friend of John's involved with Marquette's basketball team. One evening John sat next to the mayor of Detroit. Muhammad Ali, President Carter, Senate Majority Leader Robert Byrd, all manner of celebrities were there. Charlotte remembers John making a beeline to Congressman and former basketball star

Bill Bradley. Maybe those evenings fueled his discontent with a mere law practice.

"I think John was beginning to realize," says Charlotte, "that even with the money and the prestigious law firm, he wasn't happy. Maybe it's impossible to maintain the intense kinds of lives we were leading—me running around doing this, this, and this for the kids and him going up, up, up—unless you really work hard at the marriage. Maybe the great American dream—the nice, big family, successful children, money to do whatever you want, prestige job—is a farce.

"John had reached it. He was a partner in one of the city's best law firms. We were beginning to get out of debt. But he wasn't happy. That's when he started telling me he was a gypsy and wanted to move around. He thought about moving to Los Angeles and to Denver, where the firm was contemplating opening offices. He talked about being a judge, about taking some time off to coach basketball. I couldn't understand it. We were at the end of the rainbow—he had everything he had told me he wanted—and then suddenly we weren't.

"He had been in one of those silences since September. He had been coming home late, around nine, and eating only soup. I found out later that he had been having dinners with a woman lawyer at Arnold & Porter, who was going through a divorce. But they were just friends.

"Halloween night, 1978, John handed me a piece of paper with a lawyer's name on it and telephone number. He told me that she would be calling me about a divorce. That's all he said. Then he walked away. I was devastated, stunned, hurt, panicked.

"I actually stopped helping him dress in the morning. I called a lawyer, and he told me to sit tight until January, because the divorce laws were changing at the first of the year. So I waited. I was a wreck. I pleaded with John not to leave me and he laughed at me and said he had been 'dating' for years. I couln't believe it. But I asked one of his secretaries and she told me that it was true. So my lawyer hired a private detective to check out John's claims. But he never discovered anything. Later, John admitted in his deposition which was read in court to one affair that started either Christmas 1973 or 1974. I think it was at an office party to which no spouses were invited.

"In desperation I went to see our priest at Our Lady of Mercy. I sat in a big chair in his study and cried. I didn't tell him anything about the past physical abuse. I just told him about the communication problem and the divorce John wanted. I talked to him twice and he called John. I was so hopeful when he told me that John was coming to see him. I went to see the priest afterward and he told me that John didn't really want a divorce and that I should just give him time to sort things out. That I should just love him. Just love him. I thought I had been loving him.

"Meanwhile, John wasn't speaking to me and took the three oldest boys to New York City for Thanksgiving. We had won the firm's lottery to have its apartment up there over the holidays. Suddenly out of the blue, he called from the train station and begged me to come with them. To forgive him. To take him back. Then he called from the train, then from the train station in New York, then from the apartment. I couldn't believe it. But this time I resisted and said no.

"I stayed home with the baby and pampered myself by reading *The Thorn Birds*. I even read in bed, something John didn't like me to do. I had Thanksgiving dinner with my family. It was a wonderful break for me in some ways because it had been years since I had been alone with only one small, quiet baby to take care of. And I was feeling strong because somehow John had changed his mind.

"When he came home, I had made Brunswick stew and I went upstairs to ask him if he'd like some. And I don't know what happened but within a few hours we were in bed. He said that he had lied about the women to hurt me. And he was going to be so good to me from then on. Because I knew that in this frame of mind he would agree to anything, I had actually drawn up a list of rights that I wanted him to agree to. Of course, they were very little things, like being able to plant flowers if I wanted. He would later ridicule my measly demands as being my 'bill of rights.' But at the time, it felt wonderful that he said okay to them.

"That first week, when he came home, he tooted the horn and opened the garage door himself and came into the kitchen with a big 'Hi, Char,' 'Hi, boys, Dad's home.' Then he'd give us all big hugs. It was wonderful. I was so happy. Our honeymoon periods weren't the kind of wining and dining fantasies you hear about, but they were periods of really nice behavior on his part. He would say over and over again how beautiful I was. He would call me more frequently during the day and tell me all the things he had done. They were wonderful periods of real communication."

Some people, though, weren't as thrilled about their reconciliation as Charlotte was. For Charlotte's sister Martha, the disappointment was great. Ever since Pelham, she had heard Charlotte tell the same sad stories. Charlotte used her sister as a kind of wailing wall, gaining cathartic solace from releasing all her emotions. Then, renewed herself, Charlotte left her sister atremble with the weight of her sorrows, expecting Martha to still be standing strong, waiting, next time Charlotte needed her. It could be too much for Martha sometimes, particularly since Charlotte didn't seem to want to leave John. Martha felt as if she was watching Charlotte slowly die, as surely as if she had terminal cancer.

After all the frenetic closeness she and Charlotte had had during the crisis of John's announcing he wanted a divorce, Charlotte suddenly cut Martha off. Hurt and angered, Martha pulled back from her sister. The relationship between man and wife is not the only one to suffer in marital discord. Ultimately, such strains only isolate the spouse more, making her husband's influence even more profound.

"She would call me after these fights, crying," says Martha. "She'd be in pieces. I didn't know enough to say to her, 'Hey, look, this isn't normal.' I would tell her to ease up on herself, that she really wasn't an awful person at all. During these really bad periods, she needed constant attention. I was worried that she'd throw herself off a bridge or something, so I called daily, sometimes hourly, to check up on her and see how she was. Then, as soon as they made up, she'd pull away from me. After this intense period, then, you felt like she had dropped you off a cliff. You see, for her to be close with him during these honeymoon periods, to rationalize her decision to go back to him, she had to cut off the person she had told all these horrible things to. That's partly how she could deny that the bad existed. So I never got to share in any of the good times. I heard only the bad.

"And I had been bludgeoned by his comments. I had seen the silences myself. One time he came home when I was there. He walked in, didn't speak to me, to Charlotte, to the kids. He went upstairs, changed, sat down to tie his shoes in the kitchen where we all were, and went out to run without saying one word. I was gone before he got back. So I knew what her life was like. Charlotte deserved better.

"The Thanksgiving that John went to New York, I thought she had finally gotten strong enough to leave him. She talked about it with Mimi and me over Thanksgiving dinner. She had even gotten a lawyer. I thought, 'This time, this time.' Then he came home and she called me and gave me the I-can't-live-without-a-man and the Church-says-it's-wrong-to-get-divorced conversation, and told me that they were back together. I hung up the phone and went completely to pieces.

"I had to distance myself after that. I was around, but just not as much. I just felt too hypocritical trying to be friendly with John. I couldn't condone what she was doing to herself. I tried to be happy for her, but I knew the whole cycle would only repeat itself. Charlotte and I are very much alike. To have to accept the fact that she really doesn't see something your way, and especially when that something is so important, that's really hard. It's like losing someone you love, because it is their life ultimately. Charlotte just gave so much to John herself that she expected too much from other people. She expected herself to swallow things lovingly and she didn't realize that someone might finally say, 'I can't take any more of this.'

"After that phone call, I went through a real grieving process. I probably would have felt worse if she had died, but not much."

14

After John won Charlotte back in November 1978, he seemed to settle down a bit, perhaps exhausted by the fall's upheaval. He seemed to enjoy a few of the pleasures that his high-paying, high-visibility job could bring. Charlotte, in fact, remembers 1979, 1980, and the beginning of 1981 as being "peak years" of their marriage. John's salary was high enough that they could afford more treats for their children and themselves. Charlotte also recalls that she and John began to enjoy more of the social perks Arnold & Porter had to offer their partners.

In the spring of 1979, for instance, Charlotte recalls they received a refund on their income taxes because of a loss from an investment the firm had made, and John used the money to purchase a Sohmer console piano for Charlotte. On one of his business trips to Rio de Janeiro, he returned with an emerald ring for his wife.

"It was by far one of the most romantic things he ever did," says Charlotte. "He gave it to me right when he came back. I was so excited that he had brought me back something so pretty and gave it to me as a surprise. It had three emeralds and eight little diamonds in between."

At Easter, 1980, John again won the firm's lottery for the New York City apartment overlooking Central Park, and he and Charlotte took all the children to the city. They went to the Easter parade, to see *Peter Pan,* a musical starring Sandy Duncan, and to tour the Empire State Building, museums, and other sights. It was a wonderful, exciting, happy trip, as were the week-long vacations the family now took at Rehoboth Beach, Delaware. John and Charlotte also took quick jaunts to basketball tournaments in Boston; Providence, Rhode Island; and Salt Lake City, Utah.

They tried to take their sons to special events in Washington —when the Pope came to the city in October 1979, for instance, the whole family went down to the Mall to see him. They also went to the Washington Ballet's Christmas production of *The Nutcracker.*

And there were other jeweled moments that could leave Charlotte speechless with appreciation. Such as July 1980, on her parents' fortieth wedding anniversary, when John picked up a substantial bill for their surprise party in an unheralded gesture of largess.

"His picking up that check made me very happy, because I hadn't asked him to do it." says Charlotte. "He just did it and never complained about the cost. That was the kind of moment I lived for and which kept me going. And the trips were things we were just starting to be able to afford. These were the kinds of things that my father had done for us, which are so exciting for children. It may sound trite, but having the extra money to do special things for the kids and for us made it easier to excuse, to survive the bad times."

Rich on its clients' fees, Arnold & Porter also hosted special events, such as yearly picnics, for its attorneys and their families, which gave Charlotte and the boys pleasant days to look forward to. Charlotte particularly appreciated the firm-sponsored outings because they gave John an opportunity to relax and spend happy afternoons with the children.

"Those picnics were great," says Charlotte. "They rented a farm in Maryland and set up every kind of sport. There were clowns and hayrides and square dancing. The food was amazing—they had lobster and corn cooked in pits, and homemade pies. They were really wonderful events."

During those three years, Arnold & Porter arranged an annual blacktie extravaganza. "John used to call them 'the proms.' The last one we went to, at the Mayflower Hotel, was really a little too much. The hors d'oeuvres buffet included a man in a half-dinghy and a slicker shucking fresh oysters, like the old man of the sea. There were ice sculptures, and after the sit-down dinner there was a flashy, patriotic entertainment group, 'Up with America' type of kids. The other dances were more subdued and nice."

These grandiose moments, however, sometimes had their little disappointments, says Charlotte. One year, she had gone to a great deal of trouble to find a dress for the Arnold & Porter formal dinner that would be as striking as what she knew another partner's wife, whom John had always admired, would wear. But she recalls that John didn't like it and made her take it back. That hurt, because she was trying so hard to imitate a style of dressing he had always loudly complimented.

And when he brought her the emerald ring, Charlotte remembers John immediately worrying about her wearing it —telling her that she would dirty or damage it. He took the joy out of wearing it, she says, so she stopped, except on fancy occasions.

After John purchased the piano, Charlotte took lessons. She wanted to be good enough to play real music for her husband. "But that got to be unpleasant too," she says. "He became like a parent about my practicing. He'd always ask if I had practiced that day and was testy if I hadn't. And then when I did practice when he was around, I would start with scales, as my teacher taught me, and he would complain about that because they sounded boring. He'd come into the room to listen every now and then, but I would get so nervous, I couldn't do anything.

"I know I was overly sensitive about the piano, but I knew he would have liked to have had a wife talented enough to play for his guests, and I just didn't have that in me. So I felt inadequate, which again took the fun out of it for me.

"It was like a beautiful but very complicated Williamsburg needlework sampler he gave me the first or second Christmas after we married. It was tedious, difficult work. I never finished it and he never let me forget it. Or tennis. I had started tennis lessons at Congressional at John's very nice suggestion and was getting pretty good, but then I'd play with John and he'd return the ball so hard I couldn't get it. And then he'd yell at me for making mistakes. I'd leave the courts completely demoralized. He just wanted us all to be as perfect as he could be.

"But despite all that, these gifts and the happy times were enough for me to live on. They truly were grand, nice, and, I think, heartfelt gestures. And I honestly didn't mind his being a workaholic, if that had been all he was. That was the kind of relationship I had grown up with—we hadn't seen my father much and that could hurt, but the good times seemed to make up for it because they were so good. I would have been basically very satisfied and settled in the marriage had it not been for the control and for the abuse."

And there was more physical violence. On Easter 1979, John had slipped into a semi-silent mood. His parents were visiting, and feeling protected by their presence, Charlotte tried an approach that before had usually worked. She says she tried to cajole him out of his mood with sex. John had gone to bed early. He always slept more during these quiet periods. When he didn't respond to Charlotte's overture, she teased him about it. John slapped her, hard, in the face.

She went downstairs and told his parents what had happened. "I guess I wanted them to realize that their son really needed some help," says Charlotte. They went upstairs to talk to him, and he claimed that I had punched him. They believed him and said that I basically deserved what I had gotten.

"You can't believe the overwhelming rush of sickness I felt. Here were three adults who meant a lot to me telling me I deserved it. It just reinforced my belief that I was the cause of it all."

John left the house that evening and told Charlotte afterward he had checked into a hotel. He would later testify that having to discuss the incident with his parents was "very humiliating." He didn't call Charlotte until several days later.

"He said that he would come back but only on his terms," she says. "He basically read me a litany of my faults and told me what had to change. It was his way or no way, he said. And I just told him to come home. I took him back because I thought I definitely had been in the wrong this time. And I was terrified. Before I was mostly terrified of losing him. Now I was also terrified of not having a provider for my family. I had four little children, and, I thought, no skills, even though I had been trained as a nurse. He had me convinced that I was worthless. What could I do to make money? Who in the world would hire me? Once again he had me convinced that he could sell the house pretty much overnight without my consent and that I would be out on the street destitute. And I believed him.

"When he came back I tried to do anything I could to soothe him."

* * *

The year ended happily. That summer the family rented a pretty, large house at the beach for a week and Charlotte recalls that they had a pleasant time together.

She began to make some real friends, whom she held on to regardless of John's opinion of them. That fall, Charlotte joined a book club, with several of her neighborhood friends, which met once a month. She even went away to the beach with them overnight. Under their encouragement, her confidence began to grow a bit, though she still never talked to any of them after 5 PM. She started coaching one of her son's soccer teams. She was slowly carving a tiny life of her own outside her home and marriage.

John didn't mind Charlotte's coaching the boys' soccer team, she says, because that involved sports and his sons, although he was not pleased by the other flickers of independence. But Charlotte managed to genuinely please him by losing twenty pounds and successfully hostessing a sumptuous Christmas party for about seventy Arnold & Porter attorneys and wives.

The book club, however, was probably the most significant addition to Charlotte's life that year. Now she had a support group, which she had never had before during her marriage. John had always censured her friendships before, she says, mostly limiting their social acquaintances to his business or sports friends, people Charlotte would never have felt comfortable confiding in. If any of his friends became more hers, John would almost disinherit them. Years before, when Molly Head—originally exclusively John's friend from Marquette but later predominantly Charlotte's —had planned to visit them with her husband, John told Charlotte he didn't want them to stay. Charlotte remembers his making jokes that only his friends were allowed to stay overnight in their home.

The Potomac book club would nurture Charlotte and gradually wean her from total dependence on John for her self-esteem, helping to build the strength she would need to eventually stand on her own. Interestingly, the first book the women would read for shared discussion was *The Woman's Room,* a novel about a middle-aged housewife trying to piece together her life following a divorce.

"That book club was the first thing I did with just the ladies," says Charlotte. "It was a big deal because we went out to dinner and I actually spent maybe $20 on myself. John didn't like it at all. But I prepared his dinner, fed the boys, and had the house perfect before I left. I also never read any of the books around him because that would aggravate him. And I knew that he'd be in a bad mood for at least a day about it. But I didn't fight it or try to change him about it. I just did it and tried not to get upset, which actually was a big step for me.

"These nights were really good for me, because it got me dressed up and out of the house. John just assumed that this was an excuse for us to go out and talk about our husbands. But we never did. We talked about the books. The discussions were so good for me. I would be absolutely floored that these educated women I thought so highly of would actually listen to me. It was so exciting."

"I think the book club had a profound effect on Charlotte," says Denise Gogarty. "I think we gave her such different feedback from what she got from John. We were accepting and uncritical of everyone, no matter what anyone's opinion about the subject matter was. And reading prescribed books on a variety of topics allowed all of us to think about something beyond the scope of our homes and children. Also, I think it was a community in the way Scott Peck, author of *The Road Less Traveled,* defines it: it was inclusive, had a sense of commitment, was a safe place for people to be themselves, soft individualism could grow, it was immune to mob psychology, was realistic in expectations, and had a spirit of love."

Says Charlotte: "I think I did grow. Of course, I saw it

more in terms of the marriage. I was handling his disapproval about the book club, and because the evenings didn't turn into major fights I felt like we were growing. But I realize now that I was really starting to come out of my shell some. Maybe I was beginning to handle things a little better with John because I no longer made him the total center of my universe. I had the boys. I had a few friends. I was doing a lot of volunteer work at the kids' school. I was no longer quite as devastated when I felt that he rejected me.

"Sometimes I think that, had we not moved to New York right after we married and I had stayed near my family, or if we hadn't moved to Dallas just as I was starting to make friends in New York, maybe I wouldn't have felt so alone and would have had the support I needed to have gotten out of the marriage sooner."

While the book club bolstered her confidence about her intellectual capacities, Charlotte also gained some self-assurance when the Christmas party seemed to be such a success with John's friends and with John. Of course, it was much simpler to pull off, because, for the first time, John and Charlotte hired a catering company.

"It was a lovely party," says Charlotte. "John said there were no expenses barred. So we ended up spending a couple thousand dollars on it. We had printed invitations. The caterers brought waiters, a bartender, and a lady in a proper uniform to take people's coats at the door. The dining-room table was covered with food. The family room had a sweets-and-coffee table. I had given the catering firm my recipe for Brunswick stew and we gave some of the guests jars of it as they left. I didn't have to do a thing, so I could really enjoy it for a change. John was really up. He was bragging about how thin I was. It was a very elegant evening. There was not one flaw. That night we achieved the social status John had always seemed to want. I figured that this was the way the rest of our lives was going to be."

* * *

In the summer of 1980, Charlotte was asked to join the board of trustees of The Woods Academy, where three of the boys were enrolled. Right after John Michael had died, the principal, Sister Celestine, had preoccupied Charlotte with volunteer work at the school to help her cope with her baby's death. Charlotte had updated all the students' health records and had helped design the school's new uniforms. The school knew that she was a hard, dedicated worker, although Charlotte doubted their wisdom in asking her.

Charlotte told John about the request at the beach. She recalls he had just come out of a long period of semi-silence that morning. She had purposely waited until they made up to tell him, because she didn't want him to forbid her to do it. They were on the boardwalk. She remembers that John handled it well, although he did ask her, "What do you have to offer?"

But Charlotte says they discussed her involvement at the school rationally. John seemed to accept the fact that she would be going to a meeting once a month. She viewed the conversation as a victory for them both. She certainly wouldn't have been able to be that calm the night before.

The trip down to the beach had been a convulusive one, says Charlotte. The previous several weeks, in fact, had been hard. A month or so before the beach vacation, John had been speaking infrequently. Charlotte recalls that he had instructed her to buy a Bar Mitzvah gift for a friend's child. Without turning around from his desk, John told her to spend around $100. Charlotte balked at being ordered to spend a certain amount of money, especially since it was a large sum, which was often denied her or the boys, and she crumpled the invitation. John chased her downstairs to the front hall, picked up a Chinese vase, she says, and threw it to the floor, smashing it at her feet.

Another argument delayed their leaving for the beach by one day, even though they were paying more than $1,000 a

week, for a house that was only a block from the beach.
When they did leave, yet another disagreement erupted in
the car. Charlotte was driving and pulled over on River
Road's shoulder because John had her in tears. She got out
of the car, hysterical, and she says that John started to drive
away, leaving her on the highway. The children began
screaming in the back seat. John stopped. Charlotte got
back in the car and they went home.

The next morning they did manage to make the three-
hour drive to the beach, but John ignored Charlotte once
they arrived. He really didn't like the beach, anyway, she
says. He went to bed early.

Left alone and depressed, Charlotte tried to forget her
fears, her anger, her self-recriminations, her insecurities. She
sat in the living room and drank the wine. Drank and drank
until she was sick.

"I remember drinking like that only a couple of times,"
says Charlotte, "and I'm not proud of it. It was like hiding
in the closet. I was trying to escape. It hurt less after a glass
of wine. And I think I was trying to grab John's attention
without really hurting myself. I guess I thought if he knew
how affected I was by all this turmoil he'd realize how much
I needed him to help me."

That August, Charlotte was pregnant again. John was
pleased, but she was a little embarrassed about expecting a
sixth baby, which would bring a fifth living child to a family
already strained energy-wise, emotionally, and financially.
She asked that John wait to make the announcement until
she was a little further along in the pregnancy and he
agreed.

But on their way to Wisconsin for a vacation, they
stopped to visit John's parents. While there, Charlotte celebrated her thirty-seventh birthday. That night, at dinner,
John presented her with an expensive purse. Inside was a
poem he had written that she says he insisted she read

aloud. Charlotte swallowed hard, turned red, and complied. In essence, John's verse said that he hoped she'd carry the purse to the hospital when she had the baby.

"It embarrassed me," she says. "It just seemed a little devious to me."

When they returned, John again ignored her request and told Charlotte's friend Denise Gogarty.

"That time was cruel," remembers Gogarty. "They were standing in the garage, just back from their trip. John immediately said to me, 'Charlotte has a big surprise for you,' and Charlotte said, 'Oh no, John, don't.' He kept at it, saying things like 'Wait until you hear the news.' She started crying and went into the house. I guess Charlotte thought I would disapprove—I wouldn't have urged another pregnancy, but once it was a baby I would only congratulate her—so it was especially cruel of John to tell me that way."

The children, in fact, were becoming a major source of trouble between Charlotte and John. Although she thought that she was learning to cope a little better with John's demands and moods, his pressure on the boys and desire for them to be outstanding students and athletes were adding friction to their uneasy relationship.

It started with Luke. Two years earlier, following John Michael's death, Luke's schoolwork had begun to slide. His third-grade teacher had noticed that he "puts tremendous pressure on himself and seems terribly anxious for a nine-year-old," and by the fourth grade he was acting the class clown in a conservative, Catholic environment. It became a serious enough problem that Charlotte sent Luke to a therapist, Dr. Mary Donahue, who speculated that because his home life was stressful, school had become Luke's release, his time to play. Charlotte made plans to move Luke to another school and held him back a grade.

She remembers that John never seemed to believe there was anything wrong with his sons other than laziness. Like many overachieving parents who expect their children to be

as driven and competent as they had been, John rode his
boys hard, probably believing they would thank him later.
He and Charlotte enrolled Luke in soccer and basketball
camps. He wanted his firstborn to be a swimmer like he had
been and pushed him to join Congressional's team even
though Luke preferred and was better at diving.

Family meals became especially tense. In addition to quiz-
zing the boys about their schoolwork, John forced them to
eat large quantities of food. Although he was now six-foot-
ten and weighed 230 pounds, John had been thin as a teenager and he wanted his boys to be well developed.

From 1980 on, says Charlotte, most of the trouble between them resulted from her trying to relax some of his
rules for the children.

"I used to hold report cards for days at a time because he
would get so angry," she says. "It got to the point that when
I told the boys that John wasn't coming home for dinner,
they'd cheer. They just weren't pleasant times. John expected too much out of them, probably for the right kind of
reasons, but it was just too much for them. He used to force
them to eat helping after helping because he wanted them to
grow up big. It happened almost every meal. It got so that I
just gave Luke smaller helpings to begin with and wouldn't
put any extra food on the table, because John wouldn't get
up to get the seconds. In fact, the kids had to wait on him.
When he wanted water, if they didn't put in the exact number of ice cubes he wanted—I think it was four—he'd get
irritated. If I suggested that he do it himself, since he didn't
like the way they did it, he'd yell at me, calling me a 'fuck-
ing bitch' a lot of the time. I don't know how many times he
called me that in front of the children.

"The dinner conversations were rather controlled. They
weren't monologues by John, but it was mostly question and
answer. If Luke tried to tell a joke that might include something a little bit naughty or one bad word, something he had
heard at school, John would listen to it and then say, 'We

don't use that kind of language in this house; if you want to use it go out in the street.' And five minutes later, John would say 'shit.' Mostly he'd ask them, 'What did you do today?' and when they'd answer, 'Nothing,' like kids do, he'd say that he wasn't paying all this money for them to do nothing.

"When he got angry at one, he was angry at them all. Like when he was angry with me, he wouldn't talk to the whole family. They just didn't understand it, and they made it worse because my kids are fighters. They never learned to sit there prim and proper and just eat.

"They were like me. I knew that if I could just keep quiet, things would at least be quiet with John. But how can you sit still and let someone walk over you? Especially in front of the children."

Something Charlotte had written in a diary when they were vacationing in Wisconsin in 1978 was beginning to become a daily concern for her: "If I could just hear him and not let him bother me—he would be happy. Why do I have to defend myself? Why can't I let him walk over me and keep quiet. . . . I wonder what the children really think of me. I imagine they'll grow up thinking I screamed a lot, was unjust to their Dad and was usually totally unreasonable. I'm pretty good alone but can rarely handle John and his clean obsession and the boys. I do try, but I rarely remain calm. The boys will probably grow up wondering why I never stood up firm and proud to their father. They can't respect me. I love them all so much, but I sometimes feel that I'm no good for them. . . ."

Part Four

THE STING OF POWER

Washington is full of famous men and the women they married when they were young.

Mrs. Oliver Wendell Holmes, at a White
House dinner honoring her husband, 1903

15

By the end of 1980, John seemed more and more restless to Charlotte. She says he told her that he wanted to leave Arnold & Porter. He wanted to do something new. He wanted to move—all this just as Charlotte and the boys were becoming more and more attached to the community. Charlotte began to wonder if anything would ever make John really happy. He seemed naturally content when Marquette won a basketball game or when he spent quiet times with the boys, just holding their hands as they walked the canal trail next to the Potomac River. But Charlotte says that these events were rare and that he seemed to be pushing his family away from him as he grasped at some fleeting dream that he couldn't even describe to her.

Perhaps the election of Ronald Reagan in November 1980 was an answer to her prayers. Reagan favored corporate types in his administration. The Californians would need all sorts of new people, come the inauguration, people familiar with Washington. They couldn't import everyone from the West Coast. Maybe John could find a position in this administration. It might be easier than trying to secure one in Carter's since John was a registered Republican.

Of course, John wasn't talking about just any pencil-pushing bureaucrat's job. He was talking about one affecting policy, one that would be worth leaving his lucrative partnership for. The power that came with a federal job must have appealed to him, but what John told Charlotte was most attractive to him was making use of Washington's revolving-door tradition, popularized in part by the founders of his firm, whereby highranking federal officers move on to high-paying private industry jobs.

It took a few well-placed phone calls to let the appropriate people know he was willing to move from Arnold & Porter, if offered an enticing office, says Charlotte. That done, John was first considered for a position in Treasury. It didn't pan out. But within a few weeks, he was being considered for the chief of the enforcement division with the Securities and Exchange Commission (SEC). In the old game of musical chairs that happens in Washington every election, the man then holding the job decided to move over to the post of general counsel to the CIA.

With his white-collar-crime background and the fact that he had represented many corporate clients in front of the SEC, John was uniquely qualified for the job and the new emphasis of the commission—tracking down and prosecuting those engaging in financial fraud and insider trading on Wall Street. In late June 1981, John Shad, Reagan's political appointee to the SEC chairmanship, chose John over forty-nine other applicants.

John was thirty-nine years old, the first person in his position not to have been promoted to it from within the agency. A man who had never deliberately made political friends. A man who, to Charlotte's knowledge, had not given money to any campaign other than Nixon's presidential race. John had won the position on professional merit. Not that he hadn't had to do some quick lobbying. But John simply hadn't done enough within the Republican Party for the job to be returning a favor to him or to some well-placed sponsor. Charlotte was very proud of him.

There had been some tense moments during the selection process. Like when the FBI interviewed neighbors about John, asking questions to determine if John was at all corruptible and therefore unsuitable for a sensitive government post, or had any secrets that could make him vulnerable to blackmail from foreign agents. The questions included what kind of husband and father he was.

The bureau's investigator spoke to Denise Gogarty and her husband for about twenty minutes. She remembers they asked if John was honest and loyal to the country. Did he seem to have integrity in his work? Those were easy to answer yes. Then he asked if John dressed well. Her husband fielded that one: "He should, he has his suits custom made."

What kind of neighbor is he? "Fine" was the answer. Then came the hard question: "What kind of husband and father is Mr. Fedders?" Gogarty knew very much John wanted this position, how badly Charlotte wanted him to have it. Charlotte was convinced that this job would finally make John happy. But Gogarty hesitated a moment, long enough for her husband to answer for her, saying he saw John playing catch with his children all the time, that he must be a good family man. The investigator didn't pursue the line of questioning other than to ask if Charlotte was a good mother. Gogarty says she had no difficulty in answering that with a resolute affirmative.

Once in his SEC office at 450 Fifth Street, near Union Station and close to Capitol Hill, John looked at the FBI records about him. He told Charlotte that she should have seen some of the comments their neighbors made. She presumed they must have overheard some of their arguments, but John never elaborated and obviously the information didn't hamper his getting the job. Besides, Gogarty remembers that nobody other than Charlotte's neighbors across the

street, with whom Charlotte had taken refuge in 1976, really
knew about the pain inside John and Charlotte's home.
Only one neighbor had overheard a bad fight between Charlotte and John as they stood in their driveway while he
jogged past their home. He later sent some reading material
to Charlotte about how to improve Christian marriages.

So, to most McAuley Park residents, the cream brick
house on Carmelita Drive was as pristine and orderly inside
as it was outside. The Fedderses were that nice, attractive
family that came to church together every Sunday. The reality of John and Charlotte's relationship remained a well-
guarded secret, except to those she had tearfully taken into
her confidence.

How prestigious was John's new position? John told
Charlotte that his was *the* most important job in the city.
That's a bit of an exaggeration, but the person who was "top
cop" at the SEC—as business journalists nicknamed him—
wielded a powerful scepter, one that could fell some of the
richest individuals in America. John was underneath the
aegis of the five SEC commissioners, all of whom were political appointees, confirmed by the Senate. They really set the
tone of the commission's actions. But John would be the one
to implement them and the one whose staff—two hundred
lawyers, accountants, and support personnel in Washington,
plus four hundred lawyers in regional offices across the
country—would ferret out and prosecute wrongdoers.

A phone call from an SEC staffer could make a stockbro-
ker or a corporate executive tremble, although many an
American uninvolved with the stock market is unfamiliar
with its work. Charlotte certainly didn't know much about
it until John explained it to her.

The SEC was founded just over fifty years ago to keep the
stock market and large corporations honest. It ensures that
publicly traded companies disclose their finances to stock-
holders and keep clear records of dealings; that stockbrokers
are properly registered and comply with a prescribed code

of ethics; that stock prices are not manipulated by their companies or executives; and that takeovers or mergers are done openly. As one former commissioner put it, the SEC keeps "con men and pickpockets" out of the stock exchange. Its first chairman, interestingly enough, was JFK's father, the late Joseph Kennedy, who found himself constantly reprimanding old friends.

Although the commission is only one strand of a large, intricate web of federal agencies designed to catch individuals corroding American freedoms, the SEC's investigations can have far-reaching ripple effects throughout the country. It, for instance, is the federal body responsible, in late 1986, for exposing Ivan Boesky, one of the country's most successful arbitrageurs (a person who specializes in buying and selling stocks of companies about to be bought out), as being guilty of receiving inside information from companies before he bought or sold their stocks. That meant Boesky was no longer speculating when he traded, he wasn't taking any kind of risk, he had an unfair advantage. Speculation is the lifeblood of Wall Street, what keeps all investors equal and the little man willing to play the market. And that willingness of the public to keep investing in company stocks is vital in keeping the American economy healthy.

So John's job was both obscure and far-reaching, one that had a lot of pressure when he took it over in the summer of 1981, because the country was in a recession. Companies desperately needed seed money from stock sales to reinvest in new technology and training. That money would only come from Americans if their faith in the market as a safe, profitable place to invest was restored. And the SEC and John would have to restore it through prosecuting a lot of cases.

When John decided to join the SEC, he and Charlotte knew it would require some financial sacrifices. His annual salary would start just under $60,000, a hefty government wage but one that was half his salary with Arnold & Porter.

It also wasn't the best time for the family to be cutting back so drastically, either. Their sixth son, Peter, was born in April. They had five young children to raise. Four were in private Catholic schools, a type of education that Charlotte says both she and John strongly believed in, but that had large tuition costs. John promised her that the boys wouldn't have to switch to the county's public schools, which Charlotte feared were too competitive and too large for them to get individual attention. She also strongly believed that the boys should get daily religious instruction, that they couldn't really know about Catholicism by only attending Sunday school once a week.

Charlotte remembers that several people questioned her and John about the wisdom of John's career decision, considering the needs of his rather large family. But John told Charlotte that he had it all figured out. To compensate for the lost income, he arranged for a $150,000 line of credit with Washington's Madison National Bank. He also promised Charlotte that he would leave the SEC within four years, no later than January 20, 1985 (the date of the next presidential inauguration), although publicly he promised to remain until Shad left. He said to Charlotte and to friends that he'd be able to springboard to at least a $300,000 salary with a Washington law firm and he was probably right. As one *Wall Street Journal* opinion piece stated following the publicity of their divorce hearing: "It's hard to think of a government job with more lucrative revolving door potential than director of enforcement at the SEC."

John's confidence of being able to easily find a job following the SEC was boosted by the number of farewell dinner and cocktail parties Arnold & Porter colleagues threw for him. At one, a partner raised his glass in a toast, saying there would always be a candle in the window at the firm for John. With so many promises, he and Charlotte could borrow to survive until he returned to the private world, the triumphant prodigal son.

Charlotte was enthusiastic because John seemed so happy for the first time in years. Right after the announcement of his getting the job, they left to spend a week at Rehoboth Beach. She recalls that John spent most of his time reading and responding to a flood of congratulatory mail, from old Cadwalader and Dallas associates, long-lost school friends, plus current admirers. When they returned from the beach, John and Charlotte attended a neighborhood party, where John was warm and complimentary to her book club friends. He was in high spirits, indeed, and Charlotte prayed the job change would be a turning point for their marriage.

"I thought John would finally be satisfied," she says. "Money had always been a problem, so, looking down the road, it seemed that he'd be making twice as much. I was happy because we were staying in Washington after all his talk of being a gypsy. I was worried that we had no cash reserves, but John seemed to think that it was all taken care of.

"We were all very excited. The boys joked about having to give up lollipops for four years. I started packing his lunches and tucked little poems and notes in them. I'd write "Top Cop" on the bag. I even cross-stitched a paperweight for him that said 'I'm a legend in my own mind,' which he seemed to really like and put on his desk at work. And, of course, since he told me that this was the most important job in Washington, I was all set to be going to the White House for dinner.

"John wanted prestige and power, but he didn't want to kiss up to anybody. That's why he disliked Arnold & Porter. I think he always believed that his hard work would speak for itself. And, remarkably, with the SEC it did. The Midwest country boy had really made it on his own. He was giddy about it. It's just that his lack of savvy about what public figures have to do to stay in office would get him in trouble."

* * *

John's ego ballooned, Charlotte says, starting with the press conference to announce his appointment. How many of his legal peers were ever photographed and discussed in the *Wall Street Journal,* the *New York Times* and the *Washington Post* all in one day? Charlotte went to the press conference and sat quietly in the corner with John's secretary, listening to her husband answer reporters' questions. She was amazed how well he fielded them.

Although future monetary reward had been the catalyst he had stated to Charlotte for entering government employment, a new lure soon seemed to tug at John—budding celebrity. It was minor league celebrity, to be sure, compared to that of cabinet officers or congressmen, but it certainly was more than he had ever tasted since his days as a tall, cool man around Marquette University. And this was the big time—this was Washington, D.C., not a college campus.

John started checking the *Washington Post* business section each morning, says Charlotte. When his boss, John Shad, was quoted on an SEC matter and he wasn't, or if a reporter had contacted him and then not quoted him in the story, John was perturbed. He had his secretary check all the other newspapers for mentions of him. He also started keeping records of each day's happenings on legal pads. He told her that he planned to write a book when he left.

John replaced Stanley Sporkin, a man who had been with the commission a long time and was very popular with his staff. Many of the lawyers under him quit right after the changeover. Part of the disgruntlement of John's attorneys, according to press accounts, was the switch in emphasis at the SEC, from the splashy exposés of corporations' foreign slush funds and attempted briberies, for which Sporkin had been famous, to more painstaking and less flamboyant investigations of insider trading and stock manipulation. It didn't lessen the pressure on John that, at his first press conference, Sporkin made a much-quoted joke that he would be keeping an eye on John from his new post at the CIA.

The difference in style of the two enforcement chiefs was, in fact, a recurrent question during John's interviews. He constantly had to respond that he would be just as creative as Sporkin had been, the SEC just as newsworthy. But he did love the attention, says Charlotte. It wouldn't be long before he was called to appear on radio and TV talk shows —*Good Morning, America, Larry King,* and *Nightline*— however briefly. *Business Week,* the *Wall Street Journal, Legal Times, Forbes,* and *Barron's* all interviewed him. And his new entry in *Who's Who in America* was impressively long.

Almost all the newspaper stories mentioned that John had been a former basketball player, that he was unusually tall, and that he liked to run his staff as he would coach an athletic team. Of all the reports, however, the one in *Barron's* was probably the most revealing of John's private personality. In answer to a suggestion that the SEC might go soft on corporations by spending so much attention on policing illegal stock tips, John countered: "As the most severe critic of my own conduct, I see absolutely no evidence to justify that conclusion. There's nobody who's a more severe critic of himself than me. I'm always looking for avenues to criticize myself. My best friend is Al McGuire. He used to coach basketball at Marquette; he's the NBC basketball commentator now. I've known him for years. And he stops me all the time and says, 'You never stop to smell the roses.'"

The final question and answer of that interview was:

"Q. John, is there anything you see going on in the securities markets that makes you personally angry?

"A. I don't have the capacity to be angry. If you're six-foot-ten, you find that anger is not necessary."

During his first months in office, besides learning to cope with all his responsibilities and getting to know his staff across the country, John made several public-speaking appearances out of town. He often traveled to the city and back in a single day, which added to his increasing weariness. But he seemed to thrive on the attention of the events as well, since he kept a detailed file on each appearance, including letters, his speech notes, and press clips. Typically he left before the children were up and came home after they were in bed, even when he was in town, says Charlotte. Now that he was also making speeches, there seemed to be little time left for his family.

Charlotte too was becoming increasingly fatigued, taking care of a newborn, a three-year-old, a seven-year-old, an eight-year-old, and a twelve-year-old. She had four children in school—three in one, and the fourth, whom she had to pick up at lunchtime, at another. She felt she was constantly driving the car. And, despite the overload of so many children, Charlotte knew the house should be just as perfect, just as orderly as when she had only two sons to watch; that John would want his meals waiting for him when he got home, no matter what the hour.

"The major change the SEC made in John was his ego," says Charlotte. "There grew even more desire in him for power at home. And he got so that if someone got in his way, he walked right over them. People didn't seem to matter anymore."

Although John had occasionally flattered Charlotte during his last years at Arnold & Porter by asking her to proofread some of his writing, now he was more reticent to discuss his work with her, she says. Perhaps he worried that she wouldn't fully appreciate the secrecy needed when he was working on a case. And perhaps John was becoming challenged and absorbed by the work itself, liking it more than he had anticipated, and didn't want to tell his wife that he was changing his mind about leaving the SEC. Maybe he thought she couldn't appreciate how gratifying enjoying one's daily work can be, how deadening disliking it is.

So, despite her cheerleader enthusiasm about John's new life, their relationship seemed to grow even more distant, exacerbated by break-neck schedules. John and Charlotte became like two whirling tops rarely moving in the same direction, and ricocheting wildly apart when they did meet.

John hadn't hit Charlotte, that she could remember, since Easter 1979. But John's control suddenly cracked and he beat her violently in November 1981, barely five months after he became a major US law enforcer. Had Charlotte pressed charges for his actions, John could have been arrested for assault and battery, an action that is against the law, no matter who the victim, who the attacker, or what their relationship is.

"Fall was always bad for us for some reason," she recalls. "That's the time each year John slipped into a mood of some kind. That night I had been following along behind him, trying to get him to talk to me. Crying, pleading, yelling. By that point in our marriage I had really gotten so that I could argue like a truck driver. I even spit at him a couple of times, anything to get him to respond and to talk to me.

"He had been downstairs eating, and I followed him up the stairs into his study. I was verbally pushing, pushing, pushing, trying to get some kind of response. He was ignoring me completely. I guess I had finally come to realize that not being able to wear shoes in my house was weird. I had them on and I stamped my feet and said, 'And another thing: I will wear my shoes in my own house.'

"He turned, and his face was terrifying, filled with this incredible hate and wide-eyed anger. I knew I had gone too far. I ran. He came after me and caught me right outside the room, at the top of the stairwell. I ran because I was afraid. But I never expected he would try to throw me over the banister. He denies it, but I'd like to know what he thought he was trying to do. He was pushing me over the railing as he beat me. There is at least a six-foot drop straight down to the landing of the staircase from where we were. I felt I was

going to fall over backwards, so I collapsed my knees and
fell to the floor. I was trying to push him away, but he had
me by my hair. He shook me up and down, back and forth,
by my hair, like he was shaking out a towel. The fury of it
was terrifying. I think he finally realized what he was doing
and walked away.

"The first thing to ache was my scalp. It wasn't until later
that my neck began to hurt so badly. I finally had to go see
an orthopedic surgeon, it was so painful. John said he was
sorry for the incident later, because he had seriously injured
me and he could see that it gave me pain. I still have to wear
a neck brace sometimes.

"Luke and one of his brothers came out of their rooms
and saw us. Seeing the shock on their little faces hurt me
most, I think."

This time, Charlotte called the police herself. Surely they
would help her, she thought.

"I was really upset when I called them," she says. "I
asked them what I should do, what I could do. They didn't
ask if I was all right, or where he was. They didn't tell me to
leave, or give me any telephone numbers of hotlines or
counselors to call. All they said was that I could go to the
police station or the courthouse and swear out a complaint.
How could I swear out a complaint against our provider, I
asked myself. I think I knew even then that it could hurt his
career.

"And it was just too much work for the condition I was
in. I would have had to pull myself together and do something the next day. After a beating, depression takes over
immediately. All the feelings of inadequacy, of guilt, of fear,
they totally immobilize you. I had mobilized myself enough
to make the call, and maybe I'm naive, but it was crushing
to me that the police, the protectors of the innocent, weren't
going to do anything to help me."

Until very recently, because of common law, the police
simply couldn't do anything without the victim's swearing

out a complaint or without an officer's witnessing the attack. Although police officers spend about one third of their time responding to domestic violence calls, police reports indicate that they have typically made arrests in only 30 percent of those cases, mainly because women have refused to press charges. Police officers have hated responding to them, say experts, partly because it is in domestic quarrels that they are most likely to be injured.

Cultural prejudices that manipulate law enforcement also die hard. A man's right, as authority of a household, to beat his wife is embedded in Western civilization. The phrase "rule of thumb" comes from English common law, which gave the husband the right to discipline his wife with "a rod no thicker than his thumb." Typically, the justification for the punishment was that the offender was a nag, an attitude that crossed the Atlantic with the Puritans, who set up dunking stools in the New England colonies to publicly discipline shrewish women. And many states, including Maryland, where Charlotte lived, had laws allowing men "the right of chastisement" without fear of prosecution for battery, laws that were not revoked until the early 1900s. The judicial system simply did not meddle in the home's harmony and hierarchy, and that attitude trickled down to the police in trying to quell domestic violence.

But research has shown categorically that the beatings will only get worse unless some outside authority or agency intervenes. A recent study done in Kansas City found that in 50 percent of the city's domestic homicides, police had been called to the home at least five times before the spouse was killed. That information plus studies done by the Police Foundation, which prove a night in jail effectively deters aggression, has compelled lawmakers to finally make some changes. In 1984, Minneapolis was one of the first major US cities to push for arresting rather than simply talking to batterers.

Today, more than half of the states allow officers to make

arrests when they have "probable cause" to suspect a crime has been committed—such as seeing bruises or cuts on the body of a crying victim—without the victim's making a formal complaint. But as an officer in a northern Virginia police department admitted, it will take some time and training on the battering syndrome to get officers to universally use the new prerogative. It's hard to break old habits, she said, and they've seen too many hysterical wives who seem unwilling to help themselves once the police do arrive on the scene.

In 1981, however, there was no such legal safety net in place for someone like Charlotte. And as she would say, she didn't even realize that what had been done to her that day was against the law.

Ever since the beginning of their fifteen-year-old marriage, says Charlotte, she and John had had periodic flare-ups about their finances. They began arguing over spending almost immediately after he moved to the SEC. With five growing boys, a house mortgage, payments on the Virginia land, and dues at Congressional, his federal paycheck seemed a pittance after the $161,444 salary John had made one year at Arnold & Porter, when the firm's profits were exceptionally high.

Of course, elsewhere in the country a $60,000 salary would seem generous, but in Washington many complain about not being able to get by on a government paycheck because of the city's high cost of living. Several of Reagan's close friends and advisers, for instance, have left their positions in the White House complaining of being pinched by $72,000 salaries. As members of the administration, they aren't allowed to supplement their income, although congressmen, in recognition of the problem, allow themselves to collect additional monies from outside endeavors, up to 30 percent of their $75,000-plus salaries.

Much of their financial problems result from trying to maintain an image. As a 1985 article in *The Washingtonian* magazine, titled "Going Broke on $100,000 a Year," points out, visibility, Washington style, has a hefty price tag.

Not that John was expected to appear at parties in the same social stratosphere as are congressmen or cabinet officers. But a snobbishness does exist in the nation's capital about persons perceived as cheapskates. They are not tolerated—Jimmy and Rosalynn Carter's no-frills White House was mercilessly ridiculed.

John was probably also aware of another axiom, stated in *The Washingtonian:* "Visibility has a cash value once you leave the administration." He couldn't afford to slip into social obscurity, darting from his SEC office to spaghetti dinners at home. He would need the contacts he made while traveling in upper-crust society once he decided to return to private life. Besides, John was accustomed to certain luxuries for himself, says Charlotte, and he wasn't going to give them up, just as he refused to give up the fifth bedroom he used as his study, which put his five sons together in three rooms. Image had always been an essential part of his bravura, ever since he and Charlotte lived in New York City, she says. They could just borrow until he left the SEC, he told her.

The children's tuition, however, remained the top priority. Yet, that was an expensive proposition, since the combined tuitions for a year exceeded $11,000. Charlotte tried to do her part to cut back elsewhere. Just as many well-off matrons with large families do in Potomac, Charlotte had had her cleaning lady come twice a week; she trimmed that to once weekly. She learned to pump her own gas, would even drive out of Potomac to find cheaper gas stations, and shopped specials at the grocery store. But she knew that it wasn't enough.

Charlotte would later testify that they would spend $137,000 in 1982, more than double what the federal government was then paying John.

Charlotte says she urged him to cut back on some image-related expenses, and to stop entertaining, but that John wouldn't. In December, he and Charlotte hosted a Christmas party for about seventy of his SEC staff. There would be no problem paying for it, he told Charlotte, because in January he would be getting $28,283 from Arnold & Porter as a partial buy-out of his interest in the law partnership. That would more than cover the party and the boys' school and leave some cash left over. He would receive one more check of the same amount from the firm the following year, so there was nothing to worry about, he said.

"John wouldn't think about limiting our membership at Congressional. At that point the club's required food minimum alone was about $800 a year. He wouldn't cancel his expensive subscription to *Architectural Digest*. He insisted on continuing ChemLawn, plus another service to spray the bushes, on top of buying his own fertilizer. He kept Terminix. That must have totaled about $1,500 a year. It was cheaper to take the trash down to the bottom of the driveway for pickup than to leave it in the garage. He wouldn't let me change that either.

"He had been giving $1,000 a year to Marquette. I know he kept giving them some money. I don't know how much. He also stayed on their alumni council. He told me that they reimbursed him for the cost of traveling to Wisconsin and his accommodation expense for the yearly meeting, but they didn't. John also continued to give extra money to the boys' schools, so he was still playing the part of the great philanthropist.

"We spent about $600 on that Christmas party. I did most of the cooking. This was just after the banister incident, so my neck was still bothering me a little. I had a little help from a friend who ran a catering service and Sandy Oseroff, who has a florist shop. I bought a honey-baked ham, and fixed Brunswick stew. We had mini-croissants and petit fours. It was very nice. We had liquor, of course, but no bartender. And by now the boys were old enough to take coats.

"Yes, we had the money coming in from Arnold & Porter that would cover the debts we had accumulated by that point. But I was beginning to be very frustrated that, instead of saving the money, we always spent it before we even got it.

"His line to me whenever I tried to talk to him about it was: 'You gotta live.' "

In February 1982, John traveled to Switzerland to finalize an agreement that would help the SEC find and prosecute American business executives illegally stockpiling funds or trading stocks through secret Swiss bank accounts. The US ambassador to Switzerland, Faith Ryan Whittlesey, who helped negotiate the treaty, seemed impressed with the earnest young enforcement chief.

They became professional friends, and under her patronage John met some White House officials and other influential Republicans. Whittlesey was uniquely positioned to help advance John because she had high visibility within the party. She was, at the time, one of the few women politicians possessing clout with the Reagan clan. She was a lawyer, a conservative who had served two terms in the Pennsylvania legislature, and then been chairman of her county's board of commissioners. When she lost a bid for Pennsylvania's lieutenant governorship, she turned her energy to campaigning in the predominantly Democratic state for Reagan in 1980. The President rewarded her election efforts with the Swiss ambassadorship. And in early 1983, when Elizabeth Dole became Secretary of Transportation, Reagan would ask Whittlesey to return to the States and replace Dole in the White House as his assistant for public liaison.

"When he came home from Europe," remembers Charlotte, "all he could do was talk about how smart she was. He sent me to Lord & Taylor's to buy sweaters for her and her daughter and an electronic Pac-Man game for her son. He told me to spend between $175 and $200 total. It seemed crazy to me to be spending so much money on thank-you gifts, when we were so strapped financially. But I did it."

That spring, on May 1, Charlotte had been asked to speak at a farewell dinner for Sister Celestine at The Woods Academy. In her own way, Charlotte was making small steps toward leadership in her little, cloistered world. The school's board had even asked her about possibly serving as its president, but she hadn't told John about it yet. John was in a quiet mood and Charlotte didn't know if he was coming to the dinner or not. That evening, he showed up at the reception preceding the meal. As Charlotte remembers it, he spent most of the cocktail hour working the crowd and avoiding her. But once she left the podium after speaking, John did something that really pleased her.

"After I finished talking and stepped down, the master of ceremonies, who was an old friend and is rather short, said, 'Charlotte, you're the type of woman who makes me want to wear lifts in my shoes.' And with that, John, who was barely speaking to me, calls out, 'Bob, I do,' which, of course, made everyone laugh because John's so tall. But it made me really proud that he would say something kind of nice—that I was worth trying to make happy, so to speak—in front of my friends. It was wonderful.

"But I guess in the long run I would rather have had some consistency in our lives than these extreme highs and lows."

Later that month, John and Charlotte hosted a cocktail party honoring Faith Whittlesey, who was in Washington on State Department business. John had told Charlotte that he wanted it to be a "garden party."

"Having a garden party was ridiculous," says Charlotte,

"since we had no garden furniture bacause John hated to sit outside. I had to borrow furniture from a neighbor. Faith sent me a four-page list which had the names of eighty couples she wanted to invite. Thank God, they didn't all come. We spent over $500 on it, even though I tried to keep the cost down. I kept it a simple but elegant cocktail party—the best liquor, hors d'oeuvres, pastries, and coffee. I got some kids from the neighborhood to direct the parking and a son of a former congressman who lived nearby to tend bar. The Swiss ambassador to the United States arrived in a chauffeur-driven limousine and was accompanied by an aide. It was a very nice party in our backyard—but it wasn't a 'garden party.' I'm also sure the party wasn't quite the caliber of receptions she was used to going to.

"The day of the party, she sent me a huge, very formal flower arrangement as thanks, which I put on our dining-room table. She and I never had a very easy time talking, though. I guess we just had nothing at all in common. I must have seemed like a dope to her; here was this man climbing up, up, up and here his wife, seemingly stagnant in the suburbs, changing dirty diapers.

"I know she helped John. He became friendly with H. P. Goldfield, who became deputy assistant secretary of Commerce, and Craig Fuller, an assistant to the President, through her. And we were invited to some fancy parties with Faith. We went to dinner at Drew Lewis's apartment at the Watergate. He was Secretary of Transportation then. Richard Allen, the former National Security adviser, and Peter McPherson, head of the Agency for International Development, were there, too. John had told me to buy a very fancy dress for this dinner. He told me at first that it would be black tie. So I found a very dressy cocktail dress and once I got there I found I was grossly overdressed. That was embarrassing.

"That night, figuring that I was protected by the company, I told John during dinner that the board at The

Woods Academy had asked me to be its president and that I had accepted. Drew Lewis's wife thought it was wonderful and said so. John just said, 'You're kidding.' I smiled and answered that I wasn't. He was not happy when we got in the car to drive home.

"It was so confusing for me. Here he was impressed by this powerful female lawyer, but he didn't want me to grow at all. He resented all my attempts to expand myself. Yet, he would call me with disdain an 'anti-intellectual' later on, during the divorce trial.

"I think he was attracted to Faith's power. The next year, when she came back to the United States to be the White House public affairs liaison, he thought about being her assistant. I thought that would have been such a step down from being the chief enforcement at the SEC, with his own huge staff, but I know he considered taking it for a couple of days.

"I think Faith liked having John as her protégé. He would be easy to sponsor because he really can be very charming and he's very smart. She'd always say to him, 'There's someone I want you to meet.' He was this up-and-coming young man, a pretty much undiscovered Republican, a rising star who would be a sort of feather in her cap in the party."

A few months later, in September, Whittlesey was again in town, and John and Charlotte had dinner with her and the Swiss minister of finance. During the meal, as Charlotte listened to the lively, intense conversation about world politics among her husband, the diplomat, and this powerful, important woman, she says she began to feel more and more insecure about herself. John's day-to-day world seemed to be slipping further and further away from her.

Shortly thereafter, John entered a silent period. It persisted, even as he was about to leave for a week's vacation in Wyoming with his friend Al McGuire. The morning of his departure, John still wasn't talking to her. Charlotte was desperate.

"That was the final time I would ever degrade myself for him. He had barely spoken for weeks, and he was leaving for a week. He was upstairs getting ready to go, and I was following him, pleading. 'What's wrong?' I kept asking. He laughed at me. He probably told me, like he had so many times before, that I had let myself go. That my hair was a mess. I was overweight. 'Don't leave angry; give me a kiss good-bye,' I said, and he did that humiliating thing of tossing me a kiss in the air. I had been saying that we had problems, to please come with me to a marriage counselor. He said, 'Look in the mirror. There's our problem.' And he walked downstairs.

"I ran after him. I threw open my nightgown and started rubbing myself all over my body. I don't know what I was trying to do. Seduce him to stay, I guess. He looked at me and said with this icy tone of voice, 'You have proved my point. You're crazy.' And then he walked out the door. He wouldn't call even once during that entire week to check on me or on his boys, who were being cared for by a supposedly crazy person.

"When he walked out the door, with me standing there, half undressed, I had never felt that low in my life. It was worse than hitting myself or hiding in the closet. I was acting crazy. I knew I had to have help. I called my internist, the man who had measured my bruises in 1976. He was very kind. This time he told me that he could see that John had problems and that I needed to see a therapist. The idea was that I should pull myself together first and then deal with John. He suggested that I go back to see the doctor who had helped Luke in 1978."

The following Monday, Charlotte went to see Dr. Mary Donahue. She told the psychologist what had happened, how the arguments between her and John sometimes ended in violence, about the silences that either followed or precipitated those arguments. It was the first time she was totally honest with a therapist. Maybe it helped that Donahue was a woman and that Charlotte already knew and trusted her. Or maybe Charlotte just realized that she had finally hit bottom and that it was now or never to get real help.

Donahue calmed Charlotte and told her that she was obviously overworked and overburdened, that John's actions were detrimental to her mental health, and that much of what he had done was "unacceptable behavior." Unacceptable? So she wasn't entirely to blame for all their strife, Charlotte thought with some relief. It was the first time that she really got the idea that there might be something wrong with John's behavior.

Donahue probed Charlotte's present life as well as her past. Such an approach proved to be far more beneficial for Charlotte than pure analysis. Because Charlotte wanted to keep the marriage together, Donahue helped her learn to respond to John in rational, controlled ways, with the hope that she could avoid further physical confrontations.

When John returned from his vacation, he told Charlotte that she owed him a major apology, and then he fell silent again. The next weekend they attended a wedding, but John sat in a pew behind her. They had a discussion and reconciled the next day, but the peace between them lasted only a few hours.

Later that week, the baby became sick with an ear infection. Despite the baby's being ill, Charlotte tried to arrange a family celebration for John's birthday, October 21. He came home carrying balloons, a gift from his staff. But Charlotte says she had to beg him to come down to the dining room to open gifts from his family, which he then left in the dining room for weeks.

The night, the baby came down with a high fever and suffered symptoms much like those John Michael had had right before he died. Charlotte was terrified but didn't talk to John about it. Also that month, John refused to join the family for one of his sons' birthday party, and for Thanksgiving dinner, says Charlotte. On another occasion that month, John, evidently irritated that the front door was locked when he came home, smashed his briefcase through the front hall's lead-glass window.

"I was upstairs helping Luke study," says Charlotte. "I heard him ring the doorbell, but I said to Luke, 'Don't worry, he can get in by himself,' because a few days before John had actually opened the door himself. And John is a creature of habit, obviously. He always carried his house keys with him and he admitted to me later that he had them with him that night. He started ringing the doorbell more frantically, as we started down the stairs. Luke and I were halfway there when we heard the first crash. I got there to open the door for him; I was only a few steps away when he broke the glass. He walked into the house and walked right past me without saying a word. I just started to clean up the glass immediately, since I had little children around with no shoes on their feet."

For almost six weeks then, John spoke barely a word to her, says Charlotte. Although she continued to fix his breakfast and to bring in his morning paper, she stopped helping John dress. He spoke long enough, she says, to accuse her of being selfish and petty. Even so, in early December, they attended together a party hosted by the Swiss embassy, bidding farewell to Faith Whittlesey as the US ambassador to its country. She was returning to Washington to work in the White House.

"I knew that the invitation was to both of us and I just informed John that I was going," says Charlotte. "I knew that I should make an appearance. This was a big step for me, trying to be calm and assert myself where he didn't want me. I got a short black skirt and a beaded top and a black velvet jacket. He later referred to it as my plastic outfit, but I knew I looked pretty good except for my glasses, which I now wore all the time. He did drive me down there. But he got out of the car and was walking a quarter of a block ahead of me. He did have the sense to wait at the door before he rang the bell.

"John ignored me the entire reception and didn't talk on the way home either. But I stayed calm and quiet. I was learning to not panic or become argumentative or combative. And I think that evening, my seeming to be more rational and confident helped. He started to come out of the silence a little bit and a few days later called me from the office and asked me to go to a private premiere of the movie *Gandhi* that his friend, the president of Columbia Pictures, was hosting."

Charlotte let John go alone, but the brief telephone conversation and his invitation encouraged Charlotte to try to reopen communication with John. Rather than try to talk to him in person and risk yet another fight, however, Charlotte sat down and wrote a letter. In it she stressed that they needed counseling. It read, in part:

A man of 41 who is not speaking to his family should not expect them to wait up and open the front door for him just because he had been on TV. You are powerful enough in your job [that] you don't have to break leaded-glass windows to impress us. . . . Do you realize the responsibility you have to find out what your problems are to help your children now and in the future? Do you realize you are more likely to succeed further (i.e., cabinet position, etc.) if your problem is taken care of now by counseling and/or medication than if your neighbors and friends and coworkers begin talking to investigative agents about your bizarre treatment of your family? . . . We are all very proud of your success, but none of us can build our whole life around your fame and power. A well-rounded, healthy man can balance his family and business. We do not resent your long hours, if you could just be pleasant and interested in us for the short time you are home. . . . I am committed to the children and my mar-

riage and I know you are a good decent man when you
are healthy—that is the man I loved. I know he's in you
somewhere. I pray you will get the help and guidance to
free him from his prison within you.

The letter affected John enough that he agreed to talk.
Charlotte recalls that he called and asked her to go to dinner. The dinner ended up being another party in honor of
Faith Whittlesey, in a private home, so he and Charlotte
waited until they got home and then took a long walk
around the neighborhood. Charlotte stuck to the advice her
therapist had given her for having an effective discussion.
Don't get sarcastic, don't use any four-letter words even if
John does, don't keep explaining the same points over and
over, don't get hysterical even if he frightens you. She kept
the checklist in her brain as they talked.

She told John she had been seeing a therapist. She also
said that she thought they needed to see a marriage counselor together, that they obviously weren't happy and
needed to work on changing the dynamics of their relationship. No personal invectives, no pleading, no tears, she says.
Not even when John said he thought they should try separating for a while. Charlotte swallowed hard, and agreed.
They went back to the house.

That night, John woke Charlotte up to make love. They
were reconciled.

Charlotte looked forward to the holidays with a new kind
of thankfulness. Maybe if she kept going to the therapist and
could learn to have such productive discussions with John,
their marriage really could be saved.

The next few weeks were relatively tranquil. Christmas
Day seemed to go smoothly, although John would later
claim that it had been very tense. They attended a friend's
New Year's Eve party and John took her to see the movie
Tootsie on John Michael's birthday, since that was always a
particularly hard day for Charlotte. On January 25, they

attended a performance of the National Symphony Orchestra, sitting in the presidential box at the Kennedy Center's concert hall as guests of Goldfield. On the twenty-eighth, they were invited to a dinner in a private home in Kalorama, one of the city's most elegant neighborhoods, just off Embassy Row.

But the peace between them was deceptive and short-lived. John was under a lot of pressure and again became preoccupied with work. He was being questioned by two House subcommittees about his initial resistance to an SEC bribery probe involving a client of his old firm. And a former client of his, Southland Corporation, the Dallas-based owner of 7-Eleven convenience stores, was being charged with trying to bribe a state official. He could eventually be called as a witness in the case, which would probably bring a flood of press questions about his work for the company.

John was starting to eat dinner away from home, not going to Congressional as he had before because of the expense, but eating in a fast-food restaurant near the SEC. He'd come home around 10 PM, just in time to go to bed, says Charlotte. Then one night, he vented his anxieties at Luke, throwing his son's ice skates at the boy when he talked back. John accused the boys of acting "like girls" when they cried and was, Charlotte feared, beginning to turn his temper as quickly and violently on them as he did on her. It frightened and angered her, but she managed to keep her opinion to herself that evening.

"Luke and John were arguing," she says. "I heard it going on. Luke had left his ice skates hanging on his room's doorknob, where he wasn't supposed to, and was being flip to John about it. John ordered Luke to put the skates away, and like fourteen-year-olds will do, Luke asked why he should. John said, 'Because I said so,' and Luke talked back. That's when John threw the skates, just as I walked into the room to try to smooth things over. I was trying to remain calm and somewhat neutral, but seeing him throw something at Luke was frightening. I said something really ridiculous, like 'Go to your room' to John, but I was trying to not say anything accusatory. That's when John looked at Luke and said, 'Go suck on your mother's tit.' I felt like John had hit me when he said that, it seemed so sick and low a thing to say to your son, but I kept quiet and just calmed the kids down."

In mid-February, the day before Luke's birthday, a large snowfall kept John trapped in the house over the weekend when he wanted to go to his office. He and Charlotte got into a fight over the boys' shoveling the driveway, and John gave Charlotte a black eye. With that blow, Charlotte sorrowfully concluded that even though she was controlling herself better under her therapist's guidance, it didn't seem to change anything between her and John.

"It had snowed a foot or more," Charlotte remembers, "and John couldn't get in to work. We cleaned the driveway and it had taken all day basically. The boys were still young to be doing such hard work. Luke, the oldest by several years, was only fourteen. John had that look in his eye. He had actually shoved me a few times and once pushed me down into the snow as we worked, but it hadn't hurt me so I tried to pretend that it was just playing.

"It was late that Sunday afternoon and we had just gotten inside and taken our boots off and were resting. John was outside poking at the gutter over the garage, worrying about the snow on the roof. It all fell down, of course. It would have been another hour's work to shovel it. I didn't want the boys to have to go out again right away, so I said that I'd help him after dinner. That wasn't good enough for him, and he started yelling at the boys. I had just picked up a little wooden toy because it was on the floor as I tried to reason with him. He said that line to the boys again, 'Go suck on your mother's tit,' and I saw red. I threw the toy at him—it missed him—and he hit me with a clenched fist right in my eye, and broke my glasses.

"I packed the boys and left them at a friend's and this time actually went to the police station in Rockville. I don't know what I wanted to do. I wanted someone to make him stop. The bruise was beginning to show. I had my friend take a photograph of it later for proof. The police were so cold to me. They told me all they could do was issue a warrant for his arrest if I would swear out a complaint. I didn't want him hauled off to jail. I didn't want to ruin him. I just wanted someone to talk to him. They were so impersonal to me. They didn't say to me, 'Aw, honey, you're still walking, and you should see the stuff we see,' but that was the attitude. I just felt like a fool, so I left."

Charlotte went home. A few days later, John left for Florida on business. He sent flowers on Valentine's Day. But he didn't call while he was gone, says Charlotte, didn't tell her where he was staying in Florida, or when he was coming home. When his boss, John Shad, called on a Saturday morning looking for him and kept pressing Charlotte about when John was getting back, she finally blurted out that she didn't know and didn't care because he had just given her a black eye. Shad's response was that he was sorry, but that John had been under a lot of pressure recently. Charlotte responded that it had been going on a long time, but Shad didn't seem to want to discuss it further. She hung up the phone, terrified about what she had done, but hoping that Shad would talk to John.

Charlotte decided to talk to a lawyer, and on February 20, 1983, she wrote John a letter telling him she wanted a divorce:

I am writing this letter to tell you how and how much I have loved you and indeed still love you. . . . Although you deny it, I have always been intensely interested in you and your life, your work, your worries, your ups and downs. I have yearned to be included in your confidence

—you have constantly shut me out. . . . You are the major being in your life. . . . And you, like so many chose . . . your profession to devote all your being. This is not uncommon in this society—especially Washington society. The difference is that you . . . have lost much, much more than the everyday workaholic. . . . Oh, how I have wanted to believe the fact that we would always be together—you said it so many times, yet you have never been willing to help that promise live. It apparently [was] too much trouble for you to seek a concrete basis for keeping *us* alive. . . . In order to love another, one must love [him]self first. As much as I love you—and I do—I have finally learned (and it was hard) to love myself. . . . Can you possibly remember how many times you have beaten me? . . . Why didn't you believe me when I said I would never let you do that to me again? Know this—no woman deserves to be beaten by her husband, not ever. . . . The final realization is that you are incapable of showing me and my children the respect and . . . love that we deserve. . . . I have cried the entire weekend because I now have to do the only thing I can. . . . I can no longer have you living in the same house as the boys and me. . . . It is a shame because most men would kill to have children as good as yours to nurture, guide, and love. Indeed, look around you and see if you can honestly find a better wife than me. And I would caution you not to be too macho in telling all your acquaintances about our situation—the truth will come out and no one admires a wife beater.

17

John's response to Charlotte's letter was a one-page note in which he thanked her for hers, calling it "generally constructive" and asked what were the plans for informing the boys about their future and joint concern for their welfare. He commented that her threat to tell people he was a "wife beater" was "unseemly" and closed with: "If you will not do my laundry today, at least leave me written instructions for operating the washer and dryer."

By his reaction, John seemed to easily accept the idea of a divorce. And yet, she recalls that when a letter arrived from Charlotte's lawyer, Bryan Renehan, confirming that she wanted the marriage to end, John became upset. After finding him in tears as he talked to Luke, explaining the situation, Charlotte agreed to give him one more chance, but only if he saw a therapist. John had to make an appointment before Charlotte would reconcile with him.

John seemed enthusiastic from his first visit, on March 5, and made Charlotte promise that she wouldn't let him stop. He knew that he had several years of work ahead of him, but he was looking forward to it, he told her. He even told one of their friends about it over the telephone. Charlotte knew that this really was their last-ditch effort, and hoped that they were finally on the road to recovery. But quickly John's interest in psychotherapy seemed to dissolve and he stopped seeing the psychiatrist after only six sessions. By Easter Sunday, when they had friends over for dinner, John was again ordering Charlotte to get people water.

In the first week of April, yet another confrontation, over cutting the grass, finally ended Charlotte's hopes. John had always been obsessive about the grass, noting on his calendars when they cut it and what number cutting of the year it was, and had demanded the entire family participate. No matter what Charlotte was doing, she had to be available to bring water to him as he mowed, or to help bag the trimmings. But this particular incident was unusually bad. As she remembers it, John yelled at the boys for being "lazy shits," and pushed one of them off the swing in the backyard because he didn't get off it fast enough when John told him to. When the child cried, says Charlotte, John called him a "baby." All the boys ended up in tears and later that night, when Charlotte tried to discuss it with him, John roared that he wasn't raising a bunch of girls.

"It was such a quick change in attitude that day," recalls Charlotte. "He and I had driven to our accountant's and as we were coming back John said to me that he had been trying to make a list of the ten most important things in his life and that I was the top three together. I was feeling really happy and then came the grass-cutting. I saw my son on the swing. He was swinging high when John yelled at him, so he was letting the swing slow down before he got off. Had John waited a few more seconds, he would have been off. I got really upset that night, and John just went into one of his moods on me."

A week or two later, Charlotte decided that she just couldn't stand the silent treatment anymore and called John at work and told him that he had to come home that night for dinner to be a real father. John said he was too busy to leave the office, she recalls.

Charlotte told him the marriage was over. And this time she stuck to it.

"It's funny how a tiny thing can be the final straw," she says. "I guess it was all the tension building up. It was weird. His not talking to me at all was just no longer acceptable. When he said, 'Gee, hon, I just can't come home,' that it was for me. I said, 'Fine, it's over.' He called back immediately. He called and he called. Finally, when I answered, he told me to hold dinner, that he was coming home. I answered, 'Fine, but it's still over,' and this time I didn't back down. He did come home. We had a pleasant meal. Then we went upstairs. There was no fighting. I just told him that I couldn't live this way anymore and he said very calmly, 'If I ever walk out this door, I'm not coming back.' And I said, 'Fine.' It was probably one of the most adult conversations we ever had."

The civility ended there, says Charlotte. She and John would sleep in the same bed, but he didn't speak to her until six weeks later, on June 5, when Charlotte discovered he had taken all her credit cards from her wallet. He also called the gas station and told them not to allow her to charge any more fuel on his account. She was frantic. How was she going to feed the boys, drive them around, clothe them? "I called him just about every name in the book that night," says Charlotte.

John surreptitiously taped Charlotte as she yelled at him about the cards, but she found the cassette the next morning and destroyed it. Three days later, John closed their checking account. She remembers that he started taking his briefcase into the bathroom with him when he showered.

When he moved out of their home, July 2, 1983, he had not told Charlotte where he was planning to live or given her a home phone number where he could be reached. The day would bring a final, ugly brawl. Charlotte had asked two of her sisters to be present in case John threatened her, anticipating trouble. As they squabbled over possessions, John would ask Charlotte if she liked something, implying the question "Would you like to keep it?" and then dash it to the ground when she answered, "Yes."

After witnessing John's throwing a Steuben ashtray and hitting Charlotte's hip with it, her sister Mimi called the police. By the time they arrived, John's hands were bleeding from the flying bits of smashed glass. His shirt had also been torn, when Charlotte had grabbed it and pleaded with him to stop breaking things. The police read both Charlotte and John their rights and explained how each could swear out a complaint against the other. When John and Charlotte declined, the police left and John drove away shortly thereafter.

As John's marriage crumbled, his career also started developing cracks. The spring had not been an easy one for him. The press and some congressional committees were beginning to criticize and question his work at the SEC. Although he had brought more insider-trading cases than had ever been filed in the commission's fifty-year history, critics charged that he was overly sympathetic to big business, shying away from bribery cases against them. In his two years at the SEC, according to the *Wall Street Journal,* John's division had brought only one overseas bribery case.

Two House subcommittees were questioning him about his initial resistance to an SEC probe of Ashland Oil, a client of Arnold & Porter, while the company was purchasing oil in Oman. John's answer was that he simply hadn't known that his former firm represented the company.

But his real trouble came when a federal grand jury in Brooklyn indicted Southland Corporation, owners of 7-Eleven, on charges of conspiring to bribe New York state officials in a tax dispute in 1977, and subsequently trying to cover up the scheme. John was questioned as a witness by the grand jury because he, as an attorney with Arnold & Porter, had helped Southland's in-house lawyers conduct an investigation of the affair, requested by the SEC, in 1977 and 1978. John was handling most of Arnold & Porter's questionable payment cases in those days. At that time, Southland submitted its findings in a report to the SEC division that John now headed. Federal prosecutors charged that the inquiry failed to uncover the bribery scheme and might, therefore, be an illegal cover-up.

John was never accused of any wrongdoing. He was, however, called to testify as a witness about the internal investigation he, as an outside consultant, had helped the company conduct on the matter. Although John's testimony on one key matter conflicted with that of two members of the audit committee of Southland's board, according to the SEC Southland report, John said that Southland executives had lied to him during the inquiry. The *Wall Street Journal* quoted the report, signed by Atlanta regional administrator Michael Wolensky, which concluded that John had not violated any law. But because Southland was being investigated, his work with the company was under examination and he was scrutinized by the press for almost a full, nerve-racking year.

John would later testify in his divorce proceedings that the Madison National Bank cut its promised line of credit of $150,000 to a mere $35,000 because of the adverse publicity surrounding him in the summer of 1983 (although a bank official denied it had limited the funds available to John when Charlotte called to ask about it) and that the whole affair had caused him great anguish. He felt it was a witch hunt. "You don't know John Fedders," he would say, "unless you know what I've gone through on Southland." He claimed that one of the prosecutors working on the Southland case had said that he would give up everything else "to get John Fedders."

John appeared before the Senate banking subcommittee examining Southland on June 28, a few days before moving out of his home, the same day the *Wall Street Journal* ran a front-page profile under the headline "SEC's Enforcer Runs Tight Ship, But Critics Charge He's Too Soft."

In that article, which raised the possibility of his being driven from office, John said that the congressional scrutiny of him was politically motivated and that some congressional aides were out to "get" him. But, he quipped: "I hear the crack of their guns, but I don't feel their bullets." His final quote in the story: "I've always operated best under pressure."

The majority of the article discussed John's style at work, and the many pressures on him there. He claimed that his hero was General Patton, because the warrior "was the most disciplined person that ever lived" and that everything in his own life was "discipline, organization, and structure." The reporter Richard Hudson wrote: "The SEC official's fondness for 'Old Blood and Guts' Patton will come as no surprise to those he calls his 'troops' at the agency. . . . Since his appointment two years ago, an SEC staffer says, management of the enforcement division 'has been tightened up.' "

John's aggressiveness and control were already legend in the agency. According to the June 28 article, some staffers felt compelled to wear suit coats in his presence and to pursue cases they thought coincided with his priorities. John had also designed a management chart "with the chain of command clearly and rigidly established." Brooks Jackson, the *Wall Street Journal* reporter who broke the news of John's abuse of Charlotte two years later, after their divorce hearing, wrote then: "Some attorneys who have worked with Mr. Fedders concede his intelligence and drive but say he is a socially awkward and sometimes arrogant man, given to locker-room bravado and macho management that women sometimes find offensive. One SEC staff member recalls Mr. Fedders' opening a meeting of women lawyers with the remark, 'Get out your Title Seven (sex discrimination) notebooks, girls.' "

But what Charlotte read with the most avid interest in June 1983 was the paragraph about her and the boys. Despite the facts he was about to leave them that very week, John painted a molasses-sweet portrait of his family life, probably knowing how crucial a proper image was for a Washington career. "He says he keeps in touch with his origins," said the *Wall Street Journal*, "by occasionally taking his wife and four [sic] children tenting on a 70-acre spread he bought in the mountains of Virginia outside Washington. 'You can see forever from there,' he says, describing a little stream on the property and its proximity to the Appalachian Trail. 'I put on my cowboy hat and my cowboy boots. It's me. Someday I'll put a log cabin on it.' "

Charlotte resented his depiction. They had walked on the land, gotten apples nearby, and had picnics—lovely events in themselves—but they had never "tented" there. Charlotte says she called the *Wall Street Journal* to let it know that she and John were separating and that John was moving out a few days later. And ever the protective mother, she wanted to report she had five, not four, sons.

The editor she spoke with at the newspaper told her that they had already received several calls about the article on Mr. Fedders. Was it true that he had physically hurt her, the voice on the telephone asked. Charlotte gasped. "Yes," she whispered but declined to elaborate. She hung up the phone, terrified that an exposé was to follow, but nothing happened.

Charlotte didn't know how people would react if she did tell them. John was a powerful, admired man; who would ever believe her, a nobody, a little housewife in the suburbs? Certainly, although she was relieved that the newspaper had done nothing, the *Wall Street Journal*'s silence galvanized that fear, as did the response of a woman at the Congressional Country Club.

"Right when John moved out," says Charlotte, "was the first time that I ever said anything to the wife of a friend of his, a beautiful woman. They were country club friends, and we were talking around the pool. She said that she heard that we were splitting up and I said, 'Yes,' and then I broke down and cried and told her that John had been abusing me for years. Her repsonse was: 'Oh, what a shame, such a sweet guy.' That was it. That certainly took me aback and kept me from talking to anybody else about it."

Without realizing it, Charlotte had broken an unspoken Washington law. Despite the fact it has more women executives than any other US city, wives of important men, women who aren't consequential themselves in terms of employment or connections, are to be seen and not heard. (Even women in power are expected to retain certain aspects of femininity, such as tenderness and quietude. For example, one senator commented that he gladly approved the appointment of Sandra Day O'Connor to the US Supreme Court because she would bring a motherly perspective to the bench.)

With each election, a bevy of new congressmen's wives are invited to a luncheon by the Congressional Wives Club. They are informally advised by their veteran cohorts about how to be good political spouses—how to dress, who to know, what to say, and most importantly, what not to say. It is accepted convention for them to avoid having any public ego of their own; they are to be proverbial straight men for their husbands, nothing more, but nothing less either.

In Washington, a spouse can be seen more as an indicator of a VIP's taste than as person, and, therefore, as primarily an asset or a liability to his reputation. Witness a sterling exchange recorded by gossip columnist Diana McLellan in her book *Ear on Washington:*

Any wife won't do. When Carter aide Greg Schneiders' star was on the rise, columnist Rowland Evans called him on the phone [to invite him to a dinner party]. . . . [He] asked Schneiders, "So, would you like to come?"

"Sure," said Greg, an unspoiled soul. Inquired Rowly, "By the way, do you have a wife?"

"Well, yes. As a matter of fact I do."

"And is she presentable?" asked Evans, quite unselfconsciously.

Silent suffering is admired in a Washington wife. McLellan points out that Joan Kennedy was forgiven her troubles because of her steadfast support of her mate, Senator Edward Kennedy, following Chappaquiddick, and that Maureen Dean was admired for sitting quietly by her husband, John, during the Watergate hearings. Squealing on the vagaries of the important spouse is simply bad form, and ex-wives who divulge unpleasantries often become non-persons.

And Charlotte unwittingly tripped over another prejudice with her poolside conversation. At that point, she was not worldly enough to recognize that, because some people wed as much for money or social position as for love, they and their friends might resent innocents still ingenuously searching for real love. She had gotten a pretty good deal, would be the disdainful appraisal of some, mainly women, perhaps unhappy themselves.

The next time she and the country club acquaintance met, the lady would look right through Charlotte.

When John left his family, he moved to a one-bedroom apartment in a large, well-established high rise on Massachusetts Avenue in Washington. His friend Goldfield lived there as well. John's apartment had a balcony, a washer and dryer in the second bathroom, a lighted doorbell, and an arch over the door to make it look more like a house entrance. The Art Deco lobby had fresh flower arrangements and someone at a desk to take messages. The rent when he moved in was $655. It was far from Spartan housing, says Charlotte, although the press would later depict it as such.

John explained his reasons for choosing the apartment at the pendente lite hearing held in the Montgomery County courthouse on September 13, 1983. (In Maryland, pendente lite determines interim custody, support, and use of possessions until the divorce proceedings, held after a couple has been officially separated for a year. No reasons for divorce are given at the hearing.) Charlotte's attorney, Bryan Renehan, asked about the apartment because John was giving Charlotte only $450 every other week. (He also paid the $841 mortgage and the utilities.) With five boys to feed, house and car insurance payments, gas and car repair bills, and dental and medical obligations despite Blue Cross/Blue Shield, she simply couldn't survive on that amount. Wasn't the apartment a little expensive? Couldn't John have found a two-bedroom apartment in the suburb of Bethesda, for instance, for $500 or less, one that ultimately would have been more suitable for housing the children when they visited, and made more money available to his family? asked Renehan.

Answered John: "Not with the sort of cleanliness that [pause], Charlotte would tell you, I'm sort of an anal personality and I like cleanliness and neatness and things like that and the things that I've seen in Bethesda are a joke."

The hearing also revealed that John had been borrowing heavily from the bank since leaving the house. On July 5, he borrowed $6,600, which went immediately for the payment due on the Virginia land; July 20, he received $5,100; and on August 12, $1,800. All the amounts were ninety-day notes, and were in addition to $19,500 in debt accumulated before he moved out. The total accumulated: $33,000, at an interest rate of 15 percent. Since moving out, he had also acquired $1,200 of furniture at Sears.

Not so much debt really, for a well-known lawyer plan-

ning on returning to private practice within two years. But
the problem was that John testified he really liked the SEC
and didn't plan on leaving it anytime soon. He had made
some cutbacks, withdrawing completely from the Congressional Country Club, for instance, that very month. But
Charlotte still worried that John didn't seem to recognize
how pinched they all were, trying to maintain two separate
households on his government servant's paycheck, which
was then $65,500. Especially since, one time, quite by acci-
dent, she had seen John come out of a notoriously expensive
gourmet shop, with a full grocery bag, and then get into
someone's glistening Mercedes. She also knew that he had
gone to the Kennedy Center opening of *42nd Street* and
fumed, wondering if he had purchased the tickets.

Meanwhile, Charlotte says she started selling some silverware and jewelry, and borrowing money from her church to
feed the children. In her testimony at the September 13
pendente lite hearing, she said: "We have cut back on food
—no fresh vegetables, little meat. No snacks that we used
to. . . . None of us have had [our] yearly physicals. We've
cut down on activities and clothing. [One of my children]
has given up soccer and scouts. The other children gave up
all the money that they earned this summer in an attempt to
help the household run."

Despite her needs, the court acknowledged John's limited
finances and essentially kept his payments about the same,
ordering him to send $500 alimony plus $100 support per
child, for a total of $1,000 per month. She made plans to
curb everyone's wants, but Charlotte was beginning to resent John's Mercedes-driving, play-going, politically potent
friends and what she saw as his attempt to keep up with
them. She borrowed from her sister Dotti and finally asked
her parents for assistance. They contributed, but said with
exasperation that John should be forced to give more.

* * *

On January 25, 1984, Charlotte was half-listening to President Reagan give his State of the Union address when she heard him say, "This year, we will intensify our drive against . . . other horrible crimes like sexual abuse and family violence." Suddenly, she had some hope.

She may have been naive to think so, but Charlotte believed that if Ronald Reagan—a president who professed a commitment to strengthening the American family—knew about her family's plight, he would quietly force John out of the SEC and back into private practice for the good of John's children. John had told her he couldn't give her more than $12,000 a year, plus pay the mortgage and utilities, because his government salary, then up to $70,000, couldn't accommodate it. In private practice, if he could earn the $300,000 salary he had claimed he would, Charlotte knew he could afford to do more for the boys.

She says she was tired of her children going without. She couldn't believe that John seemed to equalize the needs of one with the needs of six. Even if he did like the SEC, he had to put the boys as his priority now. It was time for her to take action. President Reagan seemed so sincere, she thought; surely he would help her.

She thought carefully about her wording. The letter read in part:

Mr. Reagan, I am the victim of wife abuse. . . . It was obviously beginning to be a very threatening situation for my entire family. . . . The boys and I live in a very comfortable home in Potomac. (I know this will sound silly, but you fly right over [our] house when you go to and from Camp David and we frequently wave—honest we do.) My husband moved to a luxury high-rise (and high rent) apartment . . . in the District. . . . The schools have been wonderful and are keeping the boys. They feel strongly that these fine young men need to continue their

education and religious training. I have been working for
both schools to compensate for the tuition-free education
they are giving. These jobs are mainly done in the home
so although I am working many hours a week, I am also
able to remain as a full time Mother. . . . My husband
seems by all accounts to be living quite a charmed life. He
is seen in the finest restaurants and theaters. He travels in
the best of circles with several friends in the White House
itself. . . . In 1981, my husband left the private practice
of law. With all his family supporting him, encouraging
him, and being very proud of him, he joined the Securities
and Exchange Commission as the Director of Enforcement. My husband is John Fedders. . . . When John
took the SEC post, we had little savings, and we knew this
job would put a tremendous strain on us financially, but I
felt this was the "break" John was looking for to finally
make him happy and relaxed. . . John Fedders did not
improve while at the SEC. . . . I hope you do not feel
this letter is from a bitter and vindictive woman. I asked
John to leave. I am sure that you can see it was the only
wise choice I could make for the welfare of my children
and myself. . . . This letter is in no way meant to undermine your confidence in John's ability as a top-notch SEC
enforcer. I do not understand, however, how a man can
enforce one set of laws and abuse another. My only expla-
nation is that John must not think what he did to me was
wrong. . . . I feel strongly that a man of the caliber of
the others in your administration would have resigned by
now and returned to private practice for "personal reasons" to end the strain on his children and even on himself. I can see why he is so hateful towards me, but my
sons did nothing to deserve his behavior towards them.

Charlotte immediately had second thoughts and never
sent the letter. She gave it instead to her sister Mimi for safe-
keeping, just in case she ever needed it. But several months

later, frustrated that John continued to refuse to voluntarily increase support payments to Charlotte, her father and her sister Mimi had the letter delivered to the White House through a politically connected friend at the American Medical Association. Dr. O'Donnell, always confident he could fix matters, had decided it was time for the family to do something. He and Mimi didn't tell Charlotte.

Eventually, the letter found its way to Fred Fielding, White House chief counsel. Martha called Fielding to see what he planned to do with the information. She recalls: "He said that the President would never knowingly keep a spouse abuser in a top administration job, but that it was a private dispute and that nothing had been proven and that there were two sides to every story. Then he asked me if I had ever seen John hit Charlotte, which I hadn't, but I told him that I had seen the black eyes and bruises and the broken glasses."

John later told Charlotte that Fielding had called him to his office to discuss the matter after Martha's call. But Mimi, not knowing that and thinking Fielding planned to do nothing, contacted Richard Vilkin, a freelance reporter who had taken a fervent interest in John's work and the Southland case. Again, neither sister told Charlotte about their actions. Mimi would eventually tell Charlotte, however, that the reason she had contacted Vilkin was to add pressure to the White House, believing that if the administration discovered that a reporter was digging around in John's alleged domestic violence, during an election year, he would be quietly forced to resign from the SEC and to return to private practice.

Although John would later say that her family waged a campaign to ruin him, the O'Donnells claim all they wanted was for the job change to occur quietly, without any publicity, so that Charlotte and her sons would have enough money to go on with their lives. They knew newspaper stories could harm his career and ultimately his ability to support the boys. But they were emphatic about his returning to private practice. They didn't care how much he liked the SEC. They thought he had done enough harm to Charlotte and that it was time for him to put his children's needs first. Dr. O'Donnell was the master of pressure politics in the AMA; he knew what he was doing, he told Charlotte's sisters.

But the subtle leverage strategy didn't work. John remained at the SEC and in six months his private life became public knowledge in an open divorce hearing.

18

On January 22, 1984, three days before Charlotte heard President Reagan refer to domestic violence in his State of the Union address, she was sitting in the basement with the boys, watching the Washington Redskins play the Los Angeles Raiders in Super Bowl XVIII. After the game, she and Luke stayed put to see *60 Minutes*. The news program was featuring a seventeen-minute report, "Dirty Little Secret," about Richard and Deborah Jahnke, two teenagers in Wyoming who had been abused by their father. A little over a year before, Richard Jahnke, no longer able to stand his father's physical abuse of him and his family, had shot and killed his father.

Alan Prendergast, the author of *The Poison Tree*, an account of the teenagers and their trial, described the *60 Minutes* program: "The report's most powerful moments came in a series of tight close-ups of Richard Jahnke, who recalled his father's 'evil voice' and merciless treatment of him with the uncanny talent for mimicry he had first displayed at his trial. Angry, bitter, and occasionally sarcastic. . . . This was one Angry Young Man, gnashing his teeth and playing the crowds."

Charlotte listened with growing concern to her fourteen-year-old sputter, "That's just like Dad," when the Jahnkes described their father brushing their teeth until their gums bled. She didn't want Luke as angry as the boy on television. It couldn't be healthy.

Charlotte had known all along that John was demanding of his children, particularly of their firstborn. Luke was to be the star athlete, the star student, "another John Fedders," as Luke says. In fact, witnessing John react in sudden anger to Luke was pretty much what had pushed Charlotte to finally want a divorce the previous spring. John had thrown objects, even a small television set, to the ground near her before. But when he threw the ice skates at Luke, she says she realized that her son was no longer safe from the same kind of instantaneous retribution she had experienced with her husband, especially since Luke was becoming old enough and sassy enough to say no. Contradicting John was what had always gotten her in trouble, and what endangered Luke.

"I think John really loved Luke," says Charlotte. "They had the closest bonding of any of the children. He spent far more time with Luke than he did with his other sons. But the real trouble started when Luke started to think for himself."

Today, Luke is eighteen. He is a handsome, lanky, earnest young man. His face bears an uncanny resemblance to his father's and has an intriguing agelessness. At times, he seems twice his years, at others half. He's accustomed to answering difficult questions about his feelings, and looks his questioner straight in the eye as he talks.

In the past, he has been frustrated by his relationship with his father, but that seems to be waning, and he remains an engaging, likable boy. He wants to be a veterinarian, and is the type of teenager who constantly brings home injured animals, who hugs his youngest brother easily, and who can make his mother giggle with his stories.

After his father left home, Luke started working at a veterinary hospital, walking the dogs and doing various odd jobs. At first he say he was very afraid he would do something wrong and be fired, since mistakes had often brought serious consequences at home. But as Luke saw that the doctor he worked for was understanding when he faltered, his own confidence began to grow.

John never slapped Luke in the face, never pummeled him as he had Charlotte, but his discipline could be harsh. The main method of punishing the boys was with a fraternity paddle, say Luke and Charlotte. And his expectations and his impatience, when Luke in particular failed to achieve the goals he had set, could be high.

Charlotte recalls that John had Luke reading *Sports Illustrated* aloud to him when the boy was six years old. As Luke grew older, his free time was restricted so that he could concentrate on his schoolwork. Luke says that his father forced him to bed early and didn't allow him to play a radio at night for fear that it would make Luke forget what he had studied that evening. To try to build him into a strong, brawny athlete, John often insisted that Luke eat two helpings at dinner, and, by the time the boy was ten, had him doing push-ups. Luke remembers that it was not unusual for John to say when he entered the room, "Hi, son, why don't you drop and give me thirty?"

Luke was put on swimming teams, soccer teams, basketball teams, but wasn't particularly outstanding at any of them. The thing he did excel at was diving, an endeavor John seemed to disapprove of. To be allowed to dive competitively, Luke had to join Congressional Country Club's swim team as well. When Luke was older, John jogged with him. They ran a two-mile course that John had mapped out, even in the winter, says Luke. Athletics was serious business. When they played football or baseball in the yard, it was "not playing," says Charlotte. "They were supposed to learn how to play the game right during those sessions."

Says Luke: "He was more a coach than a father."

"The main message Luke . . . got from his father was that [he was] inadequate, inefficient, and lazy," says Dr. Mary Donahue, the psychologist who counseled Luke in 1978 when his fourth-grade work began to slide and who later helped Charlotte. "Luke was looking for more positive input from his father. . . . He went through a period of disillusionment and then just shut down when he [felt] it was hopeless."

What had struck Luke about the *60 Minutes* report was not just the strictness of the Jahnke children's father but his roughness. Luke remembers that before church John would comb the boys' hair, sometimes raking the brush so hard against their scalps that their heads pounded for minutes afterwards. When he cut their nails, he trimmed them so low that their fingertips were often sore for a day or two. Once, when Luke had smashed his finger bowling with friends, his nail turned black and looked as if in a few days it would fall off naturally. When he was showing it to his mother, John came by, grabbed Luke's hand, and pulled the nail off. "Which made it bleed considerably and kind of hurt," says Luke.

John would do similar things as coach of Luke's basketball teams. "If I jammed a finger," remembers Luke, "he'd pull it out and I had to keep playing. He'd let the other kids sit out for a while. I was the one who always seemed to do the drill wrong, all the time. Even if I did most of it right, I had to do it over. It made me feel low because he was a coach and was supposed to help me with that stuff and not have me do it over by myself in a corner, like a punishment.

"But his son had to be the best. He would criticize me on the drive home. He'd say I was doing everything wrong and that I shouldn't be on the team.

"We all played football out front, on the street. If we didn't catch the ball, or dropped it two or three times, he'd start to go inside, saying, 'I'm not going to play with someone who can't catch.' We'd beg and beg and beg, but he wouldn't come out again.

"If I didn't do real hot at a swim meet one day, he'd take me up into his room after we came home and show me pictures of him swimming. He'd tell me how he had been a coach and a star and that if he could be that good, why couldn't I?"

"I think John truly wanted Luke to be a great athlete for good reasons," says Charlotte. "He wanted him to be accomplished; what parent doesn't want that for his child? A lot of men try to achieve what they didn't themselves through their sons. It's just that Luke was never as competitive as John had been as a youth, and it was hard on him that John rarely praised him."

In fact, the best thing about the Arnold & Porter picnics, Luke says, was the fact people would applaud his abilities in some of the organized games. "I'd go and play volleyball or Frisbee and get more recognition there than I did at home. I wasn't the first person to get picked for a team, but I wasn't the last either. Somebody wanted me. That made me feel real good.

"I guess I just would have liked my father to have been around more, to be more understanding, more patient. My Dad never said 'That's great' to me. Never."

One of the major activities John did do with his sons, according to Luke, was drilling them on their push-ups. When the boys hadn't done them, he told them that their upper bodies looked weak. When Luke broke his hand, he remembers that John made him try to do a push-up to see if he could still do the exercise even in a cast.

"We did push-ups every night most of the time if he was home and in a good mood," says Luke. "He'd call all of us in and say, 'Give me thirty.' And then at the end of thirty, we'd have to hold ourselves two inches off the ground for a few seconds. I think doing the push-ups is what drove us apart from Dad the most because everyone hated it. It was a real bad time. That and the chin-ups. We did those in the summer hanging from the bar on the jungle gym outside. It wasn't a chin-up bar, it was a big, thick pole that the swings were attached to. Even now I can barely wrap my hand around it. So that made it really hard. We would have to climb up the trapeze to the bar, then he would pull that back. Sometimes he'd do it before we were set and we'd fall. I was about thirteen when we started."

Luke and Charlotte recall that John could also be brusque when helping him with his schoolwork. "Whenever we got talking, we got into a fight," says Luke. "When I had to read to him, we'd always argue that I had skipped a word or pronounced a word wrong. It was always 'Gosh, you don't know this? I'm not going to help you.' One night I had to memorize a poem for school and he came in and said, 'Well, let me hear it.' I got nervous, so I messed up. So he said, 'Stay in your room for another hour until you have it.' So, the next hour, he made me nervous again, and I messed up again. I'd get one line wrong, and he made me do it all over again.

"He came home with a guitar one night and nonchalantly talked me into taking lessons. I probably did it for two years. I never really enjoyed it; none of us are very musical. He was never pleased with me. When I started doing songs on the guitar, he'd say, 'Here, play me something,' and I'd get all nervous and I could never play like that.

"Then he brought down this old trumpet that used to be his from the attic and told me that I was going to play it. He said, 'Why don't you take lessons at school?' I didn't say no because he'd get mad, and when he got mad, he got *mad*. You knew that going along with him made him happy. As long as you did everything his way, you were safe."

* * *

John disciplined his sons with an old Sigma Delta Chi journalism fraternity paddle. He called it "the board of education." "We'd be in church sometimes," says Luke, "and if we started—we weren't fooling around—but if there was a giggle, he'd lean over and hold up his finger and that meant one hit. If we did it again, he'd hold up two fingers, then three fingers. We'd get home and you'd hear the screams upstairs in his den. He was like Big Brother in *1984*.

"Once in a while, someone would take the board and hide it so he couldn't use it. Then he'd hit us with these floppy lead weights he said he had put in his shoes when he was young."

"I remember that when John did that," says Charlotte, "or when they were roughhousing, he'd say to the kids, 'Ah, I didn't hurt you.' I think he had no idea how strong he really was and that one good swat from him could hurt a great deal."

"Toward the end," says Luke, "he used to run at me like he was going to grab me when I refused to cut the grass a second time. I'd say, 'No, we're not going to do it again today.' I was always speaking for all of us. Then he'd run at me from maybe fifty feet or so. I'd get freaked out when he did that. I'd run away, so he never caught me. I don't know what he would have done had he gotten his hands on me, but I wasn't planning to find out the hard way. It was real scary, because I knew what he was like when he was mad and from the simple fact of having a six-foot-ten guy running at you full speed.

"Yeah, I was afraid of him at the end, when he wasn't talking and stuff. Because you never knew what he was going to do next. His moods changed like the weather. You were on guard all the time. If a cop is walking his beat, he doesn't have his gun all locked up on safety; he has it unlatched and ready to fire. That's how we were around the house—waiting for it."

* * *

Charlotte tried to make the sporting events as pleasant as possible. In 1981, when John and Luke jogged together they made a bet that Luke wasn't as fast a runner as John. They set a race for Memorial Day weekend. John promised Luke $50 if he won the two-mile contest. Charlotte and the boys strung their driveway with toilet paper as a finish line and waited for the runners to appear at the bottom of the hill. The family was in a festive mood because they knew John was being considered for the SEC position and he was so happy. Charlotte took a photo as Luke, indeed, broke the paper ribbon first, to the cheers of his brothers.

John, however, never paid Luke the bet.

"I don't believe in bets or bribes for children," says Charlotte, "but if you make them, you should honor them. Several times John promised the boys a penny-an-acorn type of pay for yard work and he never paid them."

The summer of 1982, John had also promised to reward the boys monetarily for their chin-ups, if they reached his goal for them by his chosen deadline. They all did, but John still didn't pay.

"He'd always say 'later' about the money when we asked," says Luke. "One time we were at the beach and we asked him for some money to go to the boardwalk and he whips out a $100 and two $50 bills and hands one each to me and two of my brothers. We were out of that door so fast, so excited, heading for the boardwalk. And then he yells up the street for us to come back. 'Do you really think I'd do that?' he asked and then handed me a $5 bill and gave them $2 apiece.

"He was big on making promises and getting everybody excited and then never doing it. We'd go out to that farm in Virginia. We'd go up the same hill and he'd stand there and say, 'We're going to build a house right here and it'll overlook the creek.' We'd run around and be excited because all kids love woods and a creek. Then, the next time, we'd climb that same hill and he'd say the same thing. It happened over and over again. I finally starting thinking, 'Bull.' I knew it would never happen. He liked making promises. I'd never believe any of them unless he was promising something about his work—that he'd do."

John took the boys to his SEC office only a few times. Luke remembers that one Sunday afternoon John worked for over an hour while he and his brothers picked up staples in the commission's copy machine room as John told them to. (John would later have the carpet in the room removed, apparently because the staff continued to drop staples around the copying machine.)

But, for the most part, Luke remembers that he didn't see much of his father once he became SEC enforcer. "That last year he was more like a boarder than part of the family. We didn't even have to do the push-ups much then. He just came in for his meals and then went upstairs. You could always tell if he was in a bad mood by the way he sat on his couch in his study. If his feet were toward the door so you could see his face, he was okay. When he was in a bad mood, he'd face the other way, with his back to the door, ignoring you. Most of the last year he sat the other way."

John had left the house on Carmelita Drive seven months before the *60 Minutes* program was aired. When he did, Luke says he felt overwhelmed by some of his new responsibilities. He had always had more than most boys his age, changing diapers and watching his baby brothers, but now he felt he needed to be even more of a surrogate father, that he really needed to discipline them when they acted up. He says he followed the only example that he had.

"When he first left," says Luke, "I thought I had to be like a father for my brothers, and I followed his role and slapped them. The first time it happened, I felt terrible because they said, 'Get away from me.' I reacted like my father and tried to be all nice. It made me see how terrible it had been for both sides, for him and for me. So I stopped."

Luke feels that tension lightened for him after his father left, despite the household's economic paralysis. "I'm sure there were some good times with my father. It's just hard for me to remember them."

TRIAL BY FIRE

"When did you stop beating your wife?"
"Who said I did?"

Old vaudeville joke

Preparing herself for her divorce trial, scheduled for February 1985, was one of the hardest things Charlotte ever did. She spent hours with her lawyer, Bryan Renehan, telling him all the sad, all the embarrassing details of her marriage, defending herself against the accusations John made through his deposition. When giving her deposition, she tried to answer succinctly, yes or no, whenever possible even though she feared that a yes or no wouldn't tell the judge the whole story, wouldn't explain how she had felt. But she remembers that Renehan reassured her that he would bring up the gray-zone elements of incidents in the divorce trial if they needed telling. He suggested she look at the judge as she answered, even though he, Renehan, would be asking her the questions.

She trusted Renehan because he was accessible, soft-spoken, compassionate, and more respectful to her than any man had ever been. She was amazed that whenever his wife telephoned, even when they were in the middle of something, Renehan immediately took the call. He also *really* listened to Charlotte, pulling on his brown mustache or adjusting his horn rim glasses as he contemplated her answer.

"Bryan is a very empathetic, nice man," says Charlotte, "which I think I desperately needed emotionally at the time. A really cruel, cutthroat lawyer would have made me vindictive, which ultimately would have been very detrimental to my emotional health."

One of the things that terrified her was having to face John's lawyer, Hal Witt, who intimidated her. During the pendente lite hearing, in September 1983, he had rattled Charlotte with a series of questions, rather brusquely asked, she thought, about her driving abilities.

She remembers the deposition Witt took from her in fall 1984 as painstaking and difficult. For more than three hours she had sat in his office, a legal stenographer silently typing, and answered questions about her check stubs, notations on her calendars, letters she had written, the part-time job she had taken at the boys' school as a development coordinator. What was he trying to imply by some of them, she indignantly asked herself.

"His voice was very quiet," says Charlotte, "but he definitely seemed insinuating. He went through all my checks, for instance, asking about any that had a man's name on it —like one to the man who delivered my newspaper—who was he? Witt was trying to establish a connection between me and some man, I suppose. Of course, he asked me if I had ever had a relationship with another man during my marriage and when I answered no, he asked if I had been with any woman. I suppose John had told him my book club might be a group of men-hating lesbians.

"The one time I notated on my calendar my appointment with Dr. Donahue as 'Mary,' he wanted to know if I always called my therapist by her first name, I guess implying that she had become too familiar to be a credible witness. He also asked about some notes I had written to people who were primarily John's friends, informing them that we had separated and saying that I hoped they would remain supportive of both John and me and of the boys. I did state that the reason for the divorce was abuse, but that was all. I didn't elaborate at all. John claimed I had launched a letter-writing vendetta against him, so I guess what Witt was trying to find out was what I was trying to accomplish with them. Now I wouldn't even write those people. But then I was so insecure that John would tell them that I was a bad person and that they would believe him. But how could I try to explain that kind of lack of confidence to John's lawyer?"

Charlotte knew many of John's complaints about her already: that she didn't discipline the boys enough, confided too much in Luke and alienated him from his father, talked too intimately with his secretary about their problems, that her mouth was their biggest problem. But he also claimed that she hadn't been tender, that she hadn't supported him enough. She had tried so hard to be everything he wanted. Was the court going to believe that she had been a cold, spoiled brat and therefore deserved brutality?

In addition, John was pressuring her to cut the expense of sending the boys to private schools and of her seeing her psychologist. Tuition alone was up to $15,000 a year. Charlotte refused on both counts—she felt she needed to continue therapy and the boys needed to stay in their schools, where they'd get more individualized academic attention. She also felt she needed to maintain some stability in their lives. Besides, she remembered that John had always supported their private, Catholic education. Why was he changing his tune now?

Nine days before February 4, 1985, the first day set for their trial, Charlotte began saying a novena to Saint Martha, the patron saint of homemakers. Each evening she went to her parish, Our Lady of Mercy, and lit a candle before the Blessed Mother's altar, and said her prayers. The modern chapel looked particularly stark during those nine winter evenings. The larger-than-life Jesus, hanging against a cold wall of slate, was splattered with shadows cast from candles on the Blessed Mother's altar to its right, where flames flickered cool in rows of blue glasses, and from candles on the Sacred Heart's altar to its left that burned hot in blood-red glasses. Those were the only lights in the chapel. But Charlotte braved the foreboding gloom, asking the saint to protect the interests of her children. On her way out, she also said a small prayer of contrition, guilty that she didn't have enough pocket change to pay the church's suggested contribution for the candle she lit that night. She was counting every nickel these days.

The day of the trial arrived cold and clear. As she dressed, Charlotte berated herself for not losing weight. She hated the idea that John would look at her and think that she had fallen apart after he left her, that as always, she had "let herself go." She drove the twenty minutes to the Rockville courthouse by herself.

The trial was to begin at 10 AM and Charlotte met Renehan in the courthouse lobby at 9:30. About 9:40, he and Hal Witt withdrew to an antechamber to discuss a proposal he had submitted to Witt several weeks beforehand. Charlotte prayed that John had accepted her alimony and support requests so that she could just go home. She had heard tales of people "settling on the courthouse stairs," and kept hoping that Renehan would return with glad tidings. As she waited anxiously, she watched clusters of lawyers gather and lean against the walls, smoke cigarettes, peruse papers, argue, make deals. Her hopes built. Five minutes to ten, and Renehan still wasn't back. Charlotte went into the courtroom with an associate of Renehan's firm, there to help him present her case. Renehan appeared in the courtroom seconds before Judge James McAuliffe arrived. He shook his head. There were no substantive additions to John's original plan in his counterproposal.

"John had always said," recalls Charlotte, "that a man couldn't be successful and be a nice guy."

John was willing to continue paying $1,000 a month to Charlotte in alimony and child support, continue life insurance payments, health insurance for the children, plus the mortgage and house utilities (all of which he calculated totaled $2,211 a month); to give Charlotte three years' use of the house and half the proceeds from its sale; and to keep the boys on his health insurance and Charlotte as beneficiary on his life insurance policy. He based his plan on his current government salary of $72,300. After paying taxes and all his monthly obligations to Charlotte, John figured that he had about $1,086 left over for himself, from which he paid his rent, which had been raised to $720.

But Charlotte knew that she and five boys couldn't exist on $12,000 support per annum. John expected her to pay the house insurance out of that amount, which alone was more than $1,000 a year. She was spending $500 a month on food. They had already sold the Virginia property and she had used those proceeds to pay tuitions and legal and medical bills. What was she supposed to do after the house was sold? Even with half the cash from the sale of their house (which had been estimated to have a fair market value of $285,000) she wouldn't be able to find a house to accommodate six people that would have a mortgage less than the $820 John now paid. She probably wouldn't even be able to find a place to rent for that amount.

She had been working part time at The Woods Academy, producing brochures and helping recruit new students, for which she had received $3,784 the previous year. She didn't want to work full time because her youngest son was only three years old and another five. The cost of day care would almost negate whatever pay she figured she could get, even if she did renew her nursing license and found a related job. Besides, she strongly believed in full-time mothering. She reasoned that John simply had to shoulder more of the economic burden. Why didn't he just return to private practice?

Charlotte and Renehan had decided to accept what they considered reduced alimony and child support based on John's government salary until he left the SEC (probably at the end of Reagan's second term), if he would also give Charlotte the house. With those qualifiers, they asked for $2,000 a month in alimony, and $1,250 for child support ($250 per child), which would include the boys' tuition.

In Maryland, a divorce settlement is an "equitable decision"; there is no presumption of a fifty-fifty split even in cases where the separation is voluntary, as Charlotte and John's had been. If one of the parties can show the other was more at fault in causing the divorce, the less guilty party is generally awarded more.

Abuse is one of the few reasons of fault the court still takes seriously, says Renehan. He had to prove fault so that John would pay his client more than the $12,000 a year he offered. So he and Charlotte built their case around the abuse. And, in truth, given her background, Charlotte says she would never have ended her marriage had it not been for the violence and psycholigical control. Renehan planned to present only seven incidences of physical attacks, for which they had undeniable documentation—doctor's reports and records of treatment—or witnesses.

Charlotte says John knew walking into the Rockville courtroom what Renehan planned to present. Several weeks before, Renehan had disclosed his list of witnesses and evidence to Witt—there are no surprises allowed in a court proceeding despite the romanticized depictions of TV dramas. In the evidence was a photograph of Charlotte with a black eye. On the list of witnesses was the name of her therapist. Renehan was stunned that John didn't want to settle out of court.

"I think you have to know John Fedders to understand this," says Renehan. "I think he was psychologically incapable of compromise. That's what made him such a successful lawyer. He is a very hard-nosed, determined, macho kind of guy. It was always winning, winning, winning for him. He ran the SEC and his home like armed camps. I think he had come to believe that he was invincible."

"I really didn't want that much money," says Charlotte. "But what John was offering was realistically not enough for a six-person household. And because he didn't bring it up in his proposal, Bryan and I had to assume that he also wasn't planning to contribute to the boys' education, high school or college, or contribute to rehabilitative alimony for reeducating me so that I could work. Nothing.

"We truly thought that John would settle out of court. This is crazy, we kept thinking: there is no way he'd take the chance of taking it to court. Once we were there, however, I couldn't just say, 'Trust me, Your Honor, this was bad, but I don't want to publicly discuss it.'

"People have said that I murdered his career, but I think he committed professional suicide. I honestly think the man didn't think he had done anything wrong. Or that people would question whether he could do his public job well given his private problems."

The *Wall Street Journal*'s reporter Brooks Jackson approached the bench to formally announce his presence after Charlotte's testimony, when the judge called for a recess. But John later told Charlotte that he knew who Jackson was all along. When the judge returned to the courtroom following lunch, he announced that Jackson was working on a possible story and that the court would make transcripts and evidence available to him.

Charlotte cried quietly through much of her testimony. It took several hours to relate all the details of the specific seven abuse incidents, the slow breaking of her spirit by John's criticisms, his moody withdrawals, his rules, their overspending, all the shattered hopes of a marriage that Charlotte always believed should have been perfect.

Her testimony included:

> I remember trying to protect my abdomen. . . . It was just a frightening experience, because . . . I was really afraid for my life and the child I was carrying. . . . During these periods [of withdrawal) he would, when he was home, just sleep a lot. And then the next morning he would wake up and be singing in the shower. When I tried to talk to him he would laugh at me or tell me everything was fine. . . . I constantly felt that I should be doing something more . . . he made me convinced that I was causing the major problem and I really felt the responsibility . . . to get help. [But] he was bitterly against it [seeing the psychiatrist]. . . . I was losing control. I kept feeling that I should be doing more for John, because I could not make him happy. . . . I went to [John] and pleaded with him not to get a divorce. . . . I really wanted our marriage to work. He laughed at me and he said that he's been dating for years. He said: "Ask anybody at Arnold & Porter." . . . I was . . . devastated. I never denied him sex at all. . . . I'm a bit of a heavyweight myself and I figured he couldn't throw me over the banister with, you know, ease, if I was on the floor. But he had me by the hair. And . . . I was on my knees, yelling at him to stop, and he just shook me by the hair, . . . up and down and back and forth, and then just kind of . . . threw me down. . . . I threw open my nightgown . . . I guess in my mind I was trying to seduce him. . . . But he just looked at me and laughed and said that I had just proved his point, that I was crazy. And then he left. Except for when my baby died, it was one of the most horrible moments in my life. . . . He yelled at [the boys] to come on out and [when they didn't] he yelled at them, "Why don't you just suck on your mother's tit" . . . . He

stopped going to [the psychiatrist], saying [to me], "I'm not going with that attitude of yours."

Finally, Renehan asked her why she had stayed so long. She responded.

All I ever wanted to be when I was growing up was a wife and mother. I knew I was a good mother. I kept trying to be a good wife. I felt a good bit of the abuse must have been my fault. . . . My religion says [marriage] is sacred . . . I never wanted to leave him. He was just my life . . . I felt no other man would want me. I didn't feel particularly attractive when I was younger. Although John married me, he didn't encourage me to feel attractive. There was always something wrong with me. I was too fat, . . . my hair was too curly. . . . I think the only reason that I ultimately felt there was no other way [than divorce] was because of the effect it was having on my children. Even when John left I didn't have the self-esteem to think that I deserved to be treated better. But I knew my children did.

The final witness Renehan called was Charlotte's therapist, Dr. Mary Donahue, who described the dynamics of the marriage and Charlotte's resulting emotional state:

[Charlotte] has episodes of depression. . . . Mrs. Fedders never felt she had much to say about . . . how the relationship was going . . . and basically he made the decisions as to where they would go, and what they would do, and what sort of things they would buy. . . . Mrs. Fedders saw herself as submissive and dependent on Mr. Fedders. . . . She never felt that she had an equal role. . . . Mrs. Fedders presents almost a classic case of someone who is a victim in that she felt inadequate and less attractive . . . and felt that she was indeed fortunate to have someone like Mr. Fedders be attracted to her. Therefore, whatever problems existed were her responsibility. . . . She always looked to herself to see what she was doing that provoked this . . . whatever problems the children presented she felt were her fault in some way. . . . I don't think she had the ability or skills . . . to get out [of her marriage]. . . . It was only as the children got a little older and she began to move out into the community a little bit more and had some exposure to other people reacting to her [that she realized] that she could do things successfully.

While listening to Renehan's arguments, the testimony of witnesses, and even the tearful statements by his wife, John sat quietly, taking notes or looking away, not visibly showing any emotional reaction. On the stand the next day, however, John's calm failed him. His uncharacteristic lack of control started almost as soon as he took the oath on February 5. When asked where he attended college, John's voice cracked as he answered, "Marquette," and the judge asked him if he needed some water. Later, John stumbled through his testimony, sometimes repeating himself, sometimes speaking in fragmented statements, sometimes interrupting himself in a tumble of thoughts.

Charlotte stared at her husband in disbelief. She had never seen him so seemingly distraught or heard him ramble on so, this man who regularly testified in front of Senate committees and talked to the press, this man who had always been so tightly controlled with her.

He went to the SEC, John said, for "the opportunity for public service. Intellectual enrichment, to do something extremely challenging, ah, to push me every day, to put enormous amounts of pressure on me. . . . The exhilaration, and the constant challenge and the pressure was something I wanted so badly. . . . I told her that it . . . provided me two things I needed desperately in life: the combination of my management skills and my intellectual capabilities. And it was exhilarating and it was going to push me."

The judge interrupted Witt's questioning to ask: "There is an emphasis in your testimony about something you desperately needed. And you emphasize the word 'desperately.' Can you tell me what led to that desperation?"

"I'm ambitious," replied John. "I would like to excel. I have said to more than one person that . . . I would like to be recognized as . . . one of the outstanding securities lawyers in the country."

Judge: "Was it a professional desperation? Was it limited to professional matters, or did you feel a desperation about everything?"

John: "Desperation, upon reflection, as we dialogue, might be the wrong word."

Judge: "It's your term."

John: "Yeah. I wanted to be in public service very badly, because I think that no place do you get the intellectual challenge and the enrichment combined. I don't care how good you are in private practice, you don't face the same kinds of problems day in and day out that you can face in a law enforcement position of this magnitude. And, ah. It provided me. I am told I have a talent—rather than saying I have it—I have both an intellectual talent and a management talent. In a law firm you can be a lawyer, but your management is limited to the number of cases there. At the commission today I have 739 open investigations, that are in the nature of formal orders. I have hundreds of . . . inquiries going on. I have just a staff to work on so many things. . . . I never have to work on anything more than ten minutes. I can deal with things intellectually.

"The most satisfying thing is working with young people." John suddenly spoke in a torrent. "To take young students or young people two years out of law school and show them how to excel and push themselves. And I never demand anything of anybody that I don't provide ten times myself. And that's caused problems for Charlotte and me. But I would say that my greatest success there is the acquisition and management of talent. You can forget all the cases we've brought. I've transformed that into an institution—not myself; I don't like the word 'I' at the SEC—but the senior staff I've selected, into what is being called the finest law enforcement agency in the world. And I take great pride in that. I don't want to dwell on it, but it's a wonderful job."

Witt continued the examination by asking about his finances. When questioned about a deduction in his pay, John struggled as he said, "I am told that, ah, ah [pause], that when the court declares the divorce." He paused. Seeing his discomfort, Judge McAuliffe suggested a ten-minute recess, but John replied: "It's not going to get any easier, Your Honor, we might as well keep going." There seemed to be an eerie awareness in the courtroom of watching a successful man self-destruct, as John, confronted with the realities of his life, seemed to be unable to speak without great emotion. Despite his suggestion to continue, the judge declared a break to let John collect himself.

Back in the courtroom, Witt continued his questioning: "Mrs. Fedders testified that you struck her possibly on seven occasions. How do you feel about having struck your wife?"

John: "There was no justification whatsoever."

Witt: "She testified that on one occasion that you hit her in the stomach [when pregnant]. Is that true?"

John: "I don't believe so. I prayed on this last night for God's wisdom as to whether I did it. I just cannot believe that I did it." He gathered momentum as he spoke. "This occurred before the birth of our first son. I was in love with her. Nobody wanted a first son more than me. I was up there, painting his name on—we called him Oscar for a while—I painted his name across the ceiling. It is incomprehensible to me that I had that capability to say . . . that I didn't care if she died, . . . if he died, or . . . if I went to jail. I deny it vehemently."

Later, Witt asked: "Mrs. Fedders testified that in November of 1981, you tried to throw her over the banister. Did you, in fact, try to throw her over the banister?"

John: "I remember the incident. I remember it all too well, again. It was by the banister. I don't believe that I tried to throw her over the banister. I don't believe that I indicated that I wanted to throw her over the banister. I did a dumb thing. You know, I am forever remorseful about it. I did hit her. She suffered from that, but, ah [pause], and I know she was scared at the time. But I don't believe, God is my witness, that I tried to throw her over the banister. We were by the banister. My actions, pushing and shoving each other, my have been such that she said, 'Whoops, I'm going over the banister.' But that was not my intention."

About the 1983 snowfall and giving Charlotte a black eye, John struggled through his answer: "In November of 1981, when I hit her, and she suffered the back problem, I promised to her, to myself [pause], and I remember going to church and promising to God that it would never happen again, and ah, ah." His voice became hoarse. "I remember beating my arm on, I was at Saint Matthew's Cathedral, near Arnold and Porter, I went like that [he banged the witness podium] on the altar rail, and I said, 'Lord, you've got to provide me some help here. I've made a lot of mistakes. It just can't happen again.' And things were going well for a while.

"I would say from September of 1982, until the time of this incident, it's a scenario. As I told Mr. Renehan, I couldn't blame the incident on the events of that day, there were so many incidents that had occurred. I felt that she was keeping me away from the kids' education, which I cared about desperately. And I wanted to be provided report cards. I would say, 'Aren't report cards due?' and everybody would frown the other way like I was going to raise holy hell. . . . I was very demanding of the children. I am very demanding of everybody, including her, and me. . .

The Southland investigation, which had been going on, began to clearly focus in on my own conduct at that time. . . . I was very tense about that. . . . I needed a lot of support at that time and I don't think I got it. I think one of Charlotte's biggest concerns was how this would hurt the ultimate dollar-earning capacity of the stud. And on the weekend before this occurred, Charlotte accused me of taking the $96,500 bribe [involved in the Southland investigation]. . . . Christmas was a disaster. There wasn't ten minutes of peace between Christmas and then. . . . I was ready to go to work beyond belief and I wake up and there's sixteen to eighteen inches of snow on the ground. I try to go to work, down the driveway, and up the street. No work. . . . It's that sort of mid-to-late afternoon period where the snow is melting, pressuring down on the gutter. I'm worried about the house. . . . I'm out there trying to save the gutter, jiggling it around and, sure as heck, all the snow from the roof comes down, right on my good clean driveway, as one would say. . . . I go in the house, and probably carry on a little bit. 'Let's get everybody outside.' . . . [My son] is on the stairway and, uh, I said that awful stigma to him."

The judge interrupted again. "Did you mean that when you said that to your son?"

John: "I hope not, Your Honor. God, I hope not."

Judge: "Let me ask you something. . . . It became very important for you to get to the office, didn't it?"

John: "I like to work a lot, yes."

Judge: "Yes, you do. And when you couldn't, home didn't look very good, did it?"

John: "No. There was a lot of tension. And, hey, you're talking about the death of a marriage, and it's going on, and, you know, this is bizarre. . . ."

Judge: "Did you think, at the time, that it was healthy for you, to have to go to work [to find happiness] that day, to leave your home?"

John: "That wasn't the only day, Your Honor. That's the problem."

Judge: "That was the day you couldn't go. That was the day nature interceded and you couldn't go."

John: "Probably the Lord was telling me to stay home is what you're saying."

Judge: "Do you think that kind of anger, that you built in, is the kind of anger that you could have and exist within a family framework?"

John: [Pause.] "Now, that's the problem. When we talk about these periods of silence, we bred on each other. She'd get depressed, I'd get depressed. Hey, I'll take the first blame."

Judge: "All you had to do was think about each other to get angry? Is that right?"

John: "Let me tell you about a little expression I used to use about our marriage when I prayed to God. We had the capability of building the Eiffel Tower in a day together, but we also had the capability of destroying it in ten minutes together."

John continued telling the story of the February snowfall and giving Charlotte a black eye: "I did it. Hit her in the eye. You know, she was out of the house with the kids in a millisecond and I'm there alone. Jackass. And Valentine's comes and I bring her candy. . . . That's the first time I realized that it was over. There was a skit that we played out for the next couple of months, with each other, but in my own mind, it was probably over that day. [In conclusion, there were] A number of incidents. I put a different coloration on them. The only place that I'm going berserk is saying to you that I deny . . . this stuff about trying to kill her. I don't think I'm capable of doing that, or saying that even, particularly in the periods she talks about. There was too much love between us in those days. Mistakes, yeah, from day one. We did a lot of dumb things to each other. We bred on each other's hatred at times. I think we enjoyed it at times. These silent periods. Ah. I take the blame, but—"

The judge stopped him to ask: "What makes you think your wife looked at it that way? Even if you possibly did enjoy those silent periods, what makes you think she enjoyed it?"

John: "I honestly believe, as we talk about some of the taunting that went on in the marriage, that Charlotte really enjoyed it. Yes, I demeaned her. I did a lot of dumb things."

Judge: "Why did you do it? Did you lack respect for your wife?"

John: "Yes. No question about it. She didn't demand respect."

Judge: "Well, she admits that her problem was gaining self-respect. But did you help her with it?"

John: "Oh, no, I mean."

Judge: "You took it from her, didn't you?"

John: [Crying.] "Sure. We both took it . . . Anytime anybody had a bubble in life . . . we were always the thorn that pricked it. You know, it's crazy. We wouldn't be here today if we could solve it. Believe me. But there we are.

"I have tremendous remorse for this. I pray. I have remorse for Charlotte. I hurt five kids, hurt my folks, her folks, and I hurt myself enormously because of this thing."

Witt began his questioning again, focusing on the letters Charlotte had written to John's friends following their separation and the concentration on money in their marriage.

Said John: "She told me that she would ruin me. . . . There was a lot of concentration in our life on money. We are both insecure about it. I have the capability to make it. But I'm afraid of it. The things about the house. I worry about the house because I think it's all going to disappear. . . . That rug is supposed to be here until 1999. That's sort of my crazy attitude. I worry about things too much. I do."

Judge: "Was it accurate, when she testified that you asked the family to remove their shoes?"

John: "Yeah, we always took our shoes off in the house, but, I mean."

Judge: "Was that a rule?"

John: "Yeah . . . she used to call me the rule-maker. Yeah, I had a lot of rules, but at our house, it was always comfortable to take off your shoes. We had so many wonderful, nice things. . . ."

Judge: "Mr. Fedders, at the time, did you ever ask yourself . . . whether you were preserving a house or a rug or raising five children?"

John: "Yeah, we talked about it from time to time."

Judge: "That's what rugs are meant for, aren't they?"

John: [Talking over the judge's question.] The kids are terrific. Don't get me wrong. We hurt the kids. They've got some problems. . . ."

Judge: "You can tell on any given day whether you're up or down, can't you?"

John: "I don't think so. Not at the beginning. I'd really be more interested in Charlotte's answer to that than mine. [Pause.] . . . Most people have said this to me, 'The only person you're down with is Charlotte.' Everybody at the SEC, Arnold and Porter, hey, I'm the guy who's going and blowing and that's why I think this just hasn't worked. Why do I do what I do to her and not to anybody else? . . . [But] I push the kids. I push everybody, I guess. Ask [my secretary], why did she leave? 'Be there at 6:45 [AM]. Tomorrow let's be here at 6:44.' . . . But nobody could do it like [his secretary]."

Judge: "And you even exhausted her?"

John: "Yeah . . . she'll be back though."

Almost finished on the stand, John concluded about his and Charlotte's life together: "We're very very intelligent people, both of us. She was insecure, and I was dumb. We did dumb things. The only problem is we're playing ours in the circus of life, everybody else is keeping theirs under the rug."

The trial was supposed to conclude the next day, February 6, but the judge became ill and it was postponed until February 25. The *Wall Street Journal* would hold its story until then. For three anxious weeks, Charlotte waited, trying to ignore a torrent of phone calls and love letters from John. Suddenly, after one and a half years of barely speaking to her, he wanted to reconcile.

20

On February 25, 1985, the judicial system failed to let Charlotte out of her marriage. After giving his testimony, on the fifth of the month John decided to contest the divorce. He wanted Charlotte back and begged the judge to give him time to attempt a reconciliation. Perhaps impressed by how repentant he seemed, perhaps feeling sorry for him because of all the controversy now surrounding him, the judge granted John's request. He delayed what was supposed to be the last day of the divorce trial until May 21, despite Bryan Renehan's protestations. While meeting with Renehan and Hal Witt in closed chambers, Judge McAuliffe suggested to Charlotte's lawyer that she go out to dinner with John to talk things out. Charlotte was stunned when Renehan told her.

"The judge's attitude went along with all that Bryan had warned me about before the trial," says Charlotte, "that the courts tend to view abuse as a symptom rather than a cause of a bad marriage. The judge seemed to think that the guy had said he was sorry, so that everything was all right. I really think policemen and judges and lawyers should be required to read about the battered wife syndrome so that they understand the pattern, so that they know that the husband's great show of sorrow, the promises to be better are only part of a cycle. That it's not something that could be worked out over dinner, only through hard work and longtime counseling."

But Charlotte was hardly so philosophic that morning. "I felt like I was in the Twilight Zone. The judge was in effect telling me that, after all this trauma I had lived through, I didn't know what I wanted. He had been so sympathetic and concerned with John when he was on the stand, and I just felt like my pain was being ignored, that once again I wasn't as important as John Fedders. I was almost hysterical when Bryan told me. Bryan said he knew that I didn't want to have anything more to do with John but that the judge's sympathies had swung and that maybe I should consider going to dinner just to show I wasn't unreasonable. But I knew how John and I had operated in the past. I knew that any sign of an opening on my part would encourage John to push harder and harder. He had been pushing me ever since the day of his testimony. Now the judge was pressuring me as well. I felt like I was being caged.

"Then I started to doubt myself. If all these people were convinced he really was sorry, maybe John really could change. Maybe this time would be different."

This time, John seemed determined to win Charlotte back. He pursued her doggedly. It started with telephone calls and then with almost daily letters, page after page filled with his ardor for her, his remorse, his claim to have refound God, and his promises that this time, with the Lord's help, and with the help of counseling, he would change. Letters that before would have made Charlotte weep with thankfulness, but now only confused her, she says.

On Valentine's Day he sent an ardently penned card in

which he proclaimed his love and apologized to Charlotte for not showing her "love, respect, and honor." He promised that his job would never again come before his family, that he would never mistreat her again. He closed the note with: "I desperately want to hear your needs, desires, plans, and goals. . . . How God is affecting your life. I need confession. . . . But, how do we begin—we need a courtship. May I have a date with you, Char?"

His pleas became more urgent. He wrote poignantly of his sorrow and loneliness in many letters: "Charlotte, please give me a chance to prove my total commitment to you and our sons. . . . Please extend your hand and help me. . . . I so much want you as my companion and helpmate on my way back. . . . Push me. Test me. . . . Ask anything. Do you feel spring in the air?"

Also on Valentine's Day, John ordered a dozen red roses from Charlotte's friend and florist, Sandy Oseroff. As strapped financially as he and Charlotte were, "John came into my shop and handed me a $100 bill," recalls Oseroff, "to send Charlotte $80 worth of long stem roses. He said that he was going to get her back one way or another. My heart was going a mile a minute. I had just testified against him. But he was happy as a lark; it was strange, but that's John—one minute he's one way, the next he's another."

But despite his pleadings, despite his promises to do anything for Charlotte to make her happy, to make their family whole, to put the needs of their sons first, John didn't do the one thing she says she really wanted him to do, the one thing that would alleviate their crushing financial problems. He didn't voluntarily quit the SEC. He had three weeks following his February 5 testimony to leave the commission quietly and to return to a more lucrative private practice, before the publicity from the pending *Wall Street Journal* article could adversely affect his professional marketability. But John didn't, even after Brooks Jackson interviewed him regarding the trial, even after his lawyer for the Southland case, Nathan Lewin, wrote a letter, dated February 12, which later appeared in the trade paper *Legal Times,* asking the newspaper not to print the story.

Lewin's letter called a possible story on the divorce an intrusion on John's privacy and read, in part: "You cannot be oblivious, in this regard, to the self-fulfilling effect of a *Journal* article that discusses whether the 'pressure is too much' on John Fedders. Even if the article's text concludes that pressure has not affected his performance, the mere publication of an article discussing such speculation will raise doubts. The public knows only the adage that infers fire from the presence of smoke."

The *Wall Street Journal's* managing editor would later be quoted as saying that the decision to run the story was one of the hardest he ever made, but on February 25, the newspaper published Jackson's unusually long story on its front page, titling it: "Storm Center: John Fedders of SEC Is Pummeled by Legal and Personal Problems." The article detailed the events of the trial, Charlotte and John's testimony, their chronic overspending, plus recounted John's involvement with the Southland investigation. It included both criticisms and praise of his SEC administration. John, SEC chairman John Shad, White House counsel Fred Fielding, and Lewin were all interviewed for the article.

Wrote Jackson: "Nobody has accused Mr. Fedders of misfeasance in office. SEC Chairman John Shad says that despite Mr. Fedders's personal and financial problems, his work remains top-notch. He is 'doing an outstanding job,' Mr. Shad says.

"Mr. Fedders himself says his work at the SEC isn't being affected by his marital, financial, and legal problems. 'I have the unique capacity of burying myself in my work,' he says. But he also acknowledges that his hard work and burning ambition have affected his personal life. 'I've put my work in front of my family for eighteen years,' he says 'In my own mind, I was the proudest guy to take home that full brief-case.' "

In the next two paragraphs, Jackson summarized why the newspaper decided to run what seemed so intensely a pri-vate story: "Problems like Mr. Fedders's were once rou-tinely swept under the rug. Many prominent people, in and out of government, have serious marital, financial, and other personal problems. But only rarely—with film stars or occa-sionally with prominent elected officials—have such prob-lems surfaced in the press.

"There are compelling reasons, however, for telling the John Fedders story. Family violence, whether tied to pres-sures of the job or other root causes, is becoming a matter of increased national concern. So too, in a different way, are the financial problems incurred by successful people when they leave the private sector for positions in government."

Author Laurence Leamer wrote in *Playing for Keeps in Washington,* a collection of profiles of the city's powerful, that "success and prominence are Washington's true tran-sients." John was about to discover just how true that state-ment could be.

Perhaps, as Charlotte hypothesized, John hadn't realized his treatment of her was wrong. Maybe he thought he could explain it—she had pushed him to do all those horrible things, after all. She and her lawyer were exaggerating things. Besides, that was home, a separate place, a private place, where he was king. What did it have to do with him professionally? He was not being charged with a crime and there was no insinuation by the *Wall Street Journal* that his private problems were eroding his performance in his public job.

But no matter what he was thinking, John misjudged the morality of the city. There was an attitude in Washington, perhaps spawned by the heartland's idealistic expectations of its capital, that public officials should be irreproachable, that their conduct should be held to a *higher* standard than simply abiding by the law, since the law could be stretched to legally allow somewhat questionable behavior. Senator Joseph Biden, for instance, said during confirmation hearings of Edwin Meese for attorney general that: "The higher . . . the government position held, the stricter the ethical standard should be."

No, John had not been charged with a crime, although had Charlotte ever pressed charges, he could have been charged with a misdemeanor. But his conduct seemed to outrage the country's sensibilities and their attitude about what home should be—a safe harbor—especially since he was one of the nation's top law enforcement officers.

A line in Charlotte's letter to President Reagan contained a pivotal thought: "I do not understand . . . how a man can enforce one set of laws and abuse another." A paragraph from syndicated columnist Ellen Goodman neatly synthesized the attitude of much of the press and country: "Let me rephrase Charlotte Fedders' question. Should a man who has brutally violated one code of behavior have the power to enforce another? The answer is 'no.' "

Charlotte's revelations were also of overwhelming interest because they yanked family violence out of the ghetto and wedged it right into upstanding suburbia. She proved that rage and violence knew no socio-economic barriers. That in itself crushed stereotypes that before had allowed middle- and upper-class Americans to ignore the problem as being one that couldn't possibly affect them.

Two other factors, both political, contributed to the newsworthiness of John and Charlotte's saga. John worked for the Reagan administration—an administration that, more than any other, preached the sanctity of the family. Reagan had publicly declared war on domestic violence. What did it mean that he employed a man who admitted to beating his wife on seven separate occasions? And could financial pressures caused by taking a comparatively low-paying government job cause or exacerbate emotional problems? The trial's revelations that one reason John might have initially joined the SEC was as a means to leap to a higher-paying private job was mildly disturbing, particularly when coupled with the fact of the debts he had run up while working for the federal government.

News broadcasts immediately picked up on the story and reporters swarmed the Rockville courthouse, scrambling to catch up on details. More than a dozen journalists pursued Charlotte to her car following the meeting between Judge McAuliffe, Witt, and Renehan, shouting questions.

As a result of the publicity, John would probably face an official review of his marital violence. According to the *Wall Street Journal*, Fielding was expected to request Shad to conduct a factual review at the conclusion of the divorce trial when reconvened in May. White House spokesman Larry Speakes announced that President Reagan wouldn't comment while the divorce trial was pending, but added: "The President obviously does not condone or advocate or tolerate any type of abuse, whether it is [against] children, wives, husbands, whoever."

But John saved the administration and his boss the trouble of an official review. Late February 26, after two days of front-page stories, he resigned, writing in part: "Newspaper reports of yesterday and today . . . have exaggerated allegations in the divorce trial and have unfairly described occasional highly regrettable episodes in our marriage. On seven occasions during more than eighteen years of marriage, marital disputes between us resulted in violence, for which I feel, and have expressed, great remorse. These isolated events do not, however, justify the extreme characterizations made in the press. Although I am thoroughly satisfied that my private difficulties have in no way affected the execution of my duties as director of the division of enforcement of the Securites and Exchange Commission and would not do so in the future if I remained in office, the glare of publicity on my private life threatens to undermine the effectiveness of the division of enforcement and of the Commission."

SEC chairman John Shad accepted John's resignation "with regret," saying that John had done an excellent job, increasing the volume of enforcement cases by 50 percent, even though he was working with 5 percent fewer personnel than his predecessor. Shad had given him the SEC's award of excellence. He credited John with cracking the traditional secrecy of Swiss bank accounts and cracking down on corporate fraud and insider trading.

Charlotte learned of John's resignation when a television reporter called her for a comment about it. "I had felt nothing when I read the *Wall Street Journal* article, really," says Charlotte. "I was just so numb by then. But when the reporter told me that John had resigned, I felt flushed in the pit of my stomach. I wanted to call and tell him that I was sorry. But I just couldn't, because he would have seen that as the beginnings of a reconciliation. I didn't feel guilty because I knew he should never have gone into that courtroom. But I felt really, really sorry for him, for my family, for all of us."

That night John and Charlotte made the network news. CBS gave the fullest report, with reporter Lesley Stahl narrating. Footage included a view of the home at Carmelita Drive, slowly pulling back, taking full advantage of its hill to make the house appear the suburban castle, as Stahl talked about John taking a $100,000 pay cut to join the SEC. Court testimony and Lewin's statement about the case involving only seven incidents were printed on the television screen underneath an instant-logo of akimbo marriage rings encased in an outline of a courthose. CBS even interviewed Congresswoman Pat Schroeder as a voice of critics who had been calling for John to be fired. She said: "The President has been one who would have you believe that no one around him would ever do such a thing, that they are saints and that everyone else is the sinner."

In closing, Stahl stood before the White House and said: "White House officials insist that there was no pressure on Mr. Fedders to resign, although they admit that, given President Reagan's emphasis on family values, the Fedders case, if allowed to linger on, could have been politically damaging."

Following his resignation, John cloistered himself in a Trappist monastery and sought psychiatric help. He would not take a private job until May, when he joined Nathan Lewin's firm of Miller, Cassidy, Larroca, & Lewin in Washington, D.C.

Charlotte, meanwhile, tried to ignore a photographer from a grocery-store tabloid who followed her around, jumping in front of her to snap pictures as she took the children to school, went to her therapist, or ran errands. She also tried to resist the insecurity and anger she felt when watching talk shows dissect her situation and debate the press's right to report it, such as the time Lewin appeared on the *CBS Morning News* and said with indignation: "In the interest of decency, there are things which a newspaper cannot know in terms of relations that go on in the home. . . . But that doesn't mean that the public should be deprived of a superb public servant. . . . There's . . . a substantial difference between allegations of criminal conduct . . . and really what are disputes in the home . . . seven times over a long marriage—that is, I think, quite different even in degree and in kind from somebody being charged with committing a crime."

In the next weeks, it became harder and harder for Charlotte to resist John. He publicly stated he was seeking a reconciliation, and reporters kept asking her about it. The pressures on her built. John seemed so sincere about changing. And Charlotte's father was sick and was unsure if he could continue to assist her financially. She hated to keep relying on her sister Dotti and her brother-in-law Bruce, who generously gave, but who also had their own family to raise. It began to make sense to Charlotte when John said the burden of maintaining his apartment and their house was too great, especially now that he was unemployed. Charlotte felt enormous remorse about his professional status. She herself was traumatized and exhausted and here was this man she had loved so much telling her constantly that he loved her, wanted her, needed her.

In April, she hesitantly decided to give him one more try. But it lasted only three weeks.

"It all started because he came by the house to pick up the boys and I asked him about what we were going to do about the income tax," Charlotte remembers. "So he came into the house and that started this three-hour conversation. Had I not asked him that question he probably would have driven away and none of this would have happened. He came into the kitchen and we talked for hours and he kissed me and touched me and it felt good because I, of course, hadn't been with anyone other than him almost two years before. I had been through a hell of a lot and I was vulnerable. I wanted someone just to hug and comfort me.

"But I felt cornered, so I made him leave. He took two of the children for the evening. The next day was Easter, so he brought the kids back by 8 AM. He came in for breakfast. He hugged me and his whole body was shaking. I felt this overwhelming need to comfort him, and feeling him tremble like that made me think he really was sincere, that maybe he really could be different now. He had been going to therapy and he claimed he had renewed faith. We decided to go to church together. I asked that we go someplace where we didn't know people. Then we went with the kids to the restaurant Hamburger Hamlet. We had a lovely time. Then he came home and he almost forced himself on me. It just felt like what it must feel to have sex in the back of a car—the act itself might feel good, but the setting was all wrong. I wanted it to be more romantic. So I agreed to come to his apartment the next night.

"I have to be honest and say that a lot of the reconciliation had to do with sex. It had always been loving and good between us, very spontaneous. There was one time that we were even driving along the New Jersey Turnpike and just pulled off the road to a secluded spot. We had always been happy with each other through it. I missed him, so I succumbed. But I didn't want this to be a full-scale reconciliation. I wanted it to be a trial run. I knew that having sex was viewed by the court as a forgiveness of past sins and could throw off our divorce. He promised that he wouldn't tell anyone about it, in case it didn't work. I should never have believed him, because he used it against me later in court.

"I think John wanted to reconcile because when all these other people reacted so badly to what he had done, he was suddenly awakened to it. And to how much he wanted to stay with his family. And whether he was aware of ulterior motives of not, I think he knew that it would save face if I accepted him back.

"He wasn't working, so we continued to meet at his apartment for those three weeks. He was trying to please, I know, but it got to be totally overwhelming. He started calling my friends to tell them that we were back together."

Her friends were not pleased. "When they reconciled I didn't know what was happening, and I didn't hear from Charlotte at all, and I was getting concerned," says Molly Head, their Marquette friend. "I kept calling. She had her answering machine and she wouldn't call back. I finally caught one of the boys on a Sunday afternoon and he went to get Charlotte and she wouldn't come to the phone, which made me angry. Well, John was there and I didn't know it. A few days later John called me to tell me about their reconciliation and he went into lurid details about their sex life. He told me that all her friends had cut her off. I was just sick. I could see that Charlotte was falling hook, line, and sinker for all these goings on with him, and that she was dependent on him again."

But Charlotte says she soon realized on her own that John hadn't changed and that she couldn't stay with him. "Almost immediately he started causing me to question myself," says Charlotte, "telling me he really didn't like the color of my hair, chastising me about the boys' leaving fingerprints on the walls. A major stumbling block was his claiming that my family had ruined him. I just couldn't accept the blame for that. He had done it himself. I just knew that eventually his anger over that would erupt into some kind of awful confrontation.

"And he hadn't changed about the money. He went to Saks Fifth Avenue and bought me earrings with a small ruby center and diamond petals. He also wanted to look for a new house—not a smaller, more affordable one, but larger ones in Potomac, with several acres of land. There was no way we could afford that.

"I tried once more because I had loved him so much and had given him so much energy. I knew I could never love at that pace again. Plus, having six children with someone creates a very special, strong bond. And what had disappointed me most about all this was that we had the potential for a good marriage and a good family. We had good kids; I was basically a good woman; he was basically a good man. We were hardworking people. Our goals weren't that unrealistic. He didn't want to be President. All I really wanted was to be a good wife and a good mother. And I think now I was both. I just couldn't do it alone."

Because of the attempted reconciliation, the May court date was again extended, to the fall of 1985. That meant Charlotte would still be subsisting on $1,000 a month until then.

In October, Judge McAuliffe granted Charlotte a limited divorce on the grounds of cruelty. It was a limited divorce because of the brief April reconciliation attempt. Under Maryland law, an absolute divorce is not allowed if a couple has spent a night under the same roof within the preceding twelve months. According to Renehan, it was the equivalent of a judicial separation. It did not entail a final division of property and forbade Charlotte and John to remarry until a final divorce settlement could be granted, no sooner than April 29, 1986, a year after Charlotte had called an end to her and John's brief encounter.

Charlotte won full use of the house for three years, custody of their five children, and $1,500 a month in support. John was also to be responsible for paying the mortgage, house insurance, utilities, taxes, and half of the maintenance costs on the house.

Charlotte could have used more money, but there wasn't that much left to divvy up at the time of McAuliffe's decision. Although John's initial salary at Miller, Cassidy, Larroca, & Lewin had been $6,000 a month, approximately equal to his SEC pay, it had fallen to just under $800, according to John's testimony. In his financial statement, dated September 23,1985, and submitted to the court, John described the $6,000 per month as loans, and outlined his salary agreement with the firm at the time thusly: "I am entitled to receive 15 percent of the first $600,000, and 10 percent of any additional moneys, received by the firm as fees attributable to matters brought to the firm by me, and 35 percent of the fees received by the firm for time worked by me."

Judge McAuliffe's decision followed two days of testimony in September, during which Charlotte told why the reconciliation hadn't worked and why she still wanted a divorce. John continued to contest it, claiming that Charlotte had been under pressure from her "advisers" to leave him. This time there were few tears from John, says Charlotte. His self-control remained intact. He asked that the court dismiss Charlotte's petition for a divorce and to order psychiatric counseling aimed at achieving a reconciliation. He said emotionally: "We'll make it, Your Honor." But Charlotte just slowly shook her head, refusing to return John's intense stare.

In his October ruling, however, Judge McAuliffe rejected John's plea, stating that Maryland law no longer recognized the resumption of sexual relations as a conclusive reconciliation. He stated in his 95-minute oral opinion: "It was a trial run and only that and it didn't work. . . . She never manifested an intent to forgive the facts which affected the parties over many years." But it was still only a limited divorce that he could grant.

After having an individual conference with Luke, Judge McAuliffe was convinced that his relationship with his father had deteriorated perhaps beyond repair. "It is not appropriate to require him to visit with [his] father over his strongest objections," said the judge.

Finally, the judge concluded about John and Charlotte's marriage: "When you put it all together, you have as classic a situation of cruelty . . . and a classic situation of excessively vicious conduct . . . as one can find."

Epilogue

John and Charlotte's tragedy seemed to strike a motherlode of pain in American women. After the trial, Charlotte immediately received many letters and phone calls from other battered women across the country, women like herself who didn't fit previous stereotypes. They were educated, wealthy, and many were even professionals themselves.

In April 1986, *The Washingtonian* magazine published a lengthy article told from Charlotte's perspective about what had gone wrong with her marriage and her dreams, a story about—as the magazine's editor, Jack Limpert, said—"the promises Washington offers and the price people sometimes pay." Many of the city's overachievers opt to throw all their efforts into their work so that they don't have the energy or emotional suppleness to be a strong part of their families.

Limpert wrote: "Many hard-driving Washingtonians—both men and women—know how hard it can be to balance the pressures of work and family. There is also the question of control: At work a high-powered executive can hire and fire, give raises and promotions, and demand quick action and obedience. But home is a place of love and gentle persuasion. I wonder if John Fedders now understands that. I also wonder whether Charlotte Fedders won't always love him."

As Charlotte had been, the magazine was deluged with calls and letters from battered wives.

Overwhelmingly, the woman were well educated and articulate, and clearly belonged to an upper-middle-class society regarded as civilized, as arbiters of proper conduct. Many of the callers had advanced degrees, and most were mothers who say they finally found the courage to end their marriages when they saw their husbands begin to rage at their children. Their husbands were civic leaders, lawyers, journalists, physicians, university professors, politicians, even ministers, who typically had low self-esteem themselves and reacted violently to anything that questioned their authority or masculinity.

The wives told of broken limbs, of black eyes inflicted for such minor infractions as taking too long to brush their teeth, of rapes, and of threats to their lives.

But although most recounted shocking beatings, they complained more of the control their husbands demanded at home. They said that the more power the men garnered at work, the more staff under their direct command, the less tolerant they became at home, the more they wanted traditional, submissive wives. At the job, the men were privileged and pampered, and they expected the same slavish deference from their families. And the women said that, as their husbands achieved top management positions, they used the same motivation techniques at home that they used at work, granting or withholding approval to spur action or produce emotional dependency.

Most managers are not this maniacal, but somewhere in the husbands of these callers the valued American drive for achievement twisted into an obsession with power.

Stories such as these women's painfully bring home the

reality of otherwise sterile statistics: that every eighteen seconds a woman in this country is battered, that every day four are beaten to death.

But because such stories have spawned community programs designed to aid victims and their families, the pilgrimage to freedom will be a little bit easier than it has been. A decade ago, there were few places for a battered wife to run. Now there are twelve hundred shelters across the country. Demand is so great that the country could use even more facilities, though. My Sister's Place in Washington, D.C., for instance, has to turn away seven families for every one it takes in.

Law officials, as well, have started to change the way they handle spouse abusers. Now, if police officers have "probable cause" to suspect a crime has been committed against a spouse, they can arrest her assailant without her having to swear out a formal complaint. Many of these men are now jailed overnight, and crime research in Minneapolis indicates that only 19 percent of those held repeat their offense during the next six months. With previous tactics, the report found 35 percent beat their spouses again within that time.

Of course, there are still serious problems, even with the improved laws. For example, because their crimes are typically misdemeanors, not felonies, the bail for spouse abusers is low. That means they usually make bond with ease and return home the same night—which terrifies their victims. Out of fear, many women still refuse to testify against their husbands, and without a witness prosecutors simply have no case.

"Women wanting to drop charges unfortunately reinforces all the stereotypes of battered wives," says a Virginia commonwealth's attorney, who prosecutes spouse abuse cases. "It makes people take the cases less seriously. Changes won't happen unless battered women are willing to help the system change by coming forward. If we get the cases to trial, about 80 percent of the abusers are found guilty, and nationwide studies have shown that if there is court intervention a woman is 50 percent less likely to be subjected to abuse again."

Many jurisdictions divert convicted batterers to counseling programs aimed at changing their behavior rather than sentencing them to time in jail. They are sent to alcohol rehabilitation, anger management programs, or hospital psychotherapy. If they complete the required counseling, they have no criminal record.

"Typically, the woman doesn't want the man to go to jail, she wants changes in the home, and these programs really seem to help," says the Virginia prosecutor. "But without the court forcing the husbands to counseling, they rarely go and the violence only gets worse."

Other professionals serving the public and coming in contact with spouse abuse victims, however, are still hampered from helping them. Staff in hospital emergency rooms, for instance, are constantly treating battered women but are unable to report the cases to the police for fear the spouse will sue the hospital. There is no protective law to cover them, as there is when they report child abuse. More often than not, abusive husbands accompany their victims to emergency rooms and insist on staying with them throughout treatment, preventing them from asking for help.

But slowly, slowly, the country is responding to the often life-or-death needs of battered spouses and their families.

Charlotte Fedders is still not finally divorced. John continues to battle her in court, fighting for extension of his visitation rights. In his suit, he says that he loves his family and wants help in restoring and improving his relationship with it. John also wants the court to assess the detrimental emotional effects on the family that he feels are sure to result from Charlotte speaking out publicly about their marriage.

Charlotte points to a letter mailed to editors of *The Wash-*

ington Post, which was never printed. It came from a social worker, recognized in the Washington metropolitan area as an expert on family violence. "Mental health professionals who are knowledgeable about the dynamics of family violence know that physical abuse is accompanied by psychological control and that when the victim takes action to end the violence, the assailant often turns to the court system to regain control and continue the harassment."

In court, Hal Witt asked John's psychiatrist if he thought John's legal actions were "an effort to assert control or pressure his wife?" The psychiatrist answered that he thought the statement to be "nonsense" and, although John's controlling nature had been "a detriment to his functioning" in the family, that his client has worked hard to change and done so. The psychiatrist added: "I have no doubt whatsoever that he has a very sincere, very genuine, very abiding wish to do what is best."

Charlotte remembers that John once told her sister that the person who endured the most in a lawsuit won it. Her divorce lawyer's fees alone total about $30,000 now. In many ways, she feels that John still controls her life.

Her other debts mounted as well, and in May 1986, Charlotte filed for bankruptcy, listing more than thirty creditors and bills accumulated over three years that totalled nearly $130,000, which she said she could not pay. Of that amount, $16,000 consisted of loans her family made her. In the bankruptcy proceeding, Charlotte testified that she was living a hand-to-mouth existence, even though John was making all his court-ordered support payments. And although she still worked part time at The Woods Academy at the time, the boys' income from odd jobs and lawn-mowing often had to be used to pay for groceries. The court dismissed all her debts except for $10,000 to her lawyer and $5,000 to one of the boys' school, which will be paid, she says, when her Potomac home is sold.

Still, Charlotte and her family are moving on with their

lives. The boys are doing well in school, says Charlotte, and that the house is happy and loud in the way a house of boys should be.

Says Charlotte: "I want happiness for them. And my definition of happiness is very different today than it would have been five years ago. Before, I would have identified the means of happiness as being good in sports, getting into college, becoming a doctor or lawyer, having a successful career. Now, I want them to have the self-confidence that comes from liking themselves, not being afraid to try anything. To be good to their families and to really enjoy everything a family can bring. I don't agree that success and being nice are mutually exclusive. I want them to be nice because I believe the greatest success in life is being a warm person, capable of tenderness.

"We've survived. But we've not only survived; we're starting to thrive."

Charlotte, in particular, has gained confidence and often speaks to women's groups now. Also, in April 1987, she appeared as a witness before a House Education and Labor Select Subcommittee. The subcommittee was holding budgeting hearings to review the need and effectiveness of the Child Abuse Prevention and Treatment Act and the Family Violence Prevention and Services Act. The Reagan Adminstration had proposed ending the family violence act, passed by Congress in 1984, then funded at $8.7 million for counseling programs and shelters for battered wives, according to the subcommittee.

Charlotte sat in a crowded room in the Rayburn Office Building, in front of a panel of congressmen. Despite the fact the congressmen had to scatter several times during the hearing to appear on the House floor for votes and made Charlotte wait over an hour to testify, she spoke with new poise. This time, rather than recoiling from the microphone as she had two years earlier at her divorce trial, she leaned forward to meet it.

She recounted much of her experience. She told them she had once gone to the police for help only to leave the station, "feeling like a crybaby." She closed by suggesting police officers, lawmakers, and doctors should be required to read literature describing the "battered wife syndrome" so that they understand it. "The system must be changed to provide protection for the real victims," she said, "not the abusers who say they are sorry. The issue that a woman has been beaten or otherwise terrorized by a man for any reason he might feel is justified must be addressed."

Charlotte calls herself a "reluctant advocate," yet says with conviction: "I want to help other wives understand that no person has the right to make another afraid."

Authors' Note

Primary thanks must go to Jack Limpert, editor of *The Washingtonian* magazine. He had the wisdom to recognize that the saga of Charlotte and John Fedders was an allegory for overachievers as well as a story of domestic violence and, therefore, deserved a more in-depth look than that allowed by newspaper reports. Likewise, thanks to Harper & Row editor Larry Ashmead, who had exuberant faith in the book and whose trust in me gave me confidence; to our agent Gwen Edelman for her persistence and invaluable, constant encouragement; to *Washingtonian* senior editor Randy Rieland, who edited the magazine article and kept it on track; to Harper & Row's Margaret Wimberger, who made the manuscript's painstaking work less painful; to my sister and brother-in-law for their steady and steadying counsel; to George Sheanshang; and, of course, to Charlotte Fedders for her brave candor and willingness to answer my incessant and often difficult questions.

Most importantly, I thank my husband, John, whose loving support, patience, and ever-ready wit saw me through *Shattered Dreams*.

LE

Words fail me when trying to acknowledge so many. I join in Laura's praise and appreciation of Gwen Edelman, Jack Limpert, as well as Larry Ashmead and countless others at Harper & Row. In addition, I thank Mary Donahue and Bryan Renehan for their professional wisdom, patience, sensitivity, and encouragement; my parents, sisters, and wonderful friends for their amazing memories, incredible fairness, and broad shoulders; and Martha, Bruce and Dotti, Joy, Mr. B., Fr. K., and gentle "Doc," who so lovingly supplemented my parenting when I was short on time or energy. A standing ovation to Laura Elliott, whose investigative talent, amazing insight, exquisite literary style, and extraordinary compassion have made working on this book an unbelievably satisfying experience.

And above all, I thank my children for their abundant supply of laughter and love.

CF